Mastering the World of Marketing

Mastering the World of Marketing

The Ultimate Training Resource from
the Biggest Names in Marketing

ERIC TAYLOR
DAVID RIKLAN

WILEY

John Wiley & Sons, Inc.

Published by John Wiley & Sons, Inc., Hoboken, New Jersey.
Published simultaneously in Canada.

For general information on our other products and services or for technical
support, please contact our Customer Care Department within the United States
at (800) 762-2974, outside the United States at (317) 572-3993 or fax (317) 572-4002.

Wiley also publishes its books in a variety of electronic formats. Some content that
appears in print may not be available in electronic books. For more information about
Wiley products, visit our web site at www.wiley.com.

Library of Congress Cataloging-in-Publication Data:

Taylor, Eric, 1963-
  Mastering the world of marketing : the ultimate training resource from the biggest
names in marketing / Eric Taylor and David Riklan.
    p. cm.
  Includes index.
  ISBN 978-0-470-88841-4 (paper)
  ISBN 978-1-118-06168-6 (ebk)
  ISBN 978-1-118-06173-2 (ebk)
  ISBN 978-1-118-06174-9 (ebk)
  1. Marketing. 2. Success in business. I. Riklan, David, 1961- II. Title.
  HF5415.T3425 2011
  658.8'8—dc22

                                                              2011013198

Printed in the United States of America

10 9 8 7 6 5 4 3 2 1

Contents

Foreword

Isaac Asimov quite rightly said, "The only constant is change."

For anyone who lived before the twentieth century, it might have taken an entire lifetime to realize the truth of that statement. Today, it is something every Internet-connected teenager simply knows.

One simply needs to understand that the pace of change is different for different things.

While human beings as a species are also evolving and changing, the pace of that change is glacially slow. So slow that we can make meaningful observations about human nature that will remain valid until some point in the future where evolution makes them obsolete.

At the heart of it, the body of knowledge about marketing is nothing more than a collection of observations about human nature.

So, is all information about the discipline of marketing perpetually relevant?

The good stuff can then be divided into two categories: knowledge that is specific to humans (like Joe Sugarman's genius collection of "Triggers") and knowledge that is specific to a medium or industry (like Chris Brogan's social media strategies).

The specific-to-humans stuff is obviously quite perennial, but what about the stuff that is specific-to-medium?

Well, we all know that web sites and ideas that were relevant and even hot two years ago (MySpace, Friendster, etc.) are now all but completely irrelevant as I write this.

Should you then dismiss all of the chapters about online marketing in this book?

Most certainly not. And here's why . . .

There are three bits of really good news to be found in all of this chaos.

1. You need to move faster.

   While information is relevant for shorter periods of time, the answer is not to duck your head in the sand and pretend it will all go away.

   Stay on top of the trends and embrace the pace of change. Your slower competition will be constantly eating your dust as a result.

2. Most of the online tactics in this book will be relevant for at least 10 years.

   Unless the dynamics of search and social media change drastically, most of what you read here is stuff you absolutely need to know in order to capture the high-ROI opportunities available online.

3. There is one major shift the Internet caused that will remain relevant for hundreds of years (if we're lucky).

The big change is this: We are all being held much more accountable for our behavior.

So what?

Well, before the Internet allowed customers to share experiences with each other in real time, businesses didn't really have to be great at what they did. It was okay to be mediocre as long as you were excellent at shaping public perception.

People are savvier now. They know what you're doing. They see through your marketing hype.

Some see this as an impediment to marketing. If they were really smart they'd see this as an opportunity.

They'd realize that we are now freed up in a sense. Rather than worrying about playing damage control and expending our energies on creating "perceived value" we can put those same energies into more useful things:

➤ Creating greater products

➤ Providing more meaningful customer service

➤ Being more interesting

It sounds like what the overly optimistic self-help pundits of the past might have advised us, but today it is a quantifiable truth. As long as the Internet remains uncensored and free, that's a truth you can bank on for decades to come.

—Mark Joyner
Founder and Chairman of Construct Zero
www.ConstructZero.org

Introduction
Mastering the World
of Marketing

One of the single biggest challenges in running any business is knowing how to effectively market your products and services.

A great product marketed poorly will most likely fail.

Marketing is simply the primary process by which businesses generate customer interest in goods or services.

■ NO CUSTOMER INTEREST = NO CUSTOMER SALES

Marketing helps us identify our target customer, helps us to sell to the customer, and enables us to keep our customers.

It creates the strategies that underlie selling, business communication, and business development.

There is an old saying in the "World of Sales" that nothing happens until somebody sells something.

But the truth is that salespeople can't sell much until marketing creates and defines the five P's: Product, Price, Place (Distribution), Promotion, and, for some people, Positioning, Packaging, or People.

Marketing frequently begins even before the product or service is created.

Even President Barack Obama has said that the lesson of his political setbacks is that "you can't be neglecting of *marketing* and PR and public opinion."

► **The Challenge with Marketing in the Twenty-First Century**

During the course of the last 10 years, marketing has changed, and for some companies it has changed drastically.

With all of the changes come many questions:

How important is social media in marketing today?

What is the best way to define my unique selling proposition?

Is it possible to control my message and my brand?

Does e-mail marketing still work effectively?

Does Facebook and Twitter marketing really work?

How do I create a marketing budget?

Who should I seek help to develop my marketing plan?

What's the best way to get publicity for my business?

Should blogging be a part of my marketing plan?

How do I write killer copy for my marketing collateral?

Should I focus my efforts on radio, TV, print, the Internet or, word-of-mouth marketing?

The amount of information available on marketing has expanded tremendously.

A simple search for "Branding" on Amazon.com brings up 2,682 books. A search for "Facebook Marketing" brings up 449 books, and a general search for "Marketing" brings up 383,132 results.

Where do you start?

We had three specific goals in mind with *Mastering the World of Marketing*:

1. Our book is designed to provide you with a great starting point for generating ideas and insights for marketing. Our book contains more than 500 specific ideas to implement to help you with marketing your products and services.

2. Our book is designed to be a resource guide with information on 100 of the top marketing minds in the world.

3. Finally, we have sprinkled the book with great business advice from people who have fought in the trenches and succeeded.

We couldn't possible cover everything in one book. Our goal is to help you kick-start great ideas and provide you with a road map to find even more.

Our book is also a book of numbers that provides you with:

One Hundred Personal Branding Tactics Using Social Media

Twenty Ways to Generate Ideas That Will Boost Your Business

The Eight Ps of Buying Triggers

Twenty-One Creative Ways to Increase Your Facebook Fanbase

Ten Internet Marketing Rules to Live By

Five Ways to Not Screw up Your Networking Attempts

Twenty-Three Questions for Prospective Bloggers

Ten Common Mistakes Exhibitors Make

The Five Most Important Words on Your Web Site

Ten Ways to Surf for Buried Treasure in Your Market

Our book is about helping you generate ideas for your marketing plan. A great illustration of this comes from a story (of unknown origin) of a small retailer that learned about Marketing Upmanship.

This retailer was dismayed when a competitor selling the same type of product opened next door to him, displaying a large sign proclaiming: BEST DEALS.

Not long after, he was horrified to find yet another competitor move in next door, on the other side of his store. Its large sign was even more disturbing: LOWEST PRICES.

After his initial panic and concern that he would be driven out of business, he looked for a way to turn the situation to his marketing advantage. Finally, an idea came to him. The next day, he proudly unveiled a new and huge sign over his front door. It read:

MAIN ENTRANCE!

One great idea can make a tremendous difference, and you need to find yours.

It's time to make "something" happen in your business.

Mastering the World of Marketing enables *you* to do precisely that.

—Eric Taylor and David Riklan

Chapter 1

The Split-Testing Attitude

Matt Bacak

In this section, I'm going to talk about something that makes me so much money because my Web pages are so much better. If you have no idea what in the world *split testing* is then you really need to read this. (I wish someone would have told me about this early on.)

But first, here are things you can use to split test. . . .

■ GOOGLE WEB SITE OPTIMIZER

Google's free web site testing and optimization tool allows you to increase the value of your existing web sites and traffic. Go here: www.google.com/websiteoptimizer.

■ HYPERTRACKER

HyperTracker is a sophisticated tracking management system that helps you to convert more clicks into customers and save wads of cash. Go here to get started: www.hypertracker.com.

I use them both. Now let me ask you an important question.

What's more important?

"Traffic to your site" or "the conversion of your site"?

The REAL answer is BOTH.

I'm always talking about traffic strategies inside the dirt. So in this issue, I want to spend some time on split testing to increase your web site's conversion.

Imagine sending 10,000 people to a page that doesn't get one sale or one optin—that would totally suck.

So, let's think of it a little differently . . . you get 1,000 people at your site and 300 sales or optins. That's a 30 percent conversion.

That's not too bad for an optin page or freakin' killer for a sales letter.

Can you increase that number?

The answer is I don't know. You've got to test.

The one thing that I have learned . . .

What you think works doesn't and what you don't think will work will.

Sounds crazy, huh. Believe me.

That's why I put the saying "Question Everything" in the list of the month this month.

Here's something else that might shock you. There is no such thing as blanket statements. (Okay, smartass, I know that was a blanket statement itself.)

But, if somebody says, "Black background pulls better than a white background," they may be right, they may be wrong.

You don't know until *you* test it to your market. I've proven many of my friends wrong by testing. I've proven myself wrong also—*many* times. That's for dang sure.

So what site should you first test?

Well, if your business looks anything like mine.

■ TRAFFIC → OPTIN PAGE → SALES LETTER → OTOS

That's freaking easy. Test the optin page.

Why?

Because, if you don't get any optins then they'll never see your sales letter anyway. Why in the world would you even waste your time?

Then, after the optin page you test? The sales letter, then the OTOs.

Test the pages in the order that the traffic comes.

Now that you got that, I want you to understand something very important when it comes to split testing that most gurus will never tell you because they have no freaking clue. (They wouldn't have any idea anyway because they don't test or just suck at it.)

This is *important*. → Don't make your first split test be a one page testing against another with only slight changes. No. No. No.

Make the first test be *radically* different pages, maybe totally different looks, totally different feels, or better yet totally different angles. Because, you will get radically different results.

Would you rather see 10 percent versus 30 percent conversion on your split test or see 10.1 percent versus 10.15 percent conversion? I hope the answer is clear.

Let me give you an example of what I'm talking about.

Recently, I did a split test on a CD I just launched. I tested the offer as a CD with *free* shipping and handling versus a *free* CD and pay for shipping and handling.

Which one won?

If you bought it you won't really know because HyperTracker cookies you so every time you go back to the page you will always see the page you initially landed on.

■ ABOUT THE AUTHOR

Matt Bacak began investing his first earnings at the tender age of 12, a young businessman in the making. Now, 15 years later, Bacak survived failed businesses, botched partnerships, heavy credit card debt, and bankruptcy—all in preparation for the accomplishments he has achieved today as a well-established Internet marketer and best-selling author.

Matt Bacak became a millionaire at the age of 27. He currently is running three multimillion-dollar companies and each company was built using the Internet. Just by using the Internet, Matt's first company grew by 1057 percent last year alone. His second company made $500,000 in less than two months. His third company, which he built in February 2006, made its first million by the end of that year.

Matt also just had one of the largest promotions that the Internet has ever seen—he acquired over 14,897 customers in less than seven days.

Web Sites

www.articlemarketingcashcd.com

Primary Products or Books

The "Article Marketing Cash" CD

Chapter 2

Thirty-One–derfully Simple Ways to Make Your Ads Generate More Inquiries

Bob Bly

A client recently phoned with a problem I'd encountered many times before.

"Our new ad campaign's main goal is to create awareness and build image, not generate sales leads," the ad manager explained. "But my management still tends to judge ads by counting the number of inquiries they bring in. Is there some way I can increase my ad's pulling power without destroying the basic campaign concept?"

Fortunately, the answer is yes.

There are proven techniques you can use to increase *any* ad's pulling power, whether your main goal is inquiries or image. Here are 31 techniques that can work for you:

1. Ask for action. Tell the reader to phone, write, contact his sales rep, request technical literature, or place an order.

2. Offer *free* information, such as a color brochure or catalog.

3. Describe your brochure or catalog. Tell about its special features, such as a selection chart, planning guide, installation tips, or other useful information it contains.

4. Show a picture of your brochure or catalog.

5. Give your literature a title that implies value. "Product Guide" is better than "catalog." "Planning Kit" is better than "sales brochure."

6. Include your address in the last paragraph of copy and beneath your logo, in type that is easy to read. (Also place it inside the coupon, if you use one.)

7. Include a toll-free number in your ad.

8. Print the toll-free number in extra-large type.

9. Put a small sketch of a telephone next to the phone number. Also use the phrase, "Call toll-free."

10. Create a hot line. For example, a filter manufacturer might have a toll-free hot line with the numbers 1–800-FILTERS. Customers can call the hot line to place an order to get more information on the manufacturer's products.

11. For a full-page ad, use a coupon. It will increase response 25 to 100 percent.

12. Make the coupon large enough that readers have plenty of room to write in their name and address.

13. Give the coupon a headline that affirms positive action: "Yes, I'd like to cut my energy costs by 50 percent or more."

14. Give the reader multiple response options: "I'd like to see a demonstration"; "Have a salesperson call"; "Send me a free planning kit by return mail."

15. For a fractional ad—one-half page or less—put a heavy dashed border around the ad. This creates the feel and appearance of a coupon, which in turn stimulates response.

16. In the closing copy for your fractional ad, say, "To receive more information, clip this ad and mail it to us with your business card."

17. A bound-in business reply card, appearing opposite your ad, can increase response by a factor of two or more.

18. Use a direct headline—one that promises a benefit or stresses the offer of free information—rather than a headline that is cute or clever.

19. Put your offer of a free booklet, report, selection guide, or other publication in the headline of your ad.

20. Offer a free gift, such as a slide rule, metric conversion table, pocket ruler, and so forth.

21. Offer a free product sample.

22. Offer a free consultation, analysis, recommendation, study, cost estimate, computer printout, and so forth.

23. Talk about the value and benefits of your free offer. The more you stress the offer, the better your response.

24. Highlight the free offer in a copy subhead. The last subhead of your ad could read, "Get the facts—*Free.*"

25. In a two-page ad, run copy describing your offer in a separate sidebar.

26. Be sure the magazine includes a reader service number in your ad.

27. Use copy and graphics that specifically point the reader toward using the reader service number. For example, an arrow pointing to

the number and copy that says, "For more information circle reader service number below."

28. Consider using more than one reader service number. For example, one number for people who want literature, another for immediate response from a salesperson.

29. In a full-page ad for multiple products, have a separate reader service number for each product or piece of literature featured in the ad.

30. Test different ads. Keep track of how many inquiries each ad pulls. Then run only those ads that pull the best.

31. Look for a sales appeal, key benefit, or theme that may be common to all of your best-pulling ads. Highlight that theme in subsequent ads.

■ ABOUT THE AUTHOR

Bob Bly is a freelance copywriter and marketing consultant with three decades of experience in business-to-business, high tech, and direct marketing.

Web Sites

www.bly.com

Primary Products or Books

www.ctcpublishing.net

Chapter 3

100 Personal Branding Tactics Using Social Media

Chris Brogan

> You are not special. You are not a beautiful or unique snowflake. You are the same decaying organic matter as everything else.
>
> —Tyler Durden, Fight Club

Branding one's self in an online environment built on entropy and go-baby-go is difficult at best, and impossible if you forget to take your happy pills. To that end, I've come up with a quick list of 100 things you might do to help with these efforts. Feel free to add your ideas to the comments section.

If you like this one, please don't hesitate to stumble, blog, digg, bookmark, and otherwise promote the hell out of this. (That's another tactic, by the way.)

■ LISTENING

➤ Build ego searches using Technorati and Google Blogsearch.

➤ Comment frequently (and meaningfully) on blogs that write about you and your posts.

➤ Don't forget the conversations hiding in Twitter (use Summize.com) and Friendfeed. Be sure to stay aware of those.

➤ If you can afford it, buy professional listening tools, like Radian6 or others in that category.

➤ Use Google Reader to store your ego searches.

➤ Use Yahoo! Site Explorer to see who's linking to your site.

➤ Use heat map tools like CrazyEgg to see how people relate to your site.

➤ Listen to others in your area of expertise. Learn from them.

➤ Listen to thought leaders in other areas, and see how their ideas apply to you.

➤ Don't forget podcasts. Check out iTunes and see who's talking about your area of interest.

➤ Track things like audience/community sentiment (positive/negative) if you want to map effort to results.

■ HOME BASE

➤ Home base is your blog/web site. Not everyone needs a blog. But most people who want to develop a personal brand do.

➤ Buy an easy-to-remember, easy-to-spell, content-appropriate domain name if you can. Don't be *too* clever.

➤ A really nice layout doesn't have to cost a lot, and it shows you're more than a social media dabbler.

➤ Your "About" page should be about you *and* your business, should the blog be professional in nature. At least, it should be about you.

➤ Make sure it's easy to comment on your site.

➤ Make sure it's easy for people to subscribe to your site's content.

➤ Use easy-to-read fonts and colors.

➤ A site laden with ads is a site that doesn't cherish its audience. Be thoughtful.

➤ Pay attention to which widgets you use in your sidebar. Don't be frivolous.

➤ Load time is key. Test your blog when you make changes, and ensure your load times are reasonable.

➤ Register your site with all the top search engines.

➤ Claim your site on Technorati.com.

➤ Use WebsiteGrader.com to make sure your site is well built in Google's eyes.

■ PASSPORTS

➤ Passports are accounts on other social networks and social media platforms. It's a good idea to build an account on some of these sites to further extend your personal branding.

➤ Twitter.com is a must if you have a social media audience. It also connects you to other practitioners.

➤ Facebook and/or MySpace are useful social networks where you can build outposts (see next list).

➤ Get a Flickr account for photo sharing.

➤ Get a YouTube account for video uploading.

➤ Get a StumbleUpon.com account for voting.

➤ Get a Digg.com account for voting, as well.

➤ Get an Upcoming.org account to promote events.

➤ Get a del.icio.us account for social bookmarking.

➤ Get a WordPress.com account for its OpenID benefits.

➤ Get a LinkedIn account for your professional network.

➤ Take a second look at Plaxo. It's changed for the better.

➤ Get a Gmail.com account for use with reader, calendar, docs, and more.

■ OUTPOSTS

➤ Build RSS outposts on Facebook. Add Flog Blog, and several other RSS tools.

➤ Build a similar outpost on MySpace, if your audience might be there.

➤ Make sure your social media is listed in your LinkedIn profile.

➤ Add a link to your blog to your e-mail signature file (this is still an outpost).

➤ Be sure your social network profiles on all sites have your blog listed, no matter where you have to put it to list it.

➤ Make sure your passport accounts (above) point to your blog and sites.

➤ Use social networks respectfully to share the best of your content, in a community-appropriate setting.

➤ Don't forget places like Yahoo! Groups, craigslist, and online forums.

➤ E-mail newsletters with some links to your blog make for an effective outpost, especially if your audience isn't especially blog savvy.

➤ Podcast content can have links to your URL and might draw awareness back to your content, too.

■ CONTENT

➤ Create new content regularly. If not daily, then at least three times a week.

➤ The more others can use your content, the better they will adopt it.

➤ Write brief pieces with lots of visual breaks for people to absorb.

➤ Images draw people's attention. Try to add a graphic per post. (Not sure why this works, but it seems to add some level of attention.)

➤ Mix up the kinds of pieces you put on your site. Interviews, how-to, newsish information, and more can help mix and draw more attention.

➤ Limit the number of "me too" posts you do in any given month to no more than three. Be original, in other words.

➤ The occasional "list" post is usually very good for drawing attention.

➤ Write passionately, but be brief (unless you're writing a list of 100 tips).

➤ Consider adding audio and video to the mix. The occasional You-Tube video with you as the star adds to your personal branding immensely, especially if you can manage to look comfortable.

➤ Brevity rules.

■ CONVERSATION

➤ Commenting on other people's blogs builds awareness fast.

➤ The more valuable your comments, the more they reflect on your ability and your character.

➤ Use your listening tools to stay active in pertinent discussions.

➤ Try not to brag, ever. Be humble. Not falsely so, but truly, because a lot of what we do isn't as important as saving lives.

➤ Ask questions with your blog posts. Defer to experts. Learn from the conversation.

➤ Be confident. Asking for external validation often is a sign of weakness.

➤ Good conversations can be across many blogs with links to show the way.

➤ Try never to be too defensive. Don't be a pushover, but be aware of how you present yourself when defending.

➤ Disclose anything that might be questionable. Anything, and quickly!

➤ Don't delete critical blog comments. Delete only spam, abrasive language posts, and offensive material. (Have a blog comments policy handy, if you get into the deleting mode.)

■ COMMUNITY

➤ Remember that community and marketplace are two different things.

➤ Make your site and your efforts heavily about other people. It comes back.

➤ Make it easy for your community to reach you.

➤ Contribute to your community's blogs and projects.

➤ Thank people often for their time and attention.

➤ Celebrate important information in your community (like birthdays).

➤ Be human. Always.

➤ Your community knows more than you. Ask them questions often.

➤ Apologize when you mess up. Be very sincere.

➤ Treat your community like gold. Never subject them to a third party of any kind without their consent.

➤ Knowing more about your competitors' communities is a useful thing, too. Learn who visits, why they visit, and how they interact.

➤ Measuring your efforts in building community grows out your brand as a natural extension.

■ FACE TO FACE

➤ Have simple, useful, crisp business cards to share. Always.

➤ Be confident in person.

➤ Clothes and appearance *do* matter. Wish they didn't, but they do.

➤ Have a very brief introduction/elevator pitch and practice it often.

➤ Ask questions of people you meet. Get to know them.

➤ Don't seek business relationships right off. Instead, seek areas of shared interest.

➤ Know when to walk away politely.

➤ Don't try to meet everyone in a room. Meet a half-dozen or more great new people.

➤ Never doubt that you are worth it.

➤ If you're terribly shy, consider finding a "wing man" for events.

➤ Doing homework ahead of time (finding people's most recent blog posts, Googling them, and so on) helps one feel in the know.

➤ Make eye contact. It's *much* more powerful than you know.

■ PROMOTION

➤ Use Digg, StumbleUpon, Del.icio.us, and Google Reader to drive awareness.

➤ Promote others even more than you promote yourself.

➤ Bragging isn't useful to anyone besides your own ego.

➤ Linking and promoting others is a nice way to show you care about people.

➤ Don't digg/stumble/link every single post. Save it for your very best.

➤ Another promotional tool: guest blog on other sites.

➤ Another promotional tool: Make videos on YouTube with URL links.

➤ Another promotional tool: Use the status section of LinkedIn and Facebook.

➤ Try hard not to send too many self-promotional e-mails. Wrap your self-promotion in something of value to others, instead.

➤ Sometimes, just doing really good work is worthy of others promoting you. Try it.

You probably have some great ideas to add to this. I'd love to hear what you want to add, or feel free to blog your own list and add value to the project that way. In any case, I hope this was helpful, and I wish you great success in your efforts to brand yourself and show the world what a rockstar you are.

■ ABOUT THE AUTHOR

Chris Brogan consults and speaks professionally with Fortune 100 and 500 companies like PepsiCo, General Motors, Microsoft, and more, on the future of business communications, and social software technologies. He is a *New York Times* best-selling coauthor of *Trust Agents* (John Wiley & Sons, Inc., 2010), and a featured monthly columnist at *Entrepreneur Magazine*. Chris's blog chrisbrogan.com, is in the Top 5 of the *Advertising Age* Power150. He has over 11 years experience in online community, social media, and related technologies.

Chris is president of New Marketing Labs, a new media marketing agency serving primarily Fortune 100 and 500 clients, and president of Human Business Works, an online education and community company for small businesses and solo entrepreneurs.

Chris is also the cofounder of the PodCamp new media conference series, exploring the use of new media community tools to extend and build value.

He has 16 years of enterprise telecommunications and wireless experience prior to all this.

Web Sites

www.chrisbrogan.com

Primary Products or Books

Trust Agents (John Wiley & Sons, Inc., 2010)

Chapter 4

Dewey, Cheatum & Howe, Inc.

John Carlton

"Rommel, you magnificent bastard! I read your book!"

—General Patton, ambushing Nazi's before they could ambush him.

Howdy . . .

Early Halloween memory: I'm getting ready to go extort candy from the neighbors with my older sister (cuz while I'm starting to suspect that Santa Claus ain't real, I'm still pretty convinced that ghosts and witches are out there, thus requiring a bodyguard) . . .

. . . and, putting my worldly experience to work, I choose the biggest bag available to carry my haul in.

Dreams of endless sugar-rushes have my five-year-old brain twitching like a junkie as we join the throngs of vandals and kids outside, and I'm raking it in.

However, just before calling it a night and heading home, I realize that my bag was a little TOO big . . . and I'd been dragging it along the ground, and all that glorious booty had fallen out in the street somewhere behind me.

The horror.

It was unfair. It violated every code of how kids should be treated by the universe that I knew about. It was a memory-scarring traumatic event.

I felt . . .

. . . *cheated*.

And I'm pretty sure that was my first lesson in empathy. Because it *sucked* to feel like I'd been cheated out of something.

Sucked, sucked, sucked. I'd headed out that evening snickering to myself about being so clever with the big bag . . . and . . . and . . .

Well, I can't even talk about it anymore. It's just too painful a memory.

And from that moment on, I have nodded in solidarity and sympathy whenever someone else was cheated. "Yeah," I'd say to myself. "Been there."

In fact, there are *three* lessons here:

■ LOSING ALL YOUR CANDY LESSON ONE

No one wants to be cheated. The burning shame and humiliation of realizing you've been gypped, or taken for a ride, or fooled *never* loses its intensity.

In fact, I think it gets worse as you get older.

As a kid, you cry and sink into despondence.

As adults, folks have been known to even scores with violence. (Think *road rage* . . . cuz someone soiled your honor by cutting you off in traffic. You want 'em dead. Doesn't matter that they're a nice, little old lady, who just didn't realize she pulled out in front of you. The complete and utter Wrath of God wouldn't be punishment enough for their trespass. *Grrrrr* . . .)

Here's how this manifests in marketing: Perhaps the biggest, baddest, and most hard-to-beat obstacle you will encounter when trying to persuade someone to take you up on your very fair, very generous, very drop-dead bargain of an offer . . .

. . . is that many people would rather *miss out* on a killer opportunity . . .

. . . than risk being cheated.

All the wonderfulness of your completely ethical, overdelivered and super-cool product is no match for even the remote possibility of being pitied, humiliated, or laughed at by a spouse, gloating buddy, or asshole neighbor.

This is why good salesmen spend so much time shoveling benefit-laden sound bites into pitches.

You need to "arm" your prospect with simple, memorable comebacks that deflect the hall of shame he fears might be tossed at him.

Because, you know, it's no secret that *all* advertising is bogus bullshit, and *anyone* who buys *anything* online is a fool, and I cannot believe you *fell* for that marketer's obvious nonsense.

What're you, a complete *sucker?*

This is why "the more you tell, the more you sell" remains such valuable advice.

Let prospects know what other people's experience was after buying. Confirm your credibility with endorsements, and make each feature come alive with benefits that resonate and nail the sweet spots of raw need.

Help him put the price in perspective, by clearly explaining how your offer stacks up against other options and the competition. Tell him what to expect in terms of results, and when to expect them.

Give him a well-lit road map to follow to get moving as quickly as possible. If it's a bargain, tell him why. If it's an investment in his success, tell him why. If there are risks, tell him what they are, and how he can mitigate them.

If there are flaws, reveal them. It will only make your case stronger by being honest and forthcoming.

Make your guarantee *shockingly* generous.

Pile up the bonuses so the bargain is both real and tangible.

In short . . . *be* that marketer you wish other biz owners would be when you deal with them.

Heck . . . if you can, arrange it so *you're* the one at risk of being cheated. *You* take all the risk. *You* overdeliver.

You give *him* every opportunity to take advantage of *you* . . . and rely on the strength of your product or service to convince him (through action and results) that you were worthy of being given the chance to prove yourself to him.

Give *him* the unfair advantage in this deal. Allow him to realize, on his own, that this really is a smart shopping decision and a genuine not-to-be-missed opportunity.

■ LOSING ALL YOUR CANDY LESSON TWO

Don't expect "logic" to win the day.

People are *so* sensitive to being on the losing end of a humiliating experience, that they will spin facts, truth, and reality to back up their actions.

Everybody spins. You spin. I spin. Mother Teresa and Gandhi spun. We spin to our good friends, to our enemies, to strangers, lovers, pets, and inanimate objects. ("C'mon," I've said to my car on a cold morning. "Start, just start today, that's all I ask . . . and I'll wash and wax you and spit-shine your chrome and . . ." Total spin. I've never waxed a car in my life. I just want the damn thing to start.)

But the biggest spin of all . . . is the spin we deliver to *ourselves*.

That's why I chose that quote from General George Patton up top. He was a student of *The Art of War*, and also devoted to the idea of "honor" among combatants.

So when he learned that Rommel was going to ambush him, he snuck his tanks into the desert and ambushed Rommel *first*.

In the movie, this comes right after a big Patton-esque blowhard speech about him wishing he and Rommel could just duel it out

alone, the two of them shaking hands and then fighting . . . and whoever won, won the war. Very honorable.

Then he goes out and *ambushes* the dude. And is near-orgasmic
as he crushes the Nazi columns.

Everybody wants the best possible deal. Everybody.

And that makes it logically impossible to create a deal that satis-
fies everyone . . .

. . . UNLESS you know how to enable the other guy to spin
things inside his head so he believes he scored huge.

Truth is often a casualty. I remember, long ago, witnessing another musician selling his guitar to someone he knew . . . these guys
KNEW each other . . . and the axe was worth ten times what he
wanted for it. But still the buyer negotiated hard, working him down
until it wasn't even a bargain any more . . . it was financial slaugh-
ter. But the seller needed the bread, so the deal went down.

And both guys worked it out in their minds that it was fair and
satisfying.

You have to just *let go of logic* when you're finalizing a sales process. A genuine good deal will be ignored if the prospect cannot square
up the price and value in his head, outside of rational equations.

Smart salesmen know that you can obliterate every obvious
objection in a prospect's mind, and still lose the sale . . .

. . . if you somehow *miss* what may be an unconscious objection
that defies logic.

This is why the great copywriters have always shoveled massive
payloads of bullets (explaining feature-benefit stories) into pitches.

You just never can predict *which* bullet will trigger that "Okay,
what the hell, let's do this deal" response.

■ LOSING ALL YOUR CANDY LESSON THREE

It should be abundantly clear by now that people will often act
against their own best self-interest.

Salesmen have known this for ages. So have politicians.

Academic types who study this stuff have proven, over and
over, that **people will consistently avoid immediate loss or pain
. . . even at the expense of long-term gain (in health, finances,
love, all of it).**

Pay attention to this: You may have the most generous offer in the
history of business, a killer bargain that will have your accountant
yelling at you for giving away so much . . .

. . . and you can lose the sale if your prospect feels any kind
of discomfort or pain—even a slight twinge of it—at the crucial
moment of decision.

Humans are just perverse creatures. Built for the jungle, but scurrying around society and civilization constantly at war with our own brains and desires and fears.

I've seen great products bomb and wonderful businesses wither and die . . .

. . . because no one understood how to deliver a sales message that dealt with the screwy suspicions of prospects.

We're ALL vulnerable to this stuff. Knowing that you're being illogical about feeling cheated won't stop the feeling. (As an aware, frosty Zen-type dude or dudette, of course, you will nevertheless confront these cockeyed distractions . . . but that's another story, for later.)

For now, don't judge yourself or your fellow humans. We're quirky, but still lovable and fun (when not in full-on "road rage" mode).

As a marketer, just pay more attention weaving a message that can help your prospect feel illogically okay about pulling out his wallet.

Hope you got to keep your candy from trick-or-treating this year.

Stay frosty,

John

P.S. *Side story:* I come from a family that looks hard for the "best" deal out there on everything they buy. My Pop's standard-operating-procedure, in fact, is to spend 6 months researching what he wants . . . buying it at a bargain so severe that tears well up in the seller's eyes . . . and then *continuing* to research for another 6 months after buying, just to make sure a better deal didn't get past him.

You gotta admire that kind of dedication to a bargain.

What's your story about being cheated? We all have them, and they set the tone for our adult objections to buying stuff.

Comment section is open for business . . .

P.P.S. Almost forgot . . . anybody remember where the title to this post (Dewey, Cheatum & Howe) comes from?

Seriously, guys. Somebody should nail this precisely (without resorting to Mr. Google, either, which is cheating) . . .

■ ABOUT THE AUTHOR

John's sales writing has been stalked for decades by many of the best (and most successful) marketers on the Internet, who freely admit using John's ads as templates for their own breakthrough pitches. And his marketing prowess is legendary.

They copy John's stuff because it works.

As a working freelance copywriter, John is one of a handful at the top of the game—commanding fees that cause unprepared clients to choke, consulting with the best marketers in the world, and consistently writing pitches that sell like crazy.

As a teacher of marketing-that-works, and writing killer sales messages for businesses, John is responsible for helping a verifiable mob of otherwise clueless entrepreneurs and small business owners get their act together.

Web Sites

www.john-carlton.com

Primary Products or Books

Simple Writing System

Kick-Ass Copywriting Secrets of a Marketing Rebel

Freelance Copywriter Course

Chapter 5

Five Ways to Avoid Small Business Marketing Complacency

Charlie Cook

Standing still is falling behind. I hope that 2010 was your best year ever and that your marketing brought in new business every week. If so, reward yourself and your employees for your successes, but don't let success make you complacent about your small business marketing plans and strategies.

To take your business to the next level in 2011, shift your focus to what isn't working with your marketing.

In an issue of *Fast Company*, Charles Fishman describes James Wiseman's experience as a newly hired section manager at a Toyota plant in the United States.

For the first couple of weeks, Wiseman joined the weekly plant meetings and shared the successes of his team, maybe even bragging a little. Instead of congratulations, his comments were met with an awkward silence. Finally, the plant manager took Wiseman aside. "We all know you are a good manager, otherwise we wouldn't have hired you. But please talk to us about your problems so we can all work on them together."

Toyota isn't satisfied with maintaining the status quo. Whether it's the quality of their products or the number of sales, it's the company's policy to look for ways to improve.

Make continual business marketing improvement your company policy. You'll find strategies, tactics, and detail plans to better your marketing results.

■ WANT TO SEE YOUR COMPANY'S PROFITS GROW EVERY YEAR?

If you want to improve on last year's results you'll need to improve on last year's marketing strategies and techniques. To do this you need to identify what is and isn't working with your small business marketing and what to change.

The key is to constantly experiment to discover how to improve on your existing performance. Each month, test a new idea against your existing strategy to continually identify better solutions.

■ HOW TO AVOID THE TRAP OF MARKETING COMPLACENCY WITH YOUR BUSINESS

1. Turn Marketing Problems into Opportunities

    Most people's marketing strategy is far from perfect, yet they use the same old tired strategies and ideas over and over. Break out of this stagnant cycle. Identify the imperfections in your marketing; there are your areas of opportunity.

2. Reward the Identification of Problems

    Praise employees who point out the problems in your marketing. Each problem you or they identify represents an opportunity to improve your lead generation and sales.

3. Seek Solutions

    Don't try to reinvent the wheel on your own. Ask for help from the people you work with. If they don't have the answer, seek out an expert.

4. Improve Your Performance

    Based on the number of leads or sales you generated last quarter or last year, set higher, specific goals for this year. You could start with the response rate to your ads or the conversion rates of your web pages or your closing rates.

5. Make Small Fixes Every Week

    There is no magic pill for success. Companies like Toyota didn't become world leaders overnight. It took years of continual improvement. Improve your marketing each month by making small changes. Over time the small improvements will result in large increases in sales.

■ NOT SURE WHAT TO FIX?

Ready to ditch marketing complacency and embrace small business marketing perfection, but not sure where to start? Here are the most common areas of opportunity:

➤ Understand what your prospects want

    ➤ When was the last time you did a survey or asked your prospects why they buy your products or services?

➤ Lead generation

    ➤ How many did you generate last month? Do you know what's limiting the response to your marketing?

    ➤ Is your copy working?

    ➤ Is your layout effective?

    ➤ Do the images support the message?

    ➤ How could you double your response rate?

➤ Conversion rates

    ➤ What percentage of your prospects become paying clients? What's getting in the way of converting twice as many?

    ➤ Is your offer working?

    ➤ Is your follow-up system working?

    ➤ Why aren't more people buying?

If you've started off 2011 marketing the same way you did in 2010, you'll generate the same results at best.

Are you satisfied with this? Or are you one of those people who is always looking for a better way: a better way to help your clients and customers and a better way to make more money?

■ ABOUT THE AUTHOR

Back in the 1990s, Charlie Cook launched his first web site. He started researching how the search engines rank sites and how to put his sites at the top. Each time he found an idea, he tested it and looked for ways to make it work even better.

The result was one of the first books on how to market sites to the search engines. Charlie then created a web site that reviewed and ranked search engines. His reference web site Searchiq.com was featured on National Public Radio, in *Fast Company* and *USA Today*, and ranked in the top 100 web sites by *PC Magazine*.

Over the last 20 years he's been providing marketing and management consulting services to Fortune 500 companies, midsized companies, publications, and numerous small businesses.

His training manuals have been used by executives, managers, and trainers at hundreds of Fortune 500 companies including AT&T, Merck, Chevron, IBM, and Boeing.

Web Sites

www.marketingforsuccess.com

www.Searchiq.com

Primary Products or Books

Insider Secrets to 15 Second Marketing

Insider Secrets to Attracting More and Better Customers

Insider Secrets to Creating Websites that Sell

Chapter 6

Ten Internet Marketing Rules to Live By

Terry Dean

Here are 10 simple Internet marketing rules to live by. Post them to your desk. Use them every day.

1. **Invest Small When Starting Anything New**

   Always invest small when starting out. It's possible any ad you run may lose money. Always keep your risks and investment small whenever you're starting a new type of advertising. Even if you had that top-level copywriter write your ad, not everything they write will be a home run. It may need a few changes to produce the results you want. The market you're advertising to may not be perfect. There is no such thing as a Sure Thing.

2. **Test Everything**

   Only one expert is right, and it's not me. It's your own personal test results. Test headlines. Test the length of your ad copy. Test audio and video on your sales page. Test a squeeze page before visitors get to the sales site. Constantly run two ads on Adwords for every ad group. Test a "try before you buy" offer. Test telephone follow-up. Quit blindly following gurus and test everything!

3. **Be Unique**

   Don't ever be a me-too business. Take a look at everyone in your marketplace. What is different about you from them? Here's a quick exercise. Write down all the benefits someone gets from your product or service. Now cross off all the benefits they can also get from other people's products and services. What's left? If nothing is left, you may need to rethink or modify what you offer to provide something unique in your marketplace.

4. Target Your Ads Only to Buyers

You've chosen your niche, but do you write your ads to all your visitors? No. You will never achieve a 100 percent buying rate. Much more common is 1 percent . . . and 10 percent is extremely high (possible at times with strong follow-up). This means at least 90 percent of your web site visitors are *not* your target audience even though they came to your site. You're not writing to them. It doesn't matter if those people like what you write at all. You're writing only to the *buyers* . . . that 1 to 10 percent of your unique visitors who will take action.

5. Develop a Backend from the Beginning

You should already have a basic idea or outline for your next offer before your first one is done. If your first product is an ebook or CD, what will you offer next? You may start your backend by offering joint venture deals and affiliate offers from others. The money in any business comes from repeat purchases and backend sales. In fact, I'd never want to be in any business where I *had* to make money from one product. It destroys your marketing ability. If your competitor can break even or even lose money on their advertising, how can you compete if you have to make a living off the same offer?

6. Your Network Determines Your Net Worth

First heard that expression from Mark Victor Hansen. Strategic Alliances, social networking, referrals, viral marketing, and so on are the key to building your business online. Going it alone is a recipe for failure. In most businesses, affiliates make up 50 percent to 75 percent of sales. Incoming links from other sites are the key to search engine optimization. Find ways to serve the other top players in your niche. Network. Mastermind. Grow together . . . even with competitors.

7. Don't Restrict Your Business to Internet Only

You're not an Internet business. You're an Internet-based business. Develop your business model with both Internet and offline strategies. Follow up on customers by phone. Here's a quick tip—call people who just purchased from you to thank them for their order and also offer them something else at a discount price right now (I've seen people increase profits by 40 percent from that alone). Send direct mail to your customers. Rent a targeted mailing list and send postcards to drive people to sign up for your list. Use offline publicity and networking to generate leads.

8. Build Your Relationship with Your Lists

Yes, I said "lists," not "list." Concentrate on educating your list members . . . both with good content and about your products/services. Use online follow-up methods such as e-mail and be willing to use direct mail. Send thank you cards to JV partners and customers. Run a teleconference where you meet with your customers or prospects. Create a blog. Put a face on your company and let them get to know you as a person.

9. Focus on Your Gifts

Focus your time and attention on what you're best at. There's dozens of ways to market your site. Concentrate on the ones that most fit with your style and skill set. If you hate writing, then don't use writing as your primary advertising method. Or hire out the writing. Figure out what skills you have . . . and focus on those. Outsource the rest to others. If you try to force yourself to be just like "Guru Number One," it's simply going to be an exercise in frustration. You're unique. Build a unique business suited to you.

10. Plan for the Long Haul

I'm sure you've been told about instant riches overnight. Quit trying for that. And quit trying to jump on the "new thing." Pick a business and work on it. Yes, I said work . . . that dirty four-letter word so many people hate. Things might not go right when you first start. You might have to modify a few elements of your presentation. You might have to change your product. To be successful in this business requires that you have a backbone and stick to it even when things don't go your way! Develop at least a one-year plan with daily actions to push you to success. You'll make modifications along the way, but at least you have a basic road map of where you're going.

■ ABOUT THE AUTHOR

Terry Dean started his online business from scratch in 1996. He went from delivering pizzas for a living to building a million-dollar Internet business promoted primarily through the Internet. Within a few years he was also consulting with home-based businesses, local companies, and million-dollar corporations. His original company and web sites were sold in 2004, and he founded MyMarketingCoach, LLC, which is dedicated to coaching entrepreneurs in the 10 key principles of success in business and life.

Web Sites

www.terrydean.org

Primary Products or Books

Monthly Mentor Club

Blogging for Fun and Profit DVDs

Internet Lifestyle Retirement System

Chapter 7

Forget Benefits, and You Will Sell More

Michel Fortin

What's the single, most important element in copywriting?

Let me say it another way.

You've done your research. You found a starving market. Your product fills a need. And your sales copy shines with benefits. If everything is so perfect, then why is your product still *not* selling? Is it the price? The offer? The competition?

Maybe. But not necessarily.

The fact is, these things are not always to blame for being unable to sell an in-demand product, even with great copy. Too often, it has more to do with one thing:

Focus. (Or should I say, the lack thereof?)

In fact, the greatest word in copywriting is not "free." It's "focus." And what you focus on in your copy is often the single, greatest determinant of your copy's success.

In my experience, copy that brings me the greatest response is copy that focuses on:

1. One message

2. One market

3. One outcome

Here's what I mean . . .

■ ONE MESSAGE

The copy doesn't tell multiple, irrelevant stories. It doesn't make multiple offers. It doesn't go on tangential topics or provide extra information that doesn't advance the sale.

Copy should make one offer and one offer only.

Too many messages confuse the reader. And as copywriter Randy Gage once noted, "The confused mind never buys." It confuses them because they don't know which offer provides them with the best value for the amount of money they are ready to spend.

Prospects want to spend their money wisely. Lose focus, and it is harder to think clearheadedly to make a wise decision in the first place. Remember this axiom:

Give people too many choices and they won't make one.

You don't want to do what my teenage daughter does to me. When we go shopping for a dress, after hours of flipping through hangers and racks, she finally pinpoints one she likes, goes to the changing room to try it on, looks at me and asks, "How's this one?"

"Perfect!" I say. "You sure, Dad?" She asks. "Yes," I add. "I'm positive." So we head to the cash register when, suddenly, she stops along the way, picks up another dress off the rack, and says, "How about this one? Or maybe this one? Oooh, look at this other one!"

We came really close to walking out of that store without buying any of the dresses.

■ ONE MARKET

I don't want to spend the little space I have for this article to extol the virtues of niche marketing. But when it comes to writing high-converting sales messages, it goes without saying: Trying to be all things to all people is next to *impossible*.

When it is possible, then your sales message must be generic enough to appeal to everyone, causing the majority in your market to feel you're not focused on them.

(There's that word "focus" again!)

In order to appeal to everyone, your sales message will be heavily diluted. It will lose clarity. People will feel left out because you're too vague. You will appear indifferent to their situation, and to their specific needs and goals, too.

If you cater to a large, diversified market, I highly encourage that you segment your market and target each segment separately, and write copy that caters to each one.

That is, write copy for each individual and targeted group of people within your market. If your market is made up of two or three (or more) identifiable market groups, write copy for each one—even if the product is the same for everyone.

■ ONE OUTCOME

"Click here," "read my about page," "here's a link to some testimonials," "call this number," "fill out this form," "don't buy now, just think about it," "here are my other web sites," "here are 41 other products to choose from," and on and on . . . Ack!

When people read your sales copy, and if your copy is meant to induce sales, then you want one thing and one thing only: get the sale! In other words, there's only one thing your readers should do, and that's buy. Or at least your copy should lead them to buy.

In other words, the ultimate outcome should be to buy—every call to action, every piece of copy, every page, every graphic should revolve around this one outcome.

Remember K.I.S.S. (i.e., "keep it straightforwardly simple").

You would be surprised at how many salesletters I critique where the author asks the reader to do too many things, to choose from too many things, or to jump through so many hoops to get the very thing they want in the first place.

Your copy should focus on one call to action only, or one ultimate outcome. Forget links to other web sites or pages that are irrelevant to the sale. Forget irrelevant forms and distractions. Why invite procrastination with too many calls to action?

In fact, I believe that the goal is *not* to elicit action but to *prevent procrastination*.

Because when people hit your web site, whether they found you on a search engine after searching for information, were referred to you by someone else, or read about you somewhere online, then they are, in large part, interested from the get-go.

So your job is not to get them to buy, really. They're already interested. They're ready to buy. Your job (i.e., your copy's job), therefore, is to get them *not* to go away.

Ultimately, focus on the reader. One, single reader.

This is probably the thing you need to focus on the most. The most common blunders I see being committed in copy is the *lack of focus* in a sales message, particularly on the individual reading the copy and the value you specifically bring to them.

In my experience as a copywriter, I find that some people put too much emphasis on the product, the provider, and even the market (as a whole), and not enough on the most important element in a sales situation: the *customer*.

That is, the individual reading the copy at that very moment.

Don't focus your copy on your product and the features of your product—and on how good, superior, or innovative they are. And don't even focus on the benefits.

Instead, focus on *increasing perceived value* with them. Why? Because perception is personal. It's intimate. It's egocentric. Let me explain.

When you talk about your product, you're making a broad claim. Everyone makes claims, especially online. "We're number one," "we offer the highest quality," "it's our best version yet," and so on. (Often, my reaction is, "So what?")

And describing benefits is just as bad.

Benefits are too broad, in my opinion. You were probably taught that a feature is what a product *has* and a benefit is what that feature *does*. Right? But even describing benefits is, in my estimation, making a broad claim, too.

The adage goes, "Don't sell quarter-inch drills, sell quarter-inch holes."

But holes alone don't mean a thing to someone who might have different uses, reasons, or needs for that hole. So you need to translate benefits into more meaningful benefits.

You see, a claim always looks self-serving. It also puts you in a *precarious position*, as it lessens your perceived value and makes your offer suspect—the opposite of what you're trying to accomplish by making claims in the first place.

Therefore, don't focus on the benefits of a certain feature. Rather, focus on how those features *specifically benefit* the individual. Directly. Personally. Intimately.

There is a difference. A *big* difference.

The more you explain what those claims specifically mean to the prospect, the more you will sell. It's not the features that count, and it's not even benefits. It's the perceived value. *So how do you build perceived value?*

The most common problem I see when people attempt to describe benefits is when what they are really describing are advantages—or glorified features, so to speak. Real benefits are far more personal and intimate.

That's why I prefer to use this continuum:

Features → Advantages → Benefits

Of course, a feature is what a product has. And an advantage (or what most people think is a benefit) is what that feature does. But . . .

. . . *A benefit is what that feature means.*

A benefit is what a person intimately gains from a specific feature. When you describe a feature, say this: "What this means to you, Mr. Prospect, is this (. . .)," followed by a more personal gain your reader gets from using the feature.

Let me give you a real-world example.

A client once came to me for a critique of her copy. She sold an antiwrinkle facial cream. It's often referred to as "microdermabrasion."

Her copy had features and some advantages, but no benefits. In fact, here's what she had:

Features

1. It reduces wrinkles.

2. It comes in a do-it-yourself kit.

3. And it's pH-balanced.

Advantages

1. It reduces wrinkles, so it makes you look younger.

2. It comes in a kit, so it's easy to use at home.

3. And it's pH balanced, so it's gentle on your skin.

This is what people will think a benefit is, such as "younger," "easy to use," and "gentle." But they are general. Vague. They're not specific and intimate enough. So I told her to add these benefits to her copy. . . .

Benefits

1. It makes you look younger, *which means* you will be more attractive, you will get that promotion or recognition you always wanted, you will make them fall in love with you all over again, they will never guess your age, and so on.

2. It's easy to use at home, *which means* you don't have to be embarrassed—or waste time and money—with repeated visits to the doctor's office. . . . It's like a facelift in a jar done in the privacy of your own home!

3. It's gentle on your skin, *which means* there are no risks, pain, or long healing periods often associated with harsh chemical peels, surgeries, and injections.

Now, those are benefits!

Remember, copywriting is "salesmanship in print." You have the ability to put into words what you normally say in a person-to-person situation. If you were to explain what a feature means during an encounter, why not do so in copy?

The more benefit-driven you are, *the more you will sell.* In other words, the greater the perceived value you present, the greater the desire for your product will be. And if they really want your product, you'll make a lot of money.

It's that simple.

In fact, like a face-to-face, one-on-one sales situation (or as we say in sales training, being "belly to belly" with your prospect), you need to denominate as specifically as possible the *value* your offer brings to your readers.

In other words, express the benefits of your offer in *terms* that relate directly not only to your market, but also and more importantly:

1. To each individual in that market

2. To each individual's situation

Don't focus on your product. Focus on your readers. Better yet, focus on how the benefits of your offer appeal to the person that's reading them. And express how your offer benefits your prospects in terms they can intimately relate to, too.

Look at it this way:

➤ Use terms the prospect is used to, appreciates, and fully understands. (The mind thinks in relative terms. That's why the use of analogies, stories, examples, metaphors, and testimonials is so important! Like "facelift in a jar," for example.)

➤ Address your reader directly and forget third-person language. Don't be afraid to use "you," "your," and "yours," as well as "I," "me," "my," and "mine." Speak to your reader as if in a personal conversation with her.

➤ Use terms that trigger their hormones, stroke their egos, tug their heartstrings, and press their hot buttons. You don't need to use puffery with superlative-laden copy. Just speak to your reader at an intimate level. An *emotional* level.

Because the worst thing you can do, second to making broad claims, is to express those claims broadly. Instead, appeal to their ego. Why? Because . . .

. . . *We are all human beings.*

Eugene Schwartz, author of *Breakthrough Advertising* (Boardroom Classics, 1984), one of the best books on copywriting, once noted we are not far evolved from chimpanzees. "Just far enough to be dangerous to ourselves," copywriter Peter Stone once noted.

He's not alone. My friend and copywriter Paul Myers was once asked during an interview, "Why do people buy from long, hypey copy?" His short answer was, "Human beings are only two feet away from the cave."

(Speaking of Eugene Schwartz, listen to his speech. It's the best keynote speech on copywriting. *Ever*. Click here to listen to it. You can also get a copy of his book, too, called *Breakthrough Advertising* [Boardroom Classics, 1984]. I have read mine several times already.)

People buy for personal wants and desires and for selfish reasons above all. Whether you sell to consumers or businesses, *people are people are people*. It's been that way for millions of years.

And nothing's changed.

Your message is just a bunch of words. But words are symbols. Different words mean different things to different people. Look at it this way: while a picture is worth a thousand words, a word is worth a thousand pictures.

And the words you choose can also be *worth a thousand sales.*

■ ABOUT THE AUTHOR

Michel Fortin is a direct-response copywriter, author, speaker, and consultant. Visit his blog and sign up free to get blog updates by e-mail, along with response-boosting tips, tested conversion strategies, the latest news, free advice, additional resources, and a lot more! Go now to www.michelfortin.com. While you're at it, follow him on Twitter: http://twitter.com/michelfortin.

Web Sites

www.michelfortin.com

www.successdoctor.com

Primary Products or Books

The Death of the Salesletter (blog)

Chapter 8

Ten Common Mistakes Exhibitors Make

Susan Friedmann

We all make mistakes; however, if we are aware of the pitfalls that can occur, there is a better chance we can avoid errors that, more often than not, can be fairly costly. The following are 10 of the most common mistakes that exhibitors make preshow, at-show, and postshow:

■ PRESHOW

1. *Failing to set exhibiting goals.* Goals, or the purpose for exhibiting, are the essence of the whole trade show experience. Knowing what you want to accomplish at a show will help plan every other aspect—your theme, the booth layout and display, graphics, product displays, premiums, literature, and so on. Exhibiting goals should complement your corporate marketing objectives and help in accomplishing them.

2. *Forgetting to read the exhibitor manual.* The exhibitor manual is your complete reference guide to every aspect of the show and your key to saving money. Admittedly, some show managements make these easier to read than others. Albeit, everything you need to know about the show you are participating in, should be contained in the manual—show schedules, contractor information, registration, service order forms, electrical service, floor plans and exhibit specifications, shipping and freight services, housing information, advertising and promotion. Remember that the floor price for show services is normally 10 to 20 percent higher, so signing up early will always give you a significant savings.

3. *Leaving graphics to the last minute.* Rush, change, and overtime charges will add significantly to your bottom line. Planning your graphics in plenty of time—six to eight weeks before show time will be less stressful for everyone concerned and avoid many blunders that occur under time pressures.

4. *Neglecting booth staff preparation.* Enormous time, energy, and money are put into organizing show participation—display, graphics, literature, premiums, and so on. However, the people chosen to represent the entire image of the organization are often left to fend for themselves. They are just told to show up. This team consists of your ambassadors and should be briefed beforehand—why you are exhibiting, what you are exhibiting, and what you expect from them. Exhibit staff training is essential for a unified and professional image.

■ AT-SHOW

5. *Ignoring visitors' needs.* Often staff members feel compelled to give the visitor as much information as possible. They fail to ask about real needs and interest in the product/service. They lack questioning skills and often miss important qualifying information. Preshow preparation and training is the key.

6. *Handing out literature and premiums.* Staff members who are unsure of what to do in the booth environment or feel uncomfortable talking to strangers, end up handing out literature or giveaway items just to keep occupied. Literature acts as a barrier to conversation and chances are, will be discarded at the first opportunity. It is vital that people chosen to represent the organization enjoy interacting with strangers and know what is expected of them in the booth environment.

7. *Being unfamiliar with demonstrations.* Many times staffers show up for duty only to discover they are totally unfamiliar with booth demonstrations. Communicate with your team members before the show and ensure that demonstrators know what is being presented and are familiar with the equipment and how to conduct the assigned demonstrations.

8. *Overcrowding the booth with company representatives.* Companies often send several representatives to major industry shows to gather competitive and general/specific industry information. These people feel compelled to gather at the company booth not only outnumbering visitors, but also monopolizing staffer time and restricting visitor interaction. Have strict rules regarding employees visiting the show and insist staffers not scheduled for booth duty stay away until their assigned time. Company executives are often the worst offenders. Assign specific tasks to avoid them fumbling around the booth.

■ POSTSHOW

9. *Ignoring lead follow-up.* Show leads often take second place to other management activities that occur after being out of the office for several days. The longer leads are left unattended, the colder and more mediocre they become. Prior to the show, establish how leads will be handled, set timelines for follow-up, and make sales representatives accountable for leads given to them.

10. *Overlooking show evaluation.* The more you know and understand about your performance at shows, the more improvement and fine-tuning can take place for future shows. No two shows are alike. Each has its own idiosyncrasies and obstacles. There is always room for improvement. Invest the time with your staff immediately after each show to evaluate your performance. It pays enormous dividends.

■ ABOUT THE AUTHOR

For over 25 years, Susan Friedmann, CSP, has traveled the world helping companies put their best foot forward at trade shows and events. Working with organizations who want to grow their trade show marketing strategies, Susan offers trade show booth staff training programs that increase results and focus on building better relationships with customers, prospects, and advocates in the marketplace.

Susan is an exciting, dynamic speaker who delivers top-notch presentations designed to inform, excite, and motivate groups of every size.

A prolific author, Susan has written 12 books including *Meeting and Event Planning For Dummies* (For Dummies, 2003), *Riches in Niches: How to Make it BIG in a Small Market* (Career Press, May 10, 2007), made it to number one in hot business books on Amazon. com, and her latest book, *The Complete Idiot's Guide to Target Marketing* (Alpha, 2009). Many of Susan's books have been translated into several languages, and her trade show booth staff training materials are used worldwide.

Web Sites

http://thetradeshowcoach.com

http://thetradeshowcoachblog.com

Primary Products or Books

The Complete Idiot's Guide to Target Marketing (Alpha, 2009).

Riches in Niches: How to Make it BIG in a Small Market (Career Press, May 10, 2007)

Meeting and Event Planning For Dummies (For Dummies, 2003)

Chapter 9

Build a Killer Media List

Rick Frishman

Media lists are databases containing the names and information about people and organizations that can help promote your business, product, or service. They're your Rolodex, Palm Pilot, and address book. They're the roster listing who is in your network.

When it comes to media lists, collect as many names as possible. The more names included on your media list, the greater your chances of getting your story told. It's simple mathematics: If you send a press release to 200 equivalent media contacts, it's more likely that your story will be picked up than if it just goes to 20 contacts. It's the old theory of throwing lots of mud on the wall and hoping that some of it sticks . . . plus, you never know just where it will stick and which contact will be interested in your story.

Start compiling a media list by including the names of all contacts who might conceivably publicize, or help promote, your business, product, or service. Don't be overly selective. The most remote, seemingly unlikely, contacts in totally unrelated fields may fall in love with your story and move mountains to promote it. Or they may refer you to others who can help.

Your media list should contain the contact's:

- ➤ Name
- ➤ Employer
- ➤ Street address
- ➤ E-mail address
- ➤ Telephone
- ➤ Back-up telephone numbers
- ➤ Specialty area

➤ Source information such as how you got the name, how and where you met, and friends or associates in common

➤ Miscellaneous information such projects pitched, projects bought, dates you last spoke, and the results

■ START NOW

It's never too soon to start a media list. A media list is always a work in progress and is never a finished product. Your media list is something you'll always be adding to, updating, and revising.

➤ Begin creating a media list now, even though you may not even have the idea for a business. Jot down the names of members of the media and interesting people. Write down why they're of interest and how they might help.

➤ Form the habit of making notes and collecting names. Carry a small notebook or a PDA at all times and keep notebooks in your car, briefcase, and purse. Always carry a pen . . . even if you're out jogging.

➤ List the names of whoever might remotely help: writers, reporters, editors, radio and TV producers, and publicists. Study the media to discover who's covering your field and add them to your list.

➤ Ask your friends, family, and business associates for names to add to your list. Get introductions or permission to use their names when you call.

➤ Call local newspapers and magazines, as well as radio and TV stations and e-mail online publications for the names of editors, reporters, and producers who cover areas that could help you.

➤ Ask everyone you meet for their business cards.

➤ Toss all your notebook entries and business cards into a bowl, a shoe box or a file drawer. Set aside a specific time each week (for example, every Monday at 9 AM) to organize, add new entries, and revise your list. Insert comments on how you met, mutual friends or contacts, and any other information that might break the ice when you contact them.

■ UPDATE CONSTANTLY

Update your media list on an ongoing basis. Every three months, at the least, review the entire list from top to bottom. In most media jobs, the pay stinks so the turnover is huge. Unless you keep your list current, you'll end up wasting time and energy trying to contact people who have long gone.

■ ABOUT THE AUTHOR

Rick Frishman, the founder of Planned Television Arts, has been one of the leading book publicists in America for over 30 years.

He is publisher at Morgan James Publishing in New York. Rick has also appeared on hundreds of radio shows and more than a dozen TV shows nationwide including *Oprah* and *Bloomberg TV.* He has also been featured in the *New York Times,* the *Wall Street Journal, Associated Press, Selling Power Magazine, New York Post,* and scores of publications.

He is the coauthor of 10 books, including national best-sellers *Guerrilla Publicity* (SpeakerNet News, 2007) and *Networking Magic* (Adams Media, 2004). Along with Robyn Freedman Spizman, Rick also cowrote the four-book series *Author 101* (Adams Media, 2005) and *Where's Your Wow? 16 Ways to Make Your Competitors Wish They Were You!* (McGraw-Hill, 2008).

He is the cohost (with attorney Richard Solomon) of the radio show *Taking Care of Business,* which airs every Thursday from 2:00–3:00 PM on WCWP-Radio in Long Island, New York.

Web Sites

www.rickfrishman.com

Primary Products or Books

Where's Your Wow? 16 Ways to Make Your Competitors Wish They Were You! (McGraw-Hill, 2008)

Guerrilla Publicity (SpeakerNet News, 2007)

Networking Magic (Adams Media, 2004)

Chapter 10

Two Businesses, One Marketing Plan

Bob Gilbreath

Can you imagine bringing together two different businesses for a single advertisement? Say Bud Light and GEICO create a Super Bowl ad together, or a local clothing retailer and a delicatessen join up to coinvest in a Yellow Pages ad. It's a strange idea, but it's not so unusual in a world in which marketing is more about adding value to customers' lives. Many businesses are discovering a way to drive efficiency, sales, and happier customers by joining with other businesses around their common interests. This is one example of how the future of marketing will look a lot different—and a lot better—than the past.

Success with marketing increasingly does not lie in crafting new and better ways of placing advertisements in front of a customer. That traditional model is falling apart thanks to people's growing use of digital technology. In a world of growing customer control, the only thing we as businesses can do to attract people and grow sales is to create advertising that people choose to engage with and marketing that itself improves people's lives; a concept I call "Marketing with Meaning."

When you think about how your marketing can add value, seemingly strange ideas like partnering with another business suddenly make sense. Two businesses working together can create a better, combined solution or experience that benefits their joint customers and bottom lines.

For example, each year my suburban township holds a "Daddy-Daughter Dance." The dance is such a big event that it actually stretches over two nights to accommodate all of the demand. Herein lays an opportunity for relevant local businesses to band together, making the experience even greater for all and to sell heaps in the process. A men's clothier and a children's clothing store could combine to host a fashion show for fathers and daughters to pick out ties and dresses.

The core idea of marketing with meaning is that businesses must take a step back and consider the higher-level needs of your customers. People don't visit a restaurant for a meal—they actually want to have a lovely night out. Therefore a restaurant owner might partner with local theaters and babysitting services to help deliver on this need. People trust their accountant with their taxes, but they have higher-level needs for income security and professional advice on life changes. Therefore an accountant might team up with a personal attorney to offer a seminar on retirement planning and living wills.

Before moving forward with a partnership, make sure that both your target customer base and business cultures overlap. Building a strong, personal relationship with your partner business is crucial— so if you don't feel trust, back away quickly.

And don't limit yourself to other small businesses. Even large companies and brands may be willing to partner. Specifically look for those with a strong local presence and desire to bond with the community. For example, recently at my neighborhood Starbucks the store allowed a personal trainer to hand out fliers offering a free class.

Whether it's a Starbucks store manager or a fellow entrepreneur at a community luncheon, it costs nothing to reach out and pitch the possibility of partnership. Just make sure you know what's in it for them, for you and for your joint customer. You just might reach a new audience, lower your marketing costs, and create something that customers rave about.

■ ABOUT THE AUTHOR

Bob Gilbreath is chief strategy officer of Possible Worldwide, a WPP digital and relationship marketing agency, and author of the new book, *The Next Evolution of Marketing: Connect with your Customers by Marketing with Meaning* (McGraw-Hill, 2009). The Next Evolution of Marketing can be applied to billion-dollar brands or small businesses, to consumer marketers and B2B firms, in both highly developed markets and developing nations around the world. He blogs regularly at www.marketingwithmeaning.com and can be found on Twitter at @mktwithmeaning.

Bob joined Bridge Worldwide after leading a dramatic turnaround of the Mr. Clean brand at Procter & Gamble. He was recognized by *Advertising Age* as one of the Top 50 Marketers of 2004.

Web Sites

www.marketingwithmeaning.com

Primary Products or Books

The Next Evolution of Marketing: Connect with Your Customers by Marketing with Meaning (McGraw-Hill, 2009)

Relevancy Rules for Google (and for You, Too)

Aaron Goldman

Why do you Google?

Because you're looking for something, right?

Ah, but it's not that simple, is it?

Why are you looking for something?

Because you're researching a project at work?

Bored?

Maybe trying to figure out where to eat dinner tonight?

There are three main reasons we search—information, entertainment, and commerce. We're either looking for something to know, do, or buy.

Of course, there's a fourth reason that accounts for countless search queries each month—navigation. Did you mistake the search box for the address bar? Trust a search engine to get you there faster than a browser? Don't worry, you're not alone—the most popular searches each month are "Facebook," "craigslist," "YouTube," "MySpace," and, yep, "Google."

Regardless of why people search, there's one common theme—decision making.

Whether you're looking for something to know, do, or buy, or a quick way to navigate the Web, you're making a decision. Where can I find accurate information about geothermal energy? Is there a video, preferably featuring a cat, that will keep me entertained for the next five minutes? Is there a restaurant within walking distance where I can buy a hamburger? What's the fastest way to get to Facebook.com?

In each case, you're faced with a decision, and today the most popular way to make that decision—assuming you have access to a

computer or cell phone—is to Google it. In fact, according to com-
Score, 65 to 70 percent of all searches conducted around the globe
are done through Google sites.

So, if you have a decision to make, you turn to Google. More
times than not, the web sites you find via Google will help you make
that decision. Of course, who gets all the credit for having helped you
make that decision? Certainly not the keywords chosen or the web
sites listed. All praise be to Big G. Studies have shown that when people don't find what they're looking for on Google, they blame themselves and their poor query choices, not Google.

Why is this?

I can just picture Microsoft CEO Steve Ballmer channeling his
inner Jan Brady and whining, "All I hear all day long is how great
Google is at this or how wonderful Google did that. Google, Google,
Google!"

When Microsoft launched its Bing search engine in June 2009, it
was branded as a "decision engine." Clearly, the folks in Redmond
had the insight that what drives people to search is the fundamental
need to make a decision. That, along with an estimated $80 million
ad campaign, has propelled Bing to a 30 percent increase in search
market share through February 2010. However, Bing still only serves
up a little over one-tenth of the overall pie, with Google enjoying
roughly two-thirds.

So, why Google?

There's only one relevant answer—relevancy. Google simply
provides the most relevant results. Suffice it to say for now, that the
Google algorithm effectively harnesses all the collective knowledge
on the Web. But the truth is, Google doesn't show the most relevant
results for every single query. WolframAlpha often shows better
results for quick facts. Many people think Bing has better image results. And Facebook shows results from your friends' status updates.
But, generally speaking, across an aggregate of all types of searches,
Google provides the most relevant results. Accordingly, the Big G has
benefited from a strong halo effect.

Research has shown that if you put the Google logo on another
search engine's results, people will report a much higher relevancy
score. It doesn't even matter if Google provides the most relevant results. In search, as in life, perception is reality.

But Google is often credited with much more than just returning
relevant results. Google is seen as being a decision maker—or, at
least, facilitating decision making. By providing a solution to this
fundamental human need, Google makes itself relevant to the
masses.

According to Avinash Kaushik, author of *Web Analytics 2.0*,
cofounder of Market Motive Inc., and Google's "analytics evangelist," relevancy is "perhaps the singular reason for Google's success."

Avinash marvels at the fact that Google "still today continues to not show ads on a vast majority of terms [if it has] no relevant ads or show ads that might earn less money but are more relevant to the search query by the user." He astutely observes that this is "hard to imagine now in a world of companies wanting to hyper monetize every pair of eyeballs."

This is your challenge as a marketer. How do you make yourself relevant? How do you enable your customers and prospects to make better decisions?

Of course, one good way to become relevant is to get your brand to the top of Google for queries related to your business. After all, if a tree falls in a forest and no one's there to hear it, does it really make a sound? Similarly, if you offer a great product or service but no one can find you, do you really offer a great product or service?

In order to become relevant, you must show people how you can help them solve a problem or make a decision. This is what Google looks for when it decides what web sites to rank and in what order.

When a query is submitted, Google scans trillions of pages across the haystack that is the Web trying to find the ones that are most relevant to that specific topic. As part of this process, Google looks for signals of relevance across a number of different criteria—the title of that page, the copy on that page, the images on that page, the links pointing to that page, the date that page was created, the frequency at which that page is updated, and so forth.

Ultimately, what is Google looking for? A page that's been around for a while, with frequent updates, and, most important, is all about that particular topic and only that topic. Assuming all else is equal—and that's a big assumption—if two web sites cover geothermal energy but one also includes info about five other energy sources on its home page, the one that sticks to geothermal energy will get the top spot for the query "geothermal energy."

In turn, a good rule of thumb for marketers trying to get to the top of Google and build a relevant brand is to corner the market on one particular niche. Give off all the different signals of relevance. Make yourself indispensible to people trying to make a decision that involves your product or service. Make yourself the Google of your category. And then branch out from there.

■ ABOUT THE AUTHOR

Aaron Goldman is Chief Marketing Officer at Kenshoo, a digital marketing software company that engineers global technology solutions for search marketing and online advertising. Kenshoo powers 5 of the world's top 10 retailers and 8 of the 10 largest ad agency networks.

Prior to Kenshoo, Goldman founded Connectual, a digital marketing consulting and matchmaking firm, helping companies like Omnicom Media Group with marketing, business development, and recruiting.

Before starting Connectual, Goldman served as vice president of marketing and strategic partnerships at Resolution Media. During his nearly five-year tenure on the executive team, Goldman managed corporate marketing, industry relations, and new business development, working with advertisers like Bank of America and Dell while sitting on the advisory boards of Google, Yahoo!, and Microsoft.

Previously, Goldman led the Midwest sales team for MaxOnline, now a division of Ask.com.

When he's not Googling himself, Goldman enjoys spending time with his family in Chicago.

Web Sites

www.GoogleyLessons.com

www.Kenshoo.com

www.AaronGoldman.net

Primary Products or Books

Everything I Know about Marketing I Learned from Google (McGraw-Hill, 2011)

A Newbie's Field Guide to Twitter for Business

Twenty-Nine Questions (and Answers) About Starting Out

Ann Handley and Beth Harte

So you've heard that Twitter is a great tool for connecting with customers in ways that haven't been previously possible. But you still don't get it, right?

As Steven Berlin Johnson wrote in his *Time* magazine cover story on Twitter in June 2010, "The one thing you can say for certain about Twitter is that it makes a terrible first impression." The service allows you to send 140-character updates to your "followers," he writes, "and you think, Why does the world need this, exactly?"

Not only doesn't it make obvious sense, but it's also marked by protocols and terms that can be perplexing to anyone new to Twitter. With a hat tip to Forrester's Jeremiah Owyang for inspiration, below is a comprehensive field guide to Twitter for business.

1. What is Twitter?

   Twitter is a free social-messaging tool for staying connected in real time. It is sometimes called a *microblogging service* that enables its users to send and read other users' short (140-character) updates, known as tweets.

2. I don't get it. . . . What's the value?

   Twitter by itself makes little sense. Its real value comes in following others and having them follow you. When you are connected to people you know or want to know, or with whom you have something in common, the platform can offer a rich experience.

3. Why does everyone talk about what they ate for lunch?

The flexibility and openness of Twitter sometimes makes for inane conversation and comments. But answering the Twitter question "What are you doing now?" isn't necessarily the most effective way to use the tool. Instead, answer the question, "What's important to me?" or (better yet) "What's important to my followers?" Also . . . engage in dialog, ask questions, and use the reply feature to answer the questions of others.

4. Why is Twitter 140 Characters?

Twitter integrates well with mobile devices, and the size limit is 130 characters for mobile text messages using SMS.

5. So Twitter is just a communications tool?

Yes, Twitter is a communications tool. But sharing information on Twitter means engaging in dialog, and from that perspective Twitter becomes a source for creating a unique online community for your organization. It's "unique" because as an organization you determine who you follow on Twitter and who you want to follow you back.

6. How do I find people to follow that might like my product and/or service?

With Twitter's "Find People" function you can search by name, word (think about your SEO terms), location name, and more. Other great tools:

➤ Twellow: The Twitter Yellow Pages

➤ Mr. Tweet: Beware of the tweets they send, it's a bit spammy.

➤ #Hashtags: Great for following up on and keeping track of conversations.

7. What are retweets and hashtags? How can I use them?

A retweet (RT) is like forwarding an e-mail. Because not everyone has the same community (followers) on Twitter, retweeting a tweet spreads that shared information across multiple communities. Hashtags are used to keep track of conversations that are happening within Twitter.

8. How do I reply to a Tweet?

When you see someone's tweet, there's a small arrow next to their tweet. If you feel like responding to them, click that arrow and it will automatically load their name into the text box. Type your answer in 140 characters and submit. Using the reply feature will make conversations easier to track and find.

9. What's a "DM"?

DM stands for "direct messages." One person can privately message another person by using the DM messaging system. You can DM only users who are following you. You may hear individuals say

"DM me for details about [whatever]," suggesting the user wants to take the discussion private.

10. What does "RT" or "Retweet" mean?

One of the greatest aspects of Twitter is how quickly word-of-mouth spreads globally. If a user thinks another user's tweet is interesting, he or she may choose to repeat, or "retweet," or "RT," what that person says.

11. Do I need to respond to everyone who sends me a tweet?

If someone is speaking directly to you, not responding is akin to ignoring someone. If someone retweets your tweet, saying thank-you is a nice thing to do. Again, there's no perfect answer here, but keep Emily Post in mind.

12. How can I tell whether someone is talking about my industry on Twitter?

One easy way is to use the search function within Twitter or use Twitter Search (search.twitter.com) to search on your company name, employee names, product names, and your SEO keywords. The search function within Twitter allows you to save your searches, and Twitter Search provides an RSS feature that allows you to save searches right to your favorite reader.

13. Why aren't people following my Twitter account?

Well . . . ask yourself the following questions:

➤ Am I talking more than listening?

➤ Am I taking more than sharing?

➤ Have I given the community enough time to embrace my organization?

➤ Am I following a lot of people each day?

➤ Am I engaging people in conversation?

➤ Am I sharing valuable industry or educational information?

If you've answered "yes" to question 1 or 2, or "no" to any of the rest, you probably aren't engaging at a level the community expects.

14. Do I have to say anything? Can I just listen?

Yes. Engaging on Twitter doesn't mean just talking. It means listening too, and monitoring Twitter for mentions of your brand or industry. A great tool for listening is Twitter Search.

15. Can anyone read my Tweets? Will Google index them?

Yes. Your tweets, if public, are published for anyone to see, including your family, your competitors, your boss—and Google. Think of Tweeting like any other kind of online publishing or blogging. If you're still concerned about privacy, make your tweets private, which means they will be visible only by those you follow.

There are toggles on the Account page that allow you to select the "make my tweets private" option.

16. How many Twitter accounts can I have?

You can have as many as you want. Just know that each one will require the same level of engagement as the others. Unless, of course, your organization uses a Twitter account for broadcast messaging to share news, discounts, and so on (e.g., @DellChannel). Tools like TwitterFeed provide a way to auto-populate and send tweets.

17. How should I brand my company Twitter handle?

It depends on your objective. Make it clear in the profile what the objective is—customer support, news, questions, conversation, or a combination thereof. Some brands, such as Dell and Oracle, have employees who share the name of the brand (e.g., @richardatdell), which creates a unique hybrid brand. Some brands use the corporate handle and an "official spokesperson," such as @marketingprofs. Employees might create personal twitter accounts, and they may indicate their affiliation with their employer. In any case, set expectations and clarify the matter in the Twitter profile.

18. Why do I need to personalize my Twitter account? Can't I just have my brand?

Brands don't talk, people do. People want to know whom they are having a conversation with—knowing a person's name is always the first step in building a relationship.

19. Should I have business objectives for Twitter?

Yes! Twitter is a tool that could potentially be a part of your marketing or business plan. If you don't have objectives for using Twitter, how will you know whether you've been successful or might need to restructure your strategy?

20. How can a business use Twitter effectively?

There isn't a clear-cut answer for this one. Every organization will have unique needs and should determine what's best for it and its online community of customers, prospects, investors, employees, and so on before engaging on Twitter.

21. How can a business use Twitter efficiently?

There are a lot of tools to help organizations use Twitter efficiently, including TweetDeck, Twhirl, SocialToo, HootSuite, and CoTweet. Here are a couple of posts on most of the available tools:

➤ Twittermania: 140-plus Twitter Tools! from Mashable

➤ TWITTER TOOLBOX: 60-plus Twitter Tools from Mashable

22. What is "broadcasting"?

Broadcasting is when organizations share a lot of information (usually about themselves) without engaging in conversation.

23. What's wrong with using Twitter to broadcast?

There's nothing wrong with it, if it's effective. You might be wondering, "How do I know if it's effective?" See Question 2. Also, your community will let you know if it's effective by either unfollowing or following your organization. For some organizations, like CNN and Dell, having a broadcasting channel on Twitter works just fine and fits within their marketing and social media strategy.

24. I've heard about TwitterHawk and am considering it, any tips?

TwitterHawk is a tool that lets organizations monitor Twitter conversations by keyword. One of the drawbacks to TwitterHawk is that it can send an auto-Tweet based on keyword. That can feel a bit spammy and can freak people out.

25. What's the best way to use link shorteners like Ow.ly, TinyURL, and Twurl?

Because Twitter is limited to 140-characters, you want to reduce those long links as much as possible. Tools like TinyURL and is.gd are great for that.

It's also a good idea to measure, monitor, and analyze your shared links. Tools like Ow.ly, Cligs, bit.ly, and Tweetburner let you do just that.

26. What is a Tweetup?

A Tweetup is an offline meet-up of people who engage on Twitter. Tweetups are a great way to meet people and get to know them better offline.

27. I've read that I should share personal information on Twitter. Why is that necessary as a professional?

Well, some people don't really care if you went to the gym or ate a donut . . . but getting a glimpse into who you are as a person helps build business relationships. It works just like offline business development. If you know your customer likes golf, you might suggest a golf outing. If you know your customer is having a birthday, you might call and wish them a happy birthday. It works in reverse, too. Customers like to know whom they are dealing with and prefer to develop a relationship based on trust; sharing a bit about yourself is one way to do that.

28. What about mobile phone applications? Which one should I use?

A huge number of Twitter apps are available, but selecting the right one is really a matter of personal choice. A sizable selection of them is reviewed here, or you can just follow our lead and use Tweetie for the iPhone (Ann) or Twitterberry on the Blackberry (Beth).

29. WOW! This is a lot. Is there a way to manage Twitter easily?

There sure is! Seesmic Desktop, TweetDeck, and Twhirl allow you to interface with Twitter in an easier manner. You can see all of your followers' tweets, get replies and direct messages, and follow or unfollow people. You can also create groups (for your favorite people) and searches (to keep an eye on keywords and mentions). They do a lot more, but that should be enough to get you heading in the right direction.

■ ABOUT THE AUTHOR

Ann Handley is the chief content officer of MarketingProfs, a rich and trusted resource that helps businesses market their products and services smarter and better, and the coauthor of the best-selling *Content Rules: How to Create Killer Blogs, Podcasts, Videos, Ebooks, Webinars (and More) That Engage Customers and Ignite Your Business* (John Wiley & Sons, Inc., 2011) www.contentrulesbook.com.

She is a 12-year veteran of creating and managing digital content to build relationships for organizations and individuals. Also, she's a writer who blogs at her personal blog, Annarchy, as well as American Express OPEN Forum, Mashable, and The Huffington Post.

Previously, Ann was the cofounder of ClickZ, one of the first sources of interactive marketing news and commentary.

Web Sites

www.contentrulesbook.com

Primary Products or Books

Content Rules: How to Create Killer Blogs, Podcasts, Videos, Ebooks, Webinars (and More) That Engage Customers and Ignite Your Business (John Wiley & Sons, Inc., 2011)

Chapter 13

Is This a Bad Time to Market?

C.J. Hayden, MCC

All economic indicators say we are in a recession. Consumer and business spending is down; unemployment is up. It's natural to wonder whether perhaps this is a bad time to be marketing your business.

Since I've been self-employed for almost two decades now, I've seen several economic cycles come and go. What I notice about these down periods is that people who frequently struggle to get clients typically think these are bad times to market. In contrast, people who have been consistently successful at landing clients seem to believe that there is never a bad time to market. Personally, I'd vote to follow the lead of those who are succeeding.

Professionals who have built successful long-term businesses have learned that continuing to market pays off in both the best of times and the worst of times. But you may not be able to produce new results by marketing in the same old way. Here are six suggestions for how to keep your marketing up when the overall business climate is down.

1. *Turn up the volume.* When people are distracted by bad news or economic concerns, you may need to communicate more often or more visibly. Where an e-mail might have done the job before, now you may need to pick up the phone or send a postcard. Instead of just one follow-up call, you may need to make two or three. If your business is slowing down, make use of the extra time you have available to ramp up all your marketing efforts.

2. *Become a necessity.* When clients are cutting back on discretionary spending, they need to perceive your services as essential. Look for ways to "dollarize" the value of your services. How can you help your clients save money, cut expenses, or work more efficiently? Will your services help them gain more customers, increase their income,

or experience less stress in tough times? Tell your prospects exactly why they need you, and why they shouldn't wait to get started.

3. *Make use of your existing network.* It's always easier to get your foot in the door when someone is holding it open. In a slow market, referrals and introductions can be the key to getting new business. Seek out opportunities to propose repeat business with former clients, too. Uncertain times encourage more reliance on trusted sources and known quantities, so warm approaches and existing contacts will pay off better than cold calls or mass mailings.

4. *Explore partnerships.* Working with a partner can create more opportunities for both of you. By sharing contacts, you each increase the size of your network. Together, you can multiply your marketing efforts and share expenses. A partner with a complementary business can allow you to offer a more complete solution than your competitors can. A photographer could team up with a graphic designer, for example. And you can help keep each other's spirits up, too.

5. *Meet people where they are.* In a down economy, prospects are even more price-sensitive than usual. Instead of slashing your rates to get their business, propose a get-acquainted offer. A professional organizer or image consultant could offer a reduced price half-day package for new clients. A management consultant or executive coach could propose a staff seminar instead of consulting/coaching work. Once clients see you in action, they'll be more willing to spend.

6. *Find the silver linings.* When companies cut back on staff, opportunities are created. With fewer people on the payroll to handle essential tasks, downsized organizations present possibilities for project work, interim assignments, and outsourced functions. Economic changes beget other needs. People who are out of work need resume writers and career coaches. Folks concerned about their finances need investment advisors and financial planners.

Landing clients during a down period requires not just more marketing, but more strategic marketing. So instead of getting depressed by the news, get inspired by it. When you hear about coming layoffs, consider how your services could benefit those companies. When you read about negative consumer attitudes, use those words to better target your marketing copy. When prospects say, "not this year," craft a proposal that ensures your place in next year's budget.

For the successful independent professional, there's no such thing as a bad time to market.

■ ABOUT THE AUTHOR

C.J. Hayden, MCC, CPCC is the author of *Get Clients Now!* (AMACOM, 2007). Thousands of business owners and independent professionals have used her simple sales and marketing system to double or triple their income. C.J. is a business coach, trainer, and speaker who helps people make a difference doing what they love. Her company, Wings for Business, specializes in serving entrepreneurs, self-employed professionals, and people in marketing and sales. C.J. is a former corporate productivity consultant with over 30 years experience in business management. She has been a professional trainer since 1978, a business advisor since 1990, and a coach since 1992. A popular speaker and workshop leader, C.J. has presented hundreds of programs on marketing and entrepreneurship to corporate clients, professional associations, and small businesses.

Web Sites

www.getclientsnow.com

www.cjhayden.com

Primary Products or Books

Get Clients Now! (AMACOM, 2007)

Get Hired Now! (Bay Tree Books, 2005)

The One-Person Marketing Plan Workbook

Chapter 14

The Dos and Dont's to Using Article Marketing to Get Online Visibility

Jeff Herring

Article marketing is the perfect vehicle to establish your strong and dominant online visibility. This is because for each article you create, you can spread it all over the Internet in minutes a day.

What holds many people back from creating strong online visibility is the false belief that you have to be found all over the Internet. Here's the really good news: You do not have to be found all over the Internet.

The even better news is you only want to be found all over your niche. And when you combine article marketing and social marketing, you have a strategy that will get you to online visibility in a hurry.

■ STEPS TO ONLINE VISIBILITY

1. *Create a high quality article around a topic in your niche.* When you submit your article and have it published on EzineArticles, you are getting your information in front of over 30 million unique visitors a month. That's over a million a day and about 3,500 just in the time it takes you to read this article.

   That alone is some fairly significant visibility online.

   But it does not stop there. People with their own web sites, blogs, and newsletters come to EzineArticles looking for content for their sites. When they use your content, complete with links back to you, you are dramatically increasing your online visibility in front of other people's traffic and list community.

2. *Spread your article all over social media platforms.* Some of this is done for you when you sign up to have "new article alerts" sent to Twitter when a new article is published. And if you have your Twitter account properly integrated, these "new article alerts" are also seen on Facebook, LinkedIn, your blog, and other places.

The next step is to take parts of your article and syndicate and repurpose it all over the social media world.

Here are some of the parts of your article you can spread all over your social marketing sites, complete with a link to the full article:

➤ Your article title

➤ Your article description

➤ The opening sentence of your article

➤ Quotes from your article

➤ Bullet points from your article

➤ Subheadings from your article

➤ Your article resource box

And here are just a few suggestions about where you can post these parts of your article:

➤ Facebook

➤ Twitter

➤ YouTube

➤ Your blog

➤ LinkedIn

➤ StumbledUpon

➤ And many more

3. *Multiplying your results.* Now that is what you can do with just one article. I wonder what would happen when you did this with every article?

Hint: "I see you everywhere. . . ."

Now that you know where to begin, I'd like to point out that there are some common mistakes that many marketers make as they build their online visibility.

Let's take a closer look at three of the most common mistakes and what to do instead.

■ THREE DEADLY ONLINE VISIBILITY MISTAKES

➤ Online Visibility Mistake 1: "If You Build It, He Will Come"

This was a great line in a movie, but it is a deadly mistake to think it works this way in real-world marketing. This mistake is most often seen when someone puts up a web site or blog and then just expects the traffic to pour in. It just does not work that way.

What to do instead. Let people know you are out there on the Internet. Write lots of articles and get them on the Article Directories. Use them on your blog, and invite your list to read the new article. Use Facebook, Twitter, and YouTube to promote your existing articles and to repurpose your articles into different media.

➤ Online Visibility Mistake 2: Just a Few Will Do

I hear this one all the time: "I tried Article Marketing and it just doesn't work." Then I ask (although I already know the answer), "How many articles did you create and promote?" The answer is usually three to five. That just won't cut it.

What to do instead. Think of your articles as "article agents" out there working for you 24/7/365 all over the world, never asking for a raise, taking a day off, or being cranky. Now how many articles do you want out there working for you? Remember this, especially as you are beginning, or wanting to ramp things up:

An article a day keeps recession away.

And, I might add, makes for great online visibility!

➤ Online Visibility Mistake 3: Not Spreading the Word

Do not leave your marketing to someone else. You are responsible for your marketing. As my friend and colleague Alex Mandossian is fond of saying, "You must take 100 percent marketing responsibility for your message."

When you write a book, it is the responsibility of the publisher to publish it. The little known hard truth is that it is then your responsibility to market it.

What to do instead. It's the same the way with your articles. Once they are published by the Article Directories, it is then your responsibility to market your articles. Here's a short list about ways to get the word out:

- ➤ E-mail your list community
- ➤ Announce on Twitter
- ➤ Announce on Facebook
- ➤ Create a Video Article
- ➤ Hold a teleseminar based on your article

If you implement just one of these three tips, you will get more online visibility. I wonder what would happen if you implemented all three of these online visibility tips. . . .

■ ABOUT THE AUTHOR

Discover how to quickly and easily create prospect and profit pulling content, and then leverage your content for online visibility, traffic generation, list building, and product creation. Jeff has helped thousands of entrepreneurs become the recognized expert in their field and be found all over their niche.

Web Site

http://JeffHerring.com

Chapter 15

What Poker Taught Me about Business

Tony Hsieh

I'd played a little bit of poker in college, but like many people, I always just considered it to be a fun form of gambling and had never bothered to actually study it. Back in 1999, poker was not yet a mainstream activity. Most people had never heard of the World Series of Poker, and TV networks like ESPN were not yet broadcasting poker tournaments to the masses.

One night while battling insomnia, I randomly came across a web site that served as a community hub for people who played poker regularly. I was fascinated by the amount of analysis and information about playing that was freely available, and spent the entire night reading different articles about the mathematics of poker.

Like many people, I had always thought that poker was mostly about luck, being able to bluff, and reading people. I learned that for limit hold 'em poker (which was the most popular type of poker in casinos at the time), none of that really mattered much in the long run. For every hand and every round of betting, there was actually a mathematically correct way to play that took into account the "pot odds" (the ratios among the amount of the bet, the number of chips already in the pot, and the statistical chances of winning).

With the exception of poker, almost all games in a typical casino are stacked against the player, and in the long run the casino always comes out ahead. I was intrigued by poker because in poker you are playing against other players, not against the casino. Instead, the casino just takes a service fee for each hand dealt (usually from the winner of each hand).

In a casino, each poker table seats up to 10 players. As long as at least one of the players is not playing in the mathematically optimal way (and usually it's several players that aren't), the players who are playing correctly will generally end up winning in the long run.

Learning the basic math behind limit hold 'em poker was not actually that hard. I bought and studied a book called *Hold 'em Poker* and started going to card rooms in California several times a week to practice what I was learning from the book. (Although California is a generally no-gambling state, card rooms are allowed because poker is not a game against the house.) Within a few weeks, I felt that I had mastered the basics of the mathematics behind playing hold 'em.

Understanding the mathematics behind hold 'em and playing against players who didn't was like owning a coin that would land on heads one-third of the time and tails the other two-thirds of the time, and always being allowed to bet on tails. On any individual coin flip, I might lose, but if I bet on tails a thousand times, then I was more than 99.99 percent guaranteed to win in the long run.

Likewise, when playing a game against the house such as roulette or blackjack, it would be like being forced to always bet on heads: Even though you might win any individual coin flip, if you did it a thousand times, you would be more than 99.99 percent guaranteed to lose in the long run.

One of the most interesting things about playing poker was learning the discipline of not confusing the right decision with the individual outcome of any single hand, but that's what a lot of poker players do. If they win a hand, they assume they made the right bet, and if they lose a hand, they often assume they made the wrong bet. With the coin that lands on heads a third of the time, this would be like seeing the coin land on heads once (the individual outcome) and changing your behavior so you bet on heads, when the mathematically correct thing to do is to always bet on tails no matter what happened in the previous coin flip (the right decision).

For the first few months, I found poker both fun and challenging, because I was constantly learning, both through reading different books and through the actual experience of playing in the field. I started to notice similarities between what was good poker strategy and what made for good business strategy, especially when thinking about the separation between short-term thinking (such as focusing on whether I won or lost an individual hand) and long-term thinking (such as making sure I had the right decision strategy).

I noticed so many similarities between poker and business that I started making a list of the lessons I learned from playing poker that could also be applied to business:

Evaluating Market Opportunities

➤ Table selection is the most important decision you can make.

➤ It's okay to switch tables if you discover it's too hard to win at your table.

➤ If there are too many competitors (some irrational or in-experienced), even if you're the best it's a lot harder to win.

Marketing and Branding

➤ Act weak when strong, act strong when weak. Know when to bluff.

➤ Your "brand" is important.

➤ Help shape the stories that people are telling about you.

Financials

➤ Always be prepared for the worst possible scenario.

➤ The guy who wins the most hands is not the guy who makes the most money in the long run.

➤ The guy who never loses a hand is not the guy who makes the most money in the long run.

➤ Go for positive expected value, not what's least risky.

➤ Make sure your bankroll is large enough for the game you're playing and the risks you're taking.

➤ Play only with what you can afford to lose.

➤ Remember that it's a long-term game. You will win or lose individual hands or sessions, but it's what happens in the long term that matters.

Strategy

➤ Don't play games that you don't understand, even if you see lots of other people making money from them.

➤ Figure out the game when the stakes aren't high.

➤ Don't cheat. Cheaters never win in the long run.

➤ Stick to your principles.

➤ You need to adjust your style of play throughout the night as the dynamics of the game change. Be flexible.

➤ Be patient and think long term.

➤ The players with the most stamina and focus usually win.

➤ Differentiate yourself. Do the opposite of what the rest of the table is doing.

➤ Hope is not a good plan.

➤ Don't let yourself go "on tilt." It's much more cost-effective to take a break, walk around, or leave the game for the night.

Continual Learning

➤ Educate yourself. Read books and learn from others who have done it before.

➤ Learn by doing. Theory is nice, but nothing replaces actual experience.

➤ Learn by surrounding yourself with talented players.

➤ Just because you win a hand doesn't mean you're good and you don't have more learning to do. You might have just gotten lucky.

➤ Don't be afraid to ask for advice.

Culture

➤ You've gotta love the game. To become really good, you need to live it and sleep it.

➤ Don't be cocky. Don't be flashy. There's always someone better than you.

➤ Be nice and make friends. It's a small community.

➤ Share what you've learned with others.

➤ Look for opportunities beyond just the game you sat down to play. You never know who you're going to meet, including new friends for life or new business contacts.

➤ Have fun. The game is a lot more enjoyable when you're trying to do more than just make money.

Aside from remembering to focus on what's best for the long term, I think the biggest business lesson I learned from poker concerned the most important decision you can make in the game. Although it seems obvious in retrospect, it took me six months before I finally figured it out.

Through reading poker books and practicing by playing, I spent a lot of time learning about the best strategy to play once I was actually sitting down at a table. My big "ah-ha!" moment came when I finally learned that the game started even before I sat down in a seat.

In a poker room at a casino, there are usually many different choices of tables. Each table has different stakes, different players, and different dynamics that change as the players come and go, and as players get excited, upset, or tired.

I learned that the most important decision I could make was which table to sit at. This included knowing when to change tables. I learned from a book that an experienced player can make 10 times as much money sitting at a table with nine mediocre players who are tired and have a lot of chips compared with sitting at a table with nine really good players who are focused and don't have that many chips in front of them.

In business, one of the most important decisions for an entrepreneur or a CEO to make is what business to be in. It doesn't matter how flawlessly a business is executed if it's the wrong business or if it's in too small a market.

Imagine if you were the most efficient manufacturer of seven-fingered gloves. You offer the best selection, the best service, and the best prices for seven-fingered gloves–but if there isn't a big enough market for what you sell, you won't get very far.

Or, if you decide to start a business that competes directly against really experienced competitors such as Wal-Mart by playing the same game they play (for example, trying to sell the same goods at lower prices), then chances are that you will go out of business.

In a poker room, I could only choose which table I wanted to sit at. But in business, I realized that I didn't have to sit at an existing table. I could define my own, or make the one that I was already at even bigger. (Or, just like in a poker room, I could always choose to change tables.)

I realized that, whatever the vision was for any business, there was always a bigger vision that could make the table bigger.

■ ABOUT THE AUTHOR

Tony Hsieh is the author of *New York Times* number one bestseller, *Delivering Happiness*, and the CEO of Zappos. In 1999, at the age of 24, Tony Hsieh (pronounced Shay) sold LinkExchange, the company he cofounded, to Microsoft for $265 million. He then joined Zappos.com as an advisor and investor, and eventually became CEO, where he helped Zappos.com grow from almost no sales to over $1 billion in gross merchandise sales annually, while simultaneously making *Fortune* magazine's annual list of "Best Companies to Work For." In November 2009, Zappos.com was acquired by Amazon.com in a deal valued at $1.2 billion on the day of closing.

Tony's first book, *Delivering Happiness*, was published on June 7, 2010, and outlines his path from starting a worm farm to life at Zappos.com. Tony shows how a very different kind of corporate culture is a powerful model for achieving success and happiness. *Delivering Happiness* debuted at number one on the *New York Times* best-seller list and remained on the list for 27 consecutive weeks.

Web Sites

www.deliveringhappinessbook.com

www.zappos.com

Primary Products or Books

Delivering Happiness (Business Plus, 2010)

Chapter 16

How to Be Fascinating

Guy Kawasaki

The primary goal of your social media activities—whether for your personal brand or your organization's brand—is to establish yourself as a fascinating subject-matter expert. The only exception to this is if you are a household name celebrity like Lance Armstrong, Oprah, or Barack Obama. If you are this level of celebrity, then tweeting or updating, "I'm at Starbucks on the way to fly VirginAmerica to Vegas" is cool.

For the rest of us, the challenge is to achieve a consistent level of fascinating information about your area of expertise. The answer is simple. First, it helps if you actually know what you're talking about. If you don't, it may be better to let people wonder if you're clueless rather than participating in social media and removing all doubt. But let's say you've crossed the Rubicon.

Then it's all about finding good stories, videos, and blog posts about your subject and providing links to these sources. For example, if you own a restaurant, then you could post a link to The Second Annual New York Foodie Photo Scavenger Hunt, Cilantro Haters, It's Not Your Fault, and Check It Out: Get Your Groceries At The Library. Do this for a few months, and people will recognize you as a food expert. And guess what? They'll come eat at your restaurant.

Then the next question is how you can find these stories, videos, and blog posts. I have four methods for you to use:

1. *StumbleUpon.* If you sign up for the service, you can tell it the subjects you're interested in. Then when you "stumble," it will only take you to pages that other StumbleUpon users have liked in that subject. To really use StumbleUpon well, get its toolbar. Like 14,846,969 others, I use the Firefox version because it lets me pick categories and share pages via Twitter, Facebook, and e-mail.

2. *SmartBrief.* SmartBrief is a company that's in the business of providing associations with good content for its members. As such, they have subject-matter experts who search every day for good content. All you have to do is go to its web site or subscribe to its e-mail newsletters to benefit from their effort and expertise.

3. *Interns.* You could hire people—usually interns—to find stuff for you. For $10 to $20/hour, there are lots of starving, smart people who will comb the Internet to look for good content. They'll probably use StumbleUpon, SmartBrief, and other tools, but what do you care if they're doing what you could easily do for yourself? If you did everything you could do yourself, you'd be licking stamps too.

4. *Alltop.* Alltop is the online version of the magazine rack in your bookstore except that it has 900 subjects and is free. It aggregates news by topics, presents the five most recent stories from the best web sites and blogs about a subject, and gives you a preview of each story. Going back to the food example, I found all those stories using Food.alltop in less than two minutes. (Disclosure: I am the cofounder of Alltop.)

The test for your social media efforts is whether people find what you post so fascinating that they retweet it (or favor it, share it, or e-mail it). Trust me, today the sincerest form of flattery is retweeting, not imitating, you. With these four resources, you'll rock.

■ ABOUT THE AUTHOR

Guy Kawasaki is the cofounder of Alltop.com, an "online magazine rack" of popular topics on the Web, and a founding partner at Garage Technology Ventures. Previously, he was the chief evangelist of Apple.

Kawasaki is the author of 10 books including *Enchantment, Reality Check, The Art of the Start, Rules for Revolutionaries, How to Drive Your Competition Crazy, Selling the Dream,* and *The Macintosh Way.* Kawasaki has a BA from Stanford University, an MBA from UCLA, and an honorary doctorate from Babson College.

Web Sites

www.openforum.com/connectodex/how-to-change-the-world

Primary Products or Books

Enchantment: The Art of Changing Hearts, Minds, and Actions (Portfolio, 2011)

Reality Check (Portfolio, 2008)

The Art of the Start (Portfolio, 2004)

Chapter 17

Common Courtesy Is a Marketing Strategy

Dan Kennedy

The printing company's truck backed up to our warehouse door, loaded with about a hundred cartons of brochures for one of our companies. The driver got a pushcart out of the back and asked where we wanted him to take the boxes. Following our directions, he wheeled the cart full of boxes through our warehouse area and into a back office.

"Just pile them over there," I said. "We have to separate them by the title of the brochures packed inside before putting them on the shelves."

"I've already done that for you," the driver said. "And these boxes are labeled with the different titles right here on the side, to make it easier for you to access the right boxes." He then proceeded to put the boxes in the right places on the shelves.

Then, as he left the building, he closed the warehouse door behind him.

And, incidentally, he thanked us for our business.

I don't know if this surprises you or not, but that's *marketing!* I'll tell you this: This experience was a lot different from our experience with most vendors' delivery people. This driver was courteous. This deliveryman did more than was required of him. This deliveryman let us know that our business was appreciated.

Common courtesies, you say. Unfortunately, these courtesies are not very common at all. In fact, they're extremely rare. And it's worth noting that our society, our marketplace, prizes that which is rare most.

This particular experience with this particular deliveryman may have been accidental. He may just be a naturally pleasant, considerate, helpful fellow. Or he may have taken it upon himself, for some unknown reason, to develop a pleasing personality, and to practice good customer relations.

But, if this is an accident, it is a great example of an accident that should be repeated on purpose, as a marketing strategy.

■ WHAT IS MARKETING?

Most people expect an article about "marketing" to address such subjects as advertising, direct mail, increasing customer's purchasing, stimulating referrals, finding a market niche, and so on. And they should, but in this article, I want to let you know everything you think of as something other than marketing is actually marketing.

For example, most businesses think of maintenance as maintenance. The Disney parks think of maintenance as marketing, because the remarkable cleanliness of the parks is a major stimulant of positive word-of-mouth advertising. What aspects of your business aren't thought of as marketing but should be thought of as marketing, and reworked as marketing strategies?

Quality is certainly one of them. Product quality. Service quality. *In Search of Excellence* (Warner Books, 1982) author Tom Peters jokes about the retail executive who became aggravated at Peters' criticism of his industry in a seminar, and cried out, "We are no worse than anybody else." Peters had a graphic artist design a company logo with the slogan in it: We are no worse than anybody else.

Quality must be developed as marketing strategy, because no other marketing strategies can build and sustain a business without it.

Another aspect of business often overlooked as a marketing strategy is courtesy.

Courtesy can be expressed many different ways. Like the delivery man taking time to sort the boxes. Or the Horchow mail-order company sending each item ordered during the holiday season in a beautiful Christmas-green gift box, with a gold elastic ribbon, and a gift card, all at no extra cost. Or the Figi's company, a mail-order marketer of gourmet foods and gifts, sending a personalized letter acknowledging receipt of an order and reassuring the customer that it will be shipped on time. Or the doctor who calls his patient at home, the evening after treatment, just to check on him. Or even with a simple thank-you.

It's an important marketing principle: People want most what they have the least of. Today, somewhat sadly, the things most people get the least of are recognition and appreciation.

■ GRATITUDE AS A MARKETING STRATEGY

Many years ago, I took over a business with mammoth collection problems: Almost all of its customers had open accounts and paid their bills 10 to 60 days late (except those who didn't pay at all). We quickly instituted a number of corrective measures, including tighter credit controls and policies, interest charges, a sequence of past-due notices, and collection calls. However, we also instituted a positive strategy. We started sending hand-signed thank-you notes for prompt payment to anybody who did pay on time . . . those who were almost on time . . . and even late payers who responded to a past-due notice. Guess what happened? Those customers who received thank-you notes became better-paying customers.

I know a doctor who started a procedure of giving fresh, long-stemmed red roses to his women patients who showed up for their appointment on time, or paid their bills on time, or referred another patient. "Funny thing," he told me. "We no longer have patients missing appointments. Our collections have improved. Referrals are up. And, some guys are asking how they can get roses, too!"

Here are a few specific ideas you might adopt, as ways of saying thank you:

➤ Keep customers' birthdays on file and send cards and/or mail gifts.

➤ Send Thanksgiving cards or letters.

➤ Make it a habit to drop a personal thank-you note in the mail each day, to at least one customer.

➤ Send a gift certificate or discount certificate to a customer who makes an unusually large purchase.

➤ Host a "Customer Appreciation Event"—a Christmas party, a backyard barbeque.

➤ Have an occasional closed-to-the-public, preferred-customer sale.

➤ Drop in personally on your best customers, with a surprise gift.

I figured it up just the other day; in 1986, personally and for my various businesses combined, I signed checks for well over $1 million, in payment for goods and services to all sorts of people and companies. And I don't care what anybody says—a million bucks is a lot of money. Yet I can count on the fingers of one hand the number of the recipients of all that money who have expressed any gratitude in any formal kind of way. Only one of them found out and recognized my birthday.

Just saying "thanks" is a big step ahead of the competition today.

■ ABOUT THE AUTHOR

Dan Kennedy is a multimillionare, serial entrepreneur, celebrated author, speaker, marketing strategist, consultant, and coach directly influencing over one million business owners annually. His No B.S. Marketing Newsletter is the most successful paid-subscription/membership newsletter in its genre.

Web Sites

http://dankennedy.com

www.NoBSBooks.com

Primary Products or Books

My Unfinished Business (Advantage Media Group, 2009).

No B.S. Marketing to the Affluent (Entrepreneur Press, 2008).

No B.S. Ruthless Management of People and Profits (Entrepreneur Media, Inc., 2008).

Chapter 18

Two Key Elements to Article Marketing

The Perfect Title and Resource Box

Christopher Knight

Article marketing can be a key strategy for many small and midsize businesses.

Unfortunately, most authors are wasting their time producing dozens to hundreds of high quality articles that never reach a fraction of their traffic potential. It's a darn shame.

When I review the behind-the-scenes traffic statistics on over 20,000 articles that have produced over 1 million monthly page views in my article marketing lab . . . *one* thing is clear: All articles are not created equal even when everything about them is identical except for the *title*.

The reason is probably not what you think.

If you've been schooled on traditional copywriting, you know that in the offline world, the headline determines as much as 95 percent of the success of the book or article. This statistic takes into consideration what makes the book title successful: Whether a human buys it or not.

Article marketing on the Internet is a whole different story because of the way your articles reach humans who have an interest in them.

Myth: Most people will read your articles because they came to a web site and started browsing just as they would have done if they had gone to a local bookstore to find a book of personal interest.

Fact: Wrong! Most people will search the Internet using one of the major search engines, and they will be putting in between one to five keywords that are related to the topic of the article or information they are looking to locate. The search engines will then deliver results that best match the human's interest.

Your goal: To have your articles show up in the search engine results for the keywords and topics that are most related to the content of your article.

How?

You must embrace this title *creation and traffic-building truth:*

> The first three to five words of your *title* determine the success of your article in terms of how much traffic your article will generate back to your web site. Success can only be had when you create keyword-rich titles for your articles that match the most commonly searched keywords for your topic.

How to determine which keywords are rich and the right ones to use for your article?

> You'll need a keyword research tool. Some are free, and some are fee-based. Overture.com has a popular keyword research tool that shows you the most common search results from the Yahoo! search engines directory. If you want to see what's on "Google's Mind" you can try one of their current beta tools called "Google Suggest":
>
> www.google.com/webhp?hl=en&complete=1.

> Whether you use a web-based keyword research tool or invest in one of the more advanced application level software keyword research tools, it's critical that you learn know how to do keyword research.

■ A "GOOD" VERSUS "BAD" *TITLE* EXAMPLE

Here is an example of the difference between a non-keyword–rich *title* vs. a very keyword-rich *title* that is proven to perform better in terms of traffic creation:

Bad *Title* Example

"Top 9 Ways You Can Acquire Fractional Jet Ownership"

Excellent Keyword Rich *Title* Example

"Fractional Jet Ownership—9 Strategies to Help You Acquire Your Private Jet"

Why is it more effective? Because it does not waste the first three words of the title with meaningless garbage words like "top" or the number "9" or "ways" . . . and gets right to the important words that might be found when someone is using a search engine to research a topic related to your article.

You'll also notice in my example that I included the word "Private" Jet. Why? Because my keyword research said that people who search for fractional jet also search for the word "private jet" and therefore I wanted to boost the chances that my title would be found by a larger number of potential visitors to the article.

Two recommendations on what *not* to do:

1. Don't include garbage characters in your *title* such as quotes, tildes, asterisks or anything else that a search engine has to work hard to discard in order to understand the *title* of your article.

2. Do not engage in any search engine spam technique by having keyword-rich *titles* that have nothing to do with the topic of your article. You'll only be hurting yourself as the search engines already aggressively filter out bad behavior like this.

If you want to maximize your results from any article marketing strategy, you must master keyword research so that you can create keyword-rich and intelligent article *titles*. Your payoff will be massive amounts of traffic to your articles and web site thanks to the search engines who love smart keyword-rich *titles*!

However, as important as a killer title is to the success of your article, there is another crucial element on which to focus.

The other key to making your article *"sell"* lies in the art of crafting the perfect Resource Box. This is the "author bio" that is below your article body and it's also known as your "SIG" (short for SIGnature).

The Essential Items That Should Be in Your Resource Box

Your name: You'd be amazed at how many folks forget to include their name in the Resource Box. Your name and optional title should be the first thing in your resource box.

Your web site address: in valid URL form. Example: http://Your-Company-Name.com.

Your elevator pitch: This is one to three sentences that encapsulate the essence of what makes you and your offering unique. Also known as your USP (unique selling proposition).

Your call to action: You've got them warmed up, and now it's time to lead them to *buy* from you or visit your web site. This is where you "ask for the sale." Best to only give (1) specific call to action.

Optional Items You Could Include in Your Resource Box

Your ezine subscription address: While getting your interested visitor to surf your web site is nice, capturing their e-mail address can help you begin the confidence/trust process. If you're going to do this strategy, include a URL for your ezine subscription address and do not use an e-mail address for the "join" address.

Your contact information: such as your business phone number or how to reach you for interviews or your press/media kit. Keep in mind that article marketing is a timeless strategy, and you may not have an easy ability to retract what you put in your article once it hits major distribution.

A free report: This could also be part of your call to action or your free bonus report that further enhances your credibility as the expert on the topic of your article.

Your e-mail autoresponder: I'm not a big fan of this strategy due to the fact that spammers will text-extract your autoresponder address and add it to their spam list. Perhaps this strategy was best for the 1990s and has now run its course.

An anchor URL: that is related to one keyword or keyword phrase that you want to build SEO strength for. Example: if I wanted to build search engine relevance/strength for the term *article marketing*, I'd link up that term in my resource box to my web site. This is an intermediate to advanced-level strategy and should not be abused by overdoing it. Keep it simple.

What Not to Include in Your Resource Box:

A listing of every web site you own: There is no faster way to dilute your credibility than by posting a half-dozen irrelevant URLs that have nothing to do with each other. Best to only post *one* URL that is related to the topic of your article.

A listing of every accomplishment you've achieved to date: No one cares. Keep your resource box brief and to the point. Yes, your resource box should be benefit-oriented so that the reader finds value in reading it rather than your ego being justified.

Advertisements or pitches for products that are not relevant to the topic of your article.

Keep the size of your resource box so that it's no larger than 20 percent of your total article size. Too often I see resource boxes that are 50 percent of the size of the total article, and this is abusive.

The body *of your article is where you "give" and the* Resource Box *is where you get to "take" for your article marketing gift of information.* The Resource Box is the "currency of payment" you receive for giving away your article. Be sure to include your name, web site address, your unique selling proposition as briefly as possible and a simple call to action.

There are many elements that go into the creation of a quality article, but oftentimes people put so much energy into crafting the article's body that the title and resource box take a backseat. When creating your article, be sure not to overlook the importance of both the title and the resource box.

■ ABOUT THE AUTHOR

Christopher M. Knight is a seasoned entrepreneur who excels at creating and leading high-performance Internet startup companies with an obsession on delivering a fast and positive end-user–driven experience. He and his team achieve this thanks to daily innovation, creative solutions based on user feedback, and a high commitment to exceed the expectations of their stakeholders. He attracts A-level achievers to quickly execute the companies' objectives and implement quality control assurances—while he steps out of the day-to-day operations to focus on the long-term client opportunities, relationship-building, and new product development.

Web Sites

http://ezinearticles.com

http://EmailUniverse.com

http://New-List.com

Primary Products or Books

EzineArticles.com

Market with Articles Teleseminar

Top Ten Metrics for Measuring Social Media Marketing ROI

Shama Kubani

Feels good to be home! I just got back from a long speaking tour. First, I was in Nashville doing a keynote on social media for women accountants and CPAs. Then, I was in Las Vegas for a keynote at the Direct Employers Conference. I spoke about social media for recruiters. After which, I spoke at the Conquer and Grow conference. It was the shortest presentation of my life—10 minutes! Very TED-like. But, I had a blast, and was forced to really sum up my points.

Below are the main points:

■ THREE THINGS TO KEEP IN MIND WHEN MEASURING SOCIAL MEDIA MARKETING SUCCESS

1. *Measure quantitatively and qualitatively:* The quantitative is the numbers part of the game. Web site visitors, Twitter followers, Facebook fans, and so on. This makes for very pretty charts, and cool case studies. The qualitative is what can't be measured by numbers. It is essentially what is being said about you and your brand. Reputation management, anyone?

2. *Keep in mind the nonlinear benefits of social media marketing:* Small and medium-sized businesses alike have the same power afforded to bigger businesses. How? R&D. Research and development was never this quick or streamlined. The feedback you can get from an online community when done correctly can be comparable to millions of dollars worth of focus groups.

3. *Build it before your need it:* Social media marketing is akin to storing a box of Band-Aids in your medicine cabinet. You don't think about it all the time, but when you have a cut, they sure come in handy! Let's say you run a restaurant, and one customer has a bad experience and blogs about it. That can really hurt! Unless, you have 10 other customers who also blogged about their great experience. Build the networks and invest in social media marketing *before* you need it.

■ TOP 10 WAYS TO MEASURE SOCIAL MEDIA MARKETING (IN 10 MINUTES!)

1. *Sales:* Your bottom line is one of your biggest indicators. In an era of multitouch marketing (I heard about you from a friend, then saw your trade show booth, then stumbled upon your company on Twitter, and here I am), your sales shouldn't be forgotten. But, remember, social media ROI isn't visible instantly. It takes time. One of my favorite quotes comes from Jeff Bezos of Amazon. He said: "I always tell people, if we have a good quarter it's because of the work we did three, four and five years ago. It's not because we did a good job this quarter." This is the *key* to social media marketing success.

2. *Higher closing ratios:* If people trust your company the chances are that they will move forward with you much more often than not. They will choose you over your competitors. Your closing ratio can tell you a lot about your marketing—not just your sales.

3. *Shorter sales cycle:* The bigger the purchase, the longer the sales cycle. This is often true in the business-to-business (B2B) world. A big part of the sales cycle is educating the prospect. And, as prospects get smarter, they do their own research. Social media should educate your prospects, making their decision easier. Measure your sales cycle. (Run a B2B business? I just did a video on B2B web marketing.)

4. *Leads:* This is perhaps the most obvious one. Are you getting more leads? Be sure to have a phone number and contact form easily accessible on your web site.

5. *New visitors:* Are you attracting new people to your web site? I talk about this as a key strategy in my book on social media. Not only should you be strengthening relationships using social media marketing, ideally, you should be attracting an audience you couldn't otherwise engage with as much ease.

6. *Brand perception:* What are people saying about you, your brand, your industry? Check it out at www.SocialMention.com. How you are perceived can truly dictate the above.

7. *Lower bounce rate:* This is what I call the sticky factor (much to our SEO department's chagrin). They like to call it your bounce rate, and it can be found using Google Analytics. This tells you how many initial visitors hit the back button to go to a different web site versus delving deeper into yours. When visitors feel like your web site is trusted and already have an introduction to you, the chances are they will stick around. It also signifies a higher quality of visitor.

8. *Site-specific metrics:* This is what most people measure, and there is a lot of controversy here. Is it quantity or quality? It is both actually. A quantity of quality Twitter Followers, Facebook Fans, and LinkedIn Connections are all viable metrics.

9. *Newsletter and blog subscribers:* There are two types of conversions that happen online. The first is what people are familiar with—direct conversion to customers and clients. The second type of conversion is less well-known, but perhaps even more crucial. It is when someone turns into a consumer. They choose to consume your information. It is the first step toward becoming a customer or a client. I talk about this extensively in my book on social media as well. Measuring your consumers (ezine and blog subscribers for example) is an excellent strategy.

10. *Good PR:* Reporters like companies and individuals who are smart, authentic, and can strike a chord with the public. Social media makes it easy for reporters to find you. It makes it easier for you to showcase your company culture and personal brand. It allows you to build relationships with bloggers. Ignore this metric at your own peril.

■ ABOUT THE AUTHOR

Shama Kubani is a Web TV show host, best-selling author, international speaker, Award-winning CEO of The Marketing Zen Group—a global digital marketing firm. Kubani is the face of today's digital world, and represents the best her generation has to offer. She has aptly been dubbed the "master millennial of the universe" and "an online marketing shaman" by *Fast Company.*

Kubani holds a Master's degree in Organizational Communication from the University of Texas at Austin, and prides herself on being a constant learner. Through her Web marketing company, Kubani works with businesses and organizations around the world. In 2009, *BusinessWeek* honored Kubani as one of the Top 25 entrepreneurs under 25 in North America. In 2010, Kubani won the prestigious Technology Titan Emerging Company CEO award. Her first book, *The Zen of Social Media Marketing* (BenBella Books), was released in April 2010 and was an instant hit.

When not working directly with her clients or filming her show, Kubani travels the world speaking on business, entrepreneurship, and technology. On the Web, she can be found on Facebook at www.Facebook.com/ShamaKabani and on Twitter at www.Twitter.com/Shama.

Web Sites

www.marketingzen.com

http://Shama.Tv

Primary Products or Books

The Zen of Social Media Marketing (BenBella Books, 2010)

Tap into Your Think Tank

Twenty Ways to Generate Ideas That Will Boost Your Business

Jim Kukral

In today's business world, your ideas are what set you apart from your competition. Here's how to get your creative juices flowing so that you can outthink and outearn your competition.

The lightbulb. Bubble wrap. The Post-It. The iPod. The Snuggie. Facebook. Twitter. These inventions, products, and businesses all started with an idea. An idea that to anyone other than its creator(s) may have seemed like an insane thing to invest much time, money, or effort in bringing to fruition. But for the masterminds behind these great ideas, the risk paid off, and so too can your next great idea.

Now, you may be thinking, *I am not going to come up with today's equivalent of the lightbulb.* That's fine. You don't have to. Great ideas come in many shapes and sizes—whether it's something as small as a new logo for your business or something as big as rolling out a brand-new product. What's important is that you give your best ideas a shot at life.

Great ideas are like gold. Everybody hopes to find them buried under the floorboards in their house. But just like finding gold, you often need a treasure map. In fiscally constrained times such as these, ideas are what matter most. Businesses live and die from the ideas they come up with. Great ideas get attention and bring people through the doors. The tricky part is figuring out how to find them.

So what does a great idea look like in practice? Peter van Stolk, founder of Jones Soda Co., is a business owner who wasn't afraid to take his great idea and run with it.

Van Stolk took his $20 million business to $42 million in four years by coming up with an idea that generated $25 million in free publicity. Jones Soda was a small Seattle-based beverage company competing against Coca-Cola and Pepsi-Cola. Combined, those two monoliths spend a billion dollars a year on advertising.

So how did van Stolk and Jones Soda compete? In 2003 van Stolk had the idea to create a Turkey & Gravy–flavored soda to be released around Thanksgiving. Soon his brand began to get mentioned in the national media, and his product began to sell out.

Peter had the idea in his car one day, and he acted on it. Ever notice how you get your best ideas when your mind is not trying to come up with them? Think about it. How many ideas have you thrown away on the treadmill or in the shower that you should have tried that could have earned you millions?

Everyone has great ideas. The problem for most people is realizing that even the most silly or outrageous idea they come up with could in fact work. Generating ideas—useful ideas—is a skill, and, like any other skill, it can be learned. The more you practice, the easier it will be to come up with ideas whenever you need them. Read on for a few suggestions on how to generate killer ideas to jump-start your venture:

Carry a notebook. The only thing worse than not being able to come up with an idea is thinking of an amazing idea, not writing it down, and then forgetting it. You may think you will remember, but you won't. Having a small notepad or digital recorder with you at all times guarantees that those ideas will not escape. Keep one in your glove compartment, on your nightstand, and in your desk drawer. Keeping a few spare sheets of loose paper in your wallet or purse is a good idea, too!

Eavesdrop. Listen to people talking on the bus, at the coffee shop, or in the elevator at work. You'll get a good feel for what people care about: their concerns, wishes, and interests. And you may also hear a great idea or two in the mix. Build on the snippets of conversation you overhear to create a story, and let that story lead you to a brilliant idea.

Do something new. Sign up for a class, take up a new hobby, listen to a different kind of music, or do anything that is new to you. Not only will it get new parts of your brain humming, you'll meet and connect with new people—which is a great way to find great new ideas.

Hold a grudge. What annoys you? When you think about the list of things you wish were different, the chances are those things also annoy other people. Keep a running list of all things that bug you and find solutions that will make them better.

Find the peanut butter to your jelly. Take two ideas and put them together to make one new idea. After all, what is a Snuggie but the mutation of a blanket and a robe? Think beyond the obvious connections to come up with something truly innovative.

Get physical. Movement increases the flow of endorphins, as well as sending more blood to your brain. Okay, I'm not a doctor, and I don't play one on TV, so maybe I don't have all the physical stuff exactly right. However, I do know that getting active helps me think. I keep a mini-trampoline in my office and jump up and down for a few minutes to get my blood moving. Run, skip, jump, climb stairs, or otherwise get your pulse rate up to get your brain moving, too.

Get an outsider's opinion. There are times when you are so close to a project that it creates a mental block for idea generation. Bringing in a fresh perspective can make all the difference. Get someone who is not familiar with your situation to ask you questions about it. It may be over dinner with friends, with a colleague at the water cooler, or in line at the grocery store with a stranger! They may ask things that lead you to an idea that you overlooked because it was too obvious. No one around? Imagine that someone is coming to you with the problem you are trying to solve. What would you tell them? Your answer may be the solution you are looking for.

Just listen. It may sound obvious, but really listen when customers talk to you. When you do, you will hear ideas for new products and services, ways to improve customer service, and uses you never considered for your products that can open up new markets for you. Your customers may not recognize when they are giving you ideas, but you need to be able to spot them. Are several customers making the same comments or asking the same questions? Act on it! You can get great ideas this way!

Change your routine. New surroundings and new experiences can help your brain to shift gears and get you to think differently. Drive a new route to the office, try a new restaurant for lunch, start work a little earlier (or a little later), work in a different place, or anything that busts you out of your rut.

Listen to music. You may find that a little Mozart awakens your creativity, or you may respond better to a little Metallica. Whatever works for you, fire up your iPod, get into the groove, and let your mind work.

Take a shower, walk the dog, do the laundry. How many great ideas do you get in the shower? It's not a coincidence that great thinking happens in the shower. Showering is a mindless activity (the only thing you really have to think about is, *Have I already repeated, or just lathered and rinsed?*), and the warm water is relaxing. Other mindless activities are great for brainstorming too. Wash the dishes, walk the dog, or fold the laundry. If you give your mind the chance to wander, you'll free yourself to come up with a brilliant idea.

Make a list (and check it twice). This is a tried-and-true method proven to work wonders. Get out a notepad, or fire up your computer, and write down everything you can think of related to your issue. For example, if you need a new slogan for a product, write down every feature and benefit you can think of, the types of people who need the product, the problems it solves, and so on. Pull out a thesaurus and start looking up synonyms. When you are done, you will not only have your slogan, you will have a library of words and phrases you can use in your marketing and publicity campaigns.

Wear a silly hat. Use a prop when it is time to be creative. It could be anything (such as wearing a silly hat) that signals to your brain that it is time to go into idea-generating mode. Have a routine that you follow when you want to be creative. It might be to put on your hat, grab a ball to toss up in the air, and lean back in your chair with your feet on the desk. Once you are in your "Creative at Work" position, start coming up with ideas. Do this a few times, and you will be conditioned to start generating ideas as soon as you see the hat. Your brain will have been trained.

Be a bookworm. Read everything you can get your hands on: business books, novels, newspapers, magazines, blogs, and everything else. The more raw materials you take in, the more you learn, and the more you know, the better you will become at putting together seemingly unrelated concepts to create something new.

Sleep on it. Just before going to bed, think about the ideas you want to generate. Be specific: *I will come up with great ways to promote our new widget.* Tell yourself you will come up with a solution while you sleep. Keep a pad and pen or a recorder next to your bed so you can capture the ideas as soon as you wake up.

Ask the almighty Google. When you are stuck on an idea, try entering a few words related to what you are looking for. Google will try to automatically complete your query, and may come up with just what you need. Then look at some of the search results to see what inspires you.

Doodle. Make random doodles on a white board or piece of paper. Draw, jot words, make circles, or whatever you do when you doodle. As you loosen up, ideas may start to form on the page.

Forget everything you know. Too often, we let our biases creep in and influence our thinking. Start fresh, without preconceived notions of what you must do or what is impossible. Be open to anything and everything.

Borrow an idea. Everyone thinks that their business is not like anyone else's. The truth is that all of our businesses are more alike than they are different. Look at what others are doing in other industries and see how you can apply their ideas to your own business. If a solution is working for someone else, there's no reason it won't work for you, too. By the time you adapt their idea and tailor it to precisely fit your business, it will be unique.

Hire a professional. If you're really and truly stuck on something, or if a deadline is rapidly approaching, there's no shame in hiring a little outside help. Hiring a consultant can be a great investment. Often times, they don't even have to come up with the ideas for you. They simply ask the right questions that will lead you to the great idea that's buried in your brain.

I keep up with my great ideas on a Word document that I've uploaded to Google Docs. This document holds some of the most creative thoughts I've ever had. I've never shown it to anyone, nor will I, as it contains ideas that might seem silly to other people, but I value it greatly as a place where I can think freely and creatively without criticism.

That's truly the key to coming up with great ideas. You need to free yourself from worry about what other people might say. If you have a place where you can brainstorm and record some of your most outrageous thoughts for getting attention without having to worry about someone else laughing at you, then you'll find that it's much easier to be creative, and, well, outrageous. And before you know it, your great ideas will be boosting your business.

■ ABOUT THE AUTHOR

Jim Kukral is the author of *Attention! This Book Will Make You Money: How to Use Attention-Getting Online Marketing to Increase Your Revenue* (John Wiley & Sons, Inc., 2010). For over 15 years, Jim has helped small businesses and large companies like FedEx, Sherwin-Williams, Ernst & Young, and Progressive Auto Insurance understand how to find success on the Web. Jim is also a professional speaker, blogger, and Web business consultant. Jim teaches thousands of students around the globe as an adjunct professor for the University of San Francisco's Internet Marketing Program. He has been quoted or featured in some way in online and offline print publications such as *Forbes, Brandweek, Entrepreneur,* the *Wall Street Journal,* the *New York Times, BusinessWeek, Small Business Trends, FeedFront, Revenue Today, Marketing Sherpa,* and *Duct Tape Marketing Network.* Find out more by visiting www.jimkukral.com and www.AttentionTheBook.com.

Web Sites

www.jimkukral.com

Primary Products or Books

Attention! This Book Will Make You Money (John Wiley & Sons, Inc., 2010)

Chapter 21

Marketing WITHOUT Marketing

Ryan Lee

Since the name of the book is called *Mastering the World of Marketing*, it might seem strange that I am going to show you how to master the art of nonmarketing.

That's right, nonmarketing.

Ok, let me explain.

Most businesses rely extensively on bringing new clients, customers, or patients through their doors on a regular basis. Here's an example . . .

Melissa Matzel is a local massage therapist. She implemented all of the marketing she learned in this book and brought in five new clients last month. That's great. But, there's a problem . . .

Starting on the first day of the next month, she's back to zero. Meaning, if those new clients do not hire Melissa for another massage, she has to continue marketing to find new clients to fill the bucket. And the cycle never ends.

This is common in just about every business. Dry cleaners, information marketers, restaurants, personal trainers, physicians, and the list goes on and on.

So here's my simple solution: Start to focus on "continuity income."

Continuity income has many different names: recurring revenue, passive income, or residual income. But no matter what it's called, it's still the same concept.

Continuity income is having consumers on some type of plan or program where they pay ongoing fees to continue with the program.

For example, let's go back to Melissa. Instead of just charging one massage at a time for $100, she can offer a monthly plan that includes the first massage each month for just $80, then additional massages are $75 or so. The clients will be billed monthly for the $80 whether they use the first massage or not. This gives the client a nice discount (and assures they will not go to other massage therapists), plus it also gives Melissa guaranteed income each month.

When you have people paying you $XX per month, it completely takes the pressure off of always trying to find new clients.

It shifts the model from customer acquisition to customer fulfillment.

Really think about the monumental shift that occurs when this happens. You can now focus much more of your time, effort, and resources on making your customers, clients, and patients happy—instead of the pressure of constantly searching for new people.

Now, let's look at the two types of basic continuity programs . . .

■ ONLINE CONTINUITY

For most people, the idea of creating continuity programs on the Internet makes sense. It's easy to conceptualize this model online. Here are some examples of online continuity programs . . .

➤ **Paid membership site.** Everyone from Consumer Reports to the *New York Times* now offer members-only content. Members usually pay a monthly fee for exclusive content in the form of articles, audio, and/or video. Membership dues vary greatly depending on the market and topic anywhere from $5 up to $400-plus per month.

➤ **Software solutions.** Software is one of the best continuity income business models. It's no coincidence that Bill Gates is one of the richest men in the world (he's in the software business!). If you can create a Web-based software program to solve a problem in your niche market you can charge a monthly fee. And don't worry about being a "techie," you can hire people to create your software inexpensively. Check out www.guru.com, www.elance.com, or www.rentacoder.com to get bids by software developers.

➤ **Coaching program.** If you have specialized knowledge, you can create a high-end, online coaching program. I've helped all types of professionals create six-figure telephone and Web coaching programs. Everyone from personal trainers to someone who owns a dry cleaning delivery route has created high-priced coaching programs.

■ OFFLINE CONTINUITY

Now, this is where we really start having fun and have to think outside the box.

The most obvious example of a continuity program in the "offline" world is a health club. Members pay monthly dues for access to the facility. But what if you don't own a health club? Never fear, here are some ideas to get you started in the wonderful world of continuity income. . . .

➤ **VIP Club.** Imagine having people *pay* you to buy more? Just look at Barnes and Noble or Costo. Members pay an annual fee for special discounts and other privileges. There's even a new barbershop which charges a monthly fee for discounted haircuts, priority appointments, and exclusive access. Think about how you can carve out a VIP club in your business.

➤ **Maintenance Service.** If you offer a service, you can create a maintenance program. I've seen every business from pest control and landscapers to carpet cleaners offer maintenance programs so customers can get continued service at a great price. Plus, it helps you with cash flow too!

➤ **All You Can X.** How do you turn a bagel shop into a continuity program? Our local bagel shop has an "unlimited coffee refills" program. You pay around $100 per year for a special mug. Just come into the shop for your refill. The bagel shop brings in tens of thousands of dollars in income to start the New Year off right—plus when people come for coffee, they usually buy something else too. How can you create an "all you can eat" variation in your business?

■ ABOUT THE AUTHOR

Ryan Lee is one of the world's leading marketing experts and known as the "Continuity King." He's been featured on the front page of the *Wall Street Journal* and the cover of *Millionaire Blueprints* magazine. Ryan now helps over 250,000 people build smart businesses through his web site and through his free videos and popular newsletter. Get his free report "7 Ways to Instantly Double Your Income" at www .ryanlee.com.

Web Sites

www.ryanlee.com

Primary Products or Books

7 Ways to Instantly Double Your Income

Chapter 22

Where and When to Begin Marketing

Jay Conrad Levinson

Guerrillas are never stopped by analysis paralysis. Don't let it stop you.

Many business owners realize the simplicity of marketing, but just don't know where they should begin. Analysis paralysis stops them in their tracks. So many tasks. Where to start? So they don't start. They know what they must do, but don't really have a plan, so they make disconnected efforts to achieve a hazy goal. When they don't see encouraging results right off the bat, they lose confidence, if any existed in the first place.

If there's any correct time to start, it's right now. If there's any proper place, it's right where you are. You'll never feel you are completely ready, so you may as well begin immediately.

If there's any secret to be learned, it's the secret of taking action and never stopping. You've heard Diana Ross sing when she was a member of The Supremes. Hear now what she says about taking action: "You can't just sit there and wait for people to give you that golden dream; you've got to get out there and make it happen for yourself."

Guerrillas have learned that the best time to market is when they don't need any more business. They know that the best source of new clients is old clients and that the best marketing is characterized by quality and not quantity. They realize that their best marketing vehicle, and least expensive, is a satisfied customer. And they know that the two best ways to measure their marketing are by customer retention and by profits, both a part of each other.

It's wise to think of your marketing the same as you think about your rent. You pay it and never think twice. It's also wise to think of your marketing as breathing. You couldn't exist with only one breath, or even two or three. Don't think you're going to attract a new customer with only one effort, or even two or three. You keep breathing and stay alive. You keep marketing and stay profitable.

Every part of your success is dependent upon one individual. You are that individual. You're in charge. You say when to begin. You've got the insight to make the right decisions now. To succeed, you're going to need that insight, along with courage and conscientiousness. If you're frightened of making mistakes, you're sunk. Accept that you'll make mistakes. Each one has a lesson to be learned.

Michael Eisner, former chairman and CEO of Disney, and the man who propelled it to undreamt-of success, says, "At a certain level, what we do at Disney is very simple. We set our goals, aim for perfection, inevitably fall short, try to learn from our mistakes, and hope that our successes will continue to outnumber our failures." There's nothing Mickey Mouse about that kind of philosophy—because it embraces mistakes as part of the process.

There is no need to hit a home run the first time you're at bat. A single will do, then another single, then another, one following each other, none grandiose, but all bringing you closer to your goal.

As small business grows, so does the need for mastering guerrilla marketing. And small business is growing faster than ever. As entrepreneurs arise all over the globe, so does the need for mastering guerrilla marketing. Just a new kid on the block as the twentieth century headed toward its completion, guerrilla marketing is now a powerful and proven force worldwide. It must be reckoned with and best yet, utilized. Some would say it's mandatory for small business survival.

Ask any small business owner: It's far easier to employ guerrilla marketing than hope to defend yourself against it.

A whale of a lot has changed since I wrote the first guerrilla marketing book in 1984. And almost all of it favors small business. Marketing itself has changed dramatically and interactively, not to mention electronically. So has the array of weapons available to guerrillas—more powerful than ever, yet half of them completely free. That's why so many guerrillas are smiling so broadly. They also know that many things have not changed and that those things are as important as the things that have.

I'm referring to the soul and essence of guerrilla marketing, which remain as always—achieving conventional goals, such as profits and joy, with unconventional methods, such as investing energy instead of money. I'm also referring to humanity, which is relatively unchanged since the first book, indeed, since the first human.

It's not possible to ignore the fact that we're in a new century, even though if you look out the window, you can't see much that has changed. If you look into the hearts and minds of your prospects, you'll see that very little has changed there, too. Certainly, there's a growing awareness of the precious and elusive nature of time, perhaps even a bit more humanity, made possible by, of all things, technology.

The marketing world has changed because it has shrunk rather than expanded. Again, credit technology for the shrink job, accomplished not as much by the jet as the net. Marketing has also become a lot more technical. But that doesn't mean you have to be technical—because technology has met you more than halfway by becoming much easier to use and even easier to pay for.

Guerrillas welcome the changes as much as they welcome the status quos. They are fully alert to what has changed and what must never change. They know well the difference between change and improvement. Analysis paralysis is a condition that has been eliminated in their world.

■ ABOUT THE AUTHOR

Jay Conrad Levinson is "The Father of Guerrilla Marketing" and the author of the Guerrilla Marketing series of books. Guerrilla Marketing is the best-known marketing brand in history, named one of the 100 best business books ever written, with over 21 million copies sold. His Guerrilla concepts have influenced marketing so much that his books appear in 62 languages and are required reading in MBA programs worldwide.

He was born in Detroit, raised in Chicago, and graduated from the University of Colorado. His studies in psychology led him to advertising agencies, including a Directorship at Leo Burnett in London, where he served as Creative Director. Returning to the United States, he joined J. Walter Thompson as Senior VP. Jay created and taught guerrilla marketing for 10 years at the extension division of the University of California in Berkeley.

A winner of first prizes in all the media, he has been part of the creative teams that made household names of The Marlboro Man, The Pillsbury Doughboy, Allstate's Good Hands, United's Friendly Skies, the Sears Diehard Battery, Morris the Cat, Mr. Clean, Tony the Tiger, and the Jolly Green Giant.

After living in the San Francisco Bay Area for 35 years, Jay and Jeannie Levinson sold their home, bought an RV, towed a Jeep, and ended up, six years later, at their lakefront home outside Orlando, Florida, and close to their 26 grandchildren, their own personal Disney World. Nobody on earth is as qualified to tell you about Guerrilla Marketing than "The Father of Guerrilla Marketing," Jay Conrad Levinson.

Web Sites

www.gmarketing.com

http://guerrillamarketingassociation.com

Primary Products or Books

Guerrilla Marketing Goes Green (John Wiley & Sons, Inc., 2010)

Guerrilla Business Secrets: 58 Ways to Start, Build, and Sell Your Business (Morgan James Publishing, 2009)

Guerrilla Profits: 10 Powerful Strategies to Increase Cashflow, Boost Earnings & Get More Business (Morgan James Publishing, 2008)

chapter 23

Top Eleven Proven Ways to Grow Your E-Mail Marketing List

Andrew Lutts

One of the best ways to grow your business is with e-mail marketing, and one of the most important things to do in e-mail marketing is to grow your subscriber list. More subscribers on your list means more potential new customers and business, and e-mail is a great way to keep both clients and prospects current on your business offerings.

Increase the number of people that you reach.

Try these strategies to get more subscribers and do more business online. Only you can determine how much time and effort to spend on these endeavors, but these tactics can help you grow your business and separate you from your competition.

Top 11 Proven Methods

1. Optimize current customer communications
2. Convert offline prospects to online prospects
3. Make use of industry e-mail newsletters
4. Use an e-mail appending service
5. Consider coregistration vendors
6. Sponsor an online event, or use an online tie-in
7. Make use of online marketing resources
8. Give your subscribers the tools to share
9. Send a postcard and convert people to online
10. Set up comarketing and cross-promotions
11. Become an online subject-matter expert

■ PROVEN METHOD 1: OPTIMIZE CURRENT CUSTOMER COMMUNICATION

Here are several ways to make use of various forms of customer communication on contact points and opportunities in order to help you grow your list:

1. Put e-mail newsletter sign-up forms on your home page and all other web pages on your web site. Also near your web page sign-up forms you should create a link to your privacy policy, and so on to assure visitors that you will not sell or rent their e-mail address to anyone. Use a nice colorful icon newsletter graphic. You can even include a screen capture of your newsletter to show how your newsletter is professional, interesting, and desirable.

2. In the e-mail signatures of you and all your employees, add a link to get the company e-mail newsletter. Be sure that salespeople and customer service people use this strategy, as they normally generate a lot of outgoing e-mail.

3. At the receptionist desk of your office, or at your cash register, and so on, have a clipboard where people can sign up to get your free e-mail newsletter.

4. At your trade show booth, put a sign up that enters people for a free giveaway, and also subscribes them to your free e-mail newsletter.

5. Inside all outgoing postal mail from your business, include a small colorful paper insert that invites people to get your e-mail newsletter. Set up an easy-to-type-in landing page address, and offer a premium for signing up.

6. On your monthly billing statements, invoices, and receipts include a line at the bottom that tells visitors how to get your free e-mail newsletter.

7. If people on your web site order an item or fill out any form, mention your e-mail newsletter on your thank you web page and encourage them to subscribe to it.

8. When people exchange business cards with you, ask them if they would like to get on your e-mail list. When you get back to your office, add them to your list.

9. Include a link to the free newsletter in the CONTACT US section of your web site, handouts, and more.

10. Be sure to indicate the mailing frequency of your newsletter (weekly, monthly), so that people know how many newsletters to expect from you.

11. At the section of your web pages where people sign up for your newsletter, list the types of articles and information you usually include in your newsletters so that people will know what they are getting. Also, include a quote from a happy subscriber like "your newsletter is great, I look forward to it every month!"

Often the newsletter message will start with full disclosure, with something like: "As a member of the Newsletter Association of America e-mail list, you indicated that you would like to receive information about business promotions and ideas on how to grow your business." For best results, offer something of value, like a free whitepaper download, free report, free trial, initial consultation, coupon discount, or other item of value that starts the relationship with your company.

■ PROVEN METHOD 2: USE AN E-MAIL APPENDING SERVICE

You can easily turn over your lead database (without e-mail addresses) to an e-mail appending company, and get a list of updated records with e-mail addresses in return. Use this for both your current prospect list and former clients who have not heard from you for some time. Some of our favorite e-mail appending services include:

FreshAddress

www.freshaddress.com

MarketOne

www.marketone.com

Reachforce

www.reachforce.com

■ PROVEN METHOD 3: CONVERT OFFLINE PROSPECTS TO ONLINE PROSPECTS

If you are looking to grow and expand your e-mail newsletter and online prospect database, advertise to a specific vertical market or business group that you want to reach. You could do a space advertisement or direct mail piece. Send them to your web site, or a specific focused landing page with a bonus premium, or give them an e-mail address to reply to for more information and to get on the e-mail distribution list. Also, as your sales team takes incoming telephone calls, they should ask the callers if they would like to be added to the e-mail mailing list for service updates.

■ PROVEN METHOD 4: MAKE USE OF INDUSTRY E-MAIL NEWSLETTERS

Put your information or advertisement in someone else's existing e-mail newsletter, and get people to come to your web site and subscribe to your newsletter. Industry e-mail newsletters are great places to advertise in; in fact, they provide you with an implicit endorsement of your company by running your ad or whitepaper. So if there is a good trade or industry publication in your vertical market, consider advertising in it.

Less common but sometimes used, an industry e-mail newsletter will let you run a "solo ad" in which only your promotion is sent in their e-mail to their subscribers. This can be a bit expensive, but can provide great returns.

■ PROVEN METHOD 5: CONSIDER COREGISTRATION VENDORS

Buying or renting mailing lists can be a risky proposition. That said, there are reputable vendors who can and do provide list owners with opt-in subscribers who are interested in receiving e-mail on specific topics. One of the best ways to do this is with coregistration. Always considered to be a very effective way to build your mailing list, coregistration is something every mailing list owner and newsletter publisher should consider.

Definition: True coregistration is simply an agreement between you and another newsletter publisher for cross promotion. This can sometimes be done without cost to either party.

How it works: You simply place a description of each other's newsletter on your "thank you for subscribing" web page. Each time a person subscribes to your partner's newsletter, she is also given the chance to subscribe to yours at the same time. Once the subscription is confirmed (with a confirmed opt-in e-mail), you've got a new subscriber.

Costs: Some people pay from 50 cents to $3 per name for a consumer (B2C) e-mail address. Business e-mail contacts (B2B) can sell for $10 to $12 and up.

Various Coregistration Vendors

Pontiflex

www.pontiflex.com

CPL (cost per lead) marketplace for companies that want to place digital ads

Opt-Intelligence (premier hosted network for the facilitation of explicit, real-time, consumer opt-ins)

www.opt-intelligence.com

OptMedia (leading coregistrations providers, supplying over 4,000 leads a day to our top buyers)

http://opt-media.com

eTargetMedia.com (online direct marketing solutions with focus on customer acquisition goals and return on investment)

www.etargetmedia.com

CoregMedia (end-to-end coregistration and lead-generation network for online publishers and advertisers)

www.coregmedia.com

Being a key contributor or sponsor to a worthwhile cause can help put you right in front of your targeted audience. Don't forget to write some press releases on your community involvement.

■ PROVEN METHOD 6: SPONSOR AN ONLINE EVENT

In the past, event marketing has meant getting visibility at conferences, sporting events, seminars, or nonprofit or social causes. Now these same opportunities can be performed online.

➤ Sponsor an online event of a company with a closely related service or business. So, for example, if you sell car parts, then consider sponsoring an online auto show or auto enthusiast online discussion forum.

➤ Support a public television online auction or other similar nonprofit fundraising event. Donate services, money, or employee time to help the organization achieve its goal. Have fun knowing that your efforts are all for the common good, and that they might bring you new business.

➤ Try sponsoring an online webinar from a strategic partner, and share the leads generated.

➤ Become a premier sponsor of a virtual trade show, and develop leads and prospects with other vendors and sponsors of the show.

➤ Keep an eye out for product placement opportunities online, where free or paid mentions or exposure to your services are just a mouse click away.

■ PROVEN METHOD 7: MAKE USE OF ONLINE MARKETING RESOURCES

Coregistration, tell-a-friend, lead generation, and affiliate marketing resources can all bring in new leads, prospects and clients. Here's a list of resources to check out:

Focalex/TAF Master (tell-a-friend) service—www.focalex.com

LinkShare—www.linkshare.com

LinkConnector—www.linkconnector.com

ClickBank—www.clickbank.com

ShareASale—www.shareasale.com

OnResponse—www.onresponse.com

Webclients.net—www.webclients.net

Commission Junction—www.cj.com

■ PROVEN METHOD 8: GIVE YOUR SUBSCRIBERS THE TOOLS TO SHARE YOUR MESSAGE

Encourage readers of your online publications and web sites to forward-to-a-friend, promote to Digg, delicious, reddit, and other places. In the body content of your messages be sure to suggest that "if they like what they are reading to forward to others." Make sure all your newsletters have a subscribe link or instructions in case someone gave them the newsletter.

■ PROVEN METHOD 9: SEND A POSTCARD TO CONVERT PEOPLE TO ONLINE

Send a postcard out and offer a premium gift as an incentive. Offer one hour of consulting to "qualified" prospects. Present people with an offer they simply can't refuse. Again, the response to any of these promotions will probably be highest if you can offer something of value. Whether your promotion invites people to visit your home page, or links directly to a special promotional landing page, make sure that page also includes a clear and appealing invitation to subscribe to your newsletter.

■ PROVEN METHOD 10: SET UP COMARKETING AND CROSS-PROMOTIONS

Partner with other companies that have a strategic product or service. Combine budgets to create cross-promotional online advertising beyond what you might normally do on your own. Try to choose partners who have similar reputations and scope to yours.

Compile shared leads between companies, as partners, and cross-promote your solution. This will make it a softer sell, since you are not simply promoting your own solution, but those of a trusted friend.

Sometimes comarketing is a paid arrangement; other times you can set it up to be more of a reciprocal arrangement.

■ PROVEN METHOD 11: BECOME AN ONLINE SUBJECT-MATTER EXPERT

You can build your reputation and traffic to your online properties by being a subject-matter expert. How? Post to blogs, forums, and provide useful relevant content. Submit articles to online publications, and include a link or e-mail address to your online newsletter.

■ ABOUT THE AUTHOR

As founder of Net Atlantic in 1995, Andy Lutts is responsible for the vision and strategy of the company. A pioneer in the fields of web hosting and e-mail marketing, Net Atlantic has thrived under Andy's leadership to become one of the nation's premier e-mail service providers.

Prior to Net Atlantic, Andy served as the vice president of Cabot Money Management, where he managed the IT efforts and Internet-based transactions with financial institutions. Andy helped grow the company to more than 10 times its size in just eight years. Before that Andy worked in sales and marketing for a California crystal manufacturing company, working in new product development and product launches.

Andy received his bachelor's degree in professional writing from Carnegie Mellon University. He currently serves as a board member of the North Shore Technology Council, the Enterprise Center at Salem State College, and the Samaritan Society.

Web Sites

www.netatlantic.com

Primary Products or Books

Manifesting Magnificence: Consciously Creating the Life You Choose to Live (Xlibris Corporation, 2008)

Chapter 24

Setting a Marketing Budget

Scott C. Margenau

One of the most important decisions that a small or medium-size business (SMB) has to make is how much money to allocate for the marketing budget. Prospects often ask, "How much should I spend on marketing?"

The answer: "It varies by industry and business size." It is also based on how much you want to grow, and how fast. Both the Counselors to America's Small Business (SCORE) and the U.S. Small Business Administration (SBA) define the variable for a proper marketing budget to be between 2 percent and 10 percent of sales, noting that for business-to-business (B2B), retail, and pharmaceuticals it can exceed 20 percent during peak brand-building years.

Most companies underspend on their marketing budgets, thinking that to not spend is to save. This quite simply isn't true. You've heard it before, and it bears repeating: *You have to spend money to make money.* The trick is to spend your money wisely on a tailored marketing plan aimed at fulfilling your company's goals. Keep in mind that your marketing efforts have a direct bearing on your revenue, so now is not the time to be penny wise and pound foolish.

■ HOW TO SET A MARKETING BUDGET: BUDGET-SETTING GUIDELINES

Two main things should be considered when setting a marketing budget:

1. The *development or refinement of the brand* and the channels used to promote the brand. These include logos, web sites, blogs, e-mail campaigns, sales presentations, brochures, ads, and so on.

2. The *ongoing expense* of promoting and advertising your brand to your customer base and your prospects.

Less than $5 million	7–8%
$5–10 million	6–7%
$10–50 million	5–6%
$50–100 million	4–5%
More than $100 million	1–3%

FIGURE 24.1

For most SMBs, the percentage of revenue dedicated to a marketing budget is determined by industry and size. But, in general terms, Figure 24.1 shows some information we have put together based on several credible sources.

■ AN IMPORTANT CONSIDERATION (ADJUST FOR INDUSTRY!)

Every industry is different, so companies that *sell to specific government branches* or one that has an *ultraspecialized niche* may be able to deduct 1 to 2 percent from the above figures. If your company is *B2B* or *business-to-consumer (B2C)*, you may need to raise your budget by 1 to 3 percent to see solid results. *Retail* and *pharmaceuticals* lead the spending, with many of these companies spending more than 20 percent of net sales. The overall average is reported to be 4 to 6 percent. Many other circumstances will merit an increase or reduction in your marketing budget as a percentage of revenue.

Feel free to contact us to discuss this, or visit www.sba.gov/smallbusinessplanner/index.html.
Here is a great quote from SCORE:

Often, small businesses estimate their sales revenue, cost-of-goods, overhead and salaries, and then gross profit. Anything left is considered available funds for marketing support. That's not such a good idea. . . . If you are the new competitor in the marketplace, you will have to spend more aggressively to establish your market share objective.

You can find the complete article at www.score.org/m_pr_11.html.

■ CAN I STILL GROW MY COMPANY WITH "BABY STEPS"?

Sure. We call this organic growth, and it is how nearly every business starts off. Remember washing cars or mowing lawns for a few bucks?

Next thing you know, your neighbor wants it done. That neighbor refers you to another neighbor and so on. Many businesses grow their clientele by word-of-mouth alone and are very successful. *But they usually hit a brick wall.* That's where building a solid branding campaign helps. When you rely on partial branding or organic growth alone, you risk losing revenue from business you did not get because *X percent never discovered you* or did not have their interest piqued when they interacted with your brand. And you cannot tally the lost revenue from those who *perceived your current brand negatively* and left your web site without you ever knowing it. This is why it is so important to build the brand correctly. Why risk millions to save thousands?

■ WHY DO SO MANY SMBS FAIL?

One reason is that companies do not allocate enough money for marketing. Successful and highly profitable SMBs know how to allocate adequate funding to marketing each year. SMBs realize that marketing, if done properly, brings back solid returns and vice versa—whereas not allocating enough in your budget for marketing could spell disaster. Think of marketing this way: *It is a fundamental ingredient for profitability and growth.*

■ ABOUT THE AUTHOR

Scott C. Margenau is the founder and CEO of ImageWorks Studio, an award-winning web design, branding, and online marketing firm. For more advice on how to use of your marketing dollars, feel free to contact sales@imageworksstudio.com or call 800–308–8573. Image-Works Studio can be found online at www.imageworkstudio.com.

Web Sites

www.imageworksstudio.com

Chapter 25

Big-Ass Fans and the Naked Truth about Attention and Controversy

Perry Marshall

One of the advertisers that grace the pages of nearly every industrial trade magazine now is a certain company called *Big-Ass Fans*.

Ahem, they are more formally known as HVLS Inc. of Lexington, Kentucky. But whatever you choose to call them, this company makes very large fans for big industrial buildings, barns, and warehouses, and they promote themselves in a very loud, obnoxious, and funny way.

There's definitely a lesson to be learned from Big-Ass Fans.

Bill Buell, the Big-Ass Fan Guy continues to astound and amaze. I went to see his entourage at the National Manufacturing show in Chicago, where he had a prominent booth near the front of the exhibit hall and a big long line of customers waiting to get autographs from NFL star Refrigerator Perry.

This Bill Buell character is no slouch. Because he was bringing an NFL football star to the show, he was able to negotiate a really sweet deal with the trade show promoters on booth space. His spacious booth was right behind Grainger's, and he got it for a song.

So here he is with cheap space and a mile of prospects wrapped around his display, waiting to get autographs and chatting with his Big-Ass salespeople about their heating and cooling problems.

Not bad, eh?

I asked Bill about his background. During most of the nineties, he published a trade journal in the agriculture industry, a high quality mag that required subscribers to fill out a thoroughly exhaustive two-page application in order to get on the list. (Compare that to the six or eight questions most trade mags require.)

Vendors desperately wanted to rent his list, which if I recall was fewer than 50,000 highly targeted prospects. But his list was *not* for sale. He meticulously groomed it and continued to run his magazine, all the while besieged with requests for access to his customer base.

Eventually one of those vendors bought his company outright for a hefty sum of money, just so they could own that list. (Note the lesson here, and my contention that your most valuable asset is your customer list. Even a reason for somebody to pay you millions of dollars for what you've built.)

A friend had a company called HVLS (High Velocity Low Speed), which had been taking a too-boring approach to selling their large fans, and the rest, as they say, is history.

Big-Ass Fans is now advertising in over 60 industrial and agricultural trade magazines, and is growing faster than any other industrial company that I'm aware of.

Let me repeat myself. At a time when everyone's griping and groaning about the woes of the economy, competition from the Asians, etc., etc., these guys are making a killing. Triple-digit growth rates. Right here in our own industrial sandbox.

Bill's brilliant combination: a product with broad appeal (just about every large building has unsolved cooling and heating problems) and an incredibly unique identity in the marketplace. People walk up to Bill all day long at the trade show and tell them how they've ripped his ads out of magazines and showed them to their wives and kids, just because they're so outrageous.

About Refrigerator Perry: I have no idea whatsoever, how much it costs to have him as a spokesman. However, it's probably less than you might guess, especially considering they've got an extended contract with him. There's a very large number of famous people, former athletes, movie stars, and so on who are eager to find such work, and agencies who specialize in making the deals. Don't overlook the possibility of doing the same thing in your business.

■ LOVE LETTERS AND HATE MAIL

Big-Ass Fans has a *Rants & Raves* section on their web site where they post comments they get on their Big-Ass marketing. Here's a sampling:

> As a professional organization, we feel the choice of your solicitations is inappropriate and crass. The use of profanity in publications for shock value is very risky when dealing with corporations who value respect and decency, such as we do. While you are certainly entitled to your

marketing tactics, we are highly offended, and will not be purchasing your material.

You may not care, but I too am disgusted with the name of your company and your advertising. I am currently in the market for some air moving equipment, but would not even consider buying from you because of your choice of names. Change that and I might consider you. Otherwise, I'll find someone else.

I was just perusing the site and started to read the comments & kudos section. Boy, some people are really anal (no pun intended). A little fun and a sense of humor goes a long way. If the folks that are offended can't see the fun and the marketing genius in your name, then you don't need them as customers.

You guys rock. This might be the coolest name for a company ever. How can you forget a name like BIGASSFANS!!!!!! Whoever the marketing person is, is a god. I saw your bumper sticker on a guys car leaving Target and fell on the ground laughing going is this for real . . . and here I am. If you guys have any promo stuff . . . bumper sticks, hats, shirts whatever I will be happy to promote you. By the way if you ever need a HR Manager let me know. I would love to put on my resume that I worked for Big-Ass Fans Inc . . . and oh yeah "The Fridge" is the spokesman. By far I bet this is one HELL of a fun company to work for. I wish you the best of luck in your business.

Listen up: *You have two choices, and only two.*

1. You can be normal, acceptable, boring, and quickly forgotten.
2. Or you can be bold, flamboyant, *offensive to some*, loved by others, and long remembered.

Understand this: You will *not* be loved by some unless you are willing to be resented by others. You will not endear yourself to one crowd without antagonizing another. It ain't never going to happen.

Take a look at any influential, famous, or successful person you care to name. Bill Clinton. Mick Jagger. Gandhi. Britney Spears. Nelson Mandela. Christopher Columbus. Pee Wee Herman. Gloria Steinem. Steve Jobs. Mother Teresa. Ralph Nader.

Every one of these people has a polarizing effect on the world around them. People either love 'em or hate 'em. These are people who have boldly presented themselves, their ideas, and accomplishments to the world and ignored the naysayers.

So the question for you is: What bold, controversial, and decisive stand can you take, that will polarize people—that will repel some and attract others?

Success lies on the other side of your answer to that question.

■ IF YOU DON'T WANT TO GET CUT, DON'T GET INTO A SWORD FIGHT

A parting comment before I go.

My four-year-old son, Cuyler, *loves* swords. Just about every morning you can find him in the living room, standing there in his underwear, swinging his plastic swords all over the place and jousting with imaginary foes.

Today his friend Jack was over, and they were playing swords in the backyard. Cuyler suddenly came running in the house, crying.

"Jack hurt my finger!"

"What were you doing?"

"We were playing swords."

"Well, Cuyler, that's what happens when you play swords."

Most people are just like my four-year-old when it comes to rocking the boat among their friends, industry, and peers. They like to *talk* about sword fighting. They like to watch it. They like to strut around and act like a gladiator in the safety and comfort of their living room.

But when their pinky gets cut, they start crying and run back into the house.

There are a lot of people who are living the professional version of Cuyler's sword fighting—it's all pretend, and they actually have no intention of making a difference, standing up for anything, challenging anyone, or championing any cause. They just stare blankly at the car ahead of them during their morning commute, they submissively comply with whatever corporate BS comes down the pipe, and they carefully avoid making any waves.

What a crummy way to go through life. If you do anything well, there are some people who aren't going to like it. Heck, if you look on the Internet, you can even find people who are against Mother Teresa. So whether you're selling fans in Kentucky, installing conveyor systems in Winnipeg, or saving the world in Calcutta, if you're going to do it, do it in a big-ass way.

■ ABOUT THE AUTHOR

Perry Marshall is the best-selling author and most quoted authority in the world on the subject of Google advertising. He has helped over 100,000 advertisers save billions of dollars in *AdWords'* "stupidity tax."

His Chicago company, Perry S. Marshall & Associates, consults online and brick-and-mortar companies on generating sales leads, web traffic, and maximizing advertising results.

Prior to his consulting career, he helped grow a tech company from $200,000 to $4 million in sales in four years, and the firm was sold to a public company for $18 million.

He's published hundreds of articles on sales, marketing, and technology, including *The Ultimate Guide to Google AdWords* (Entrepreneur Press, 2010), which is the world's most popular book on Google advertising. He is also author of *Industrial Ethernet* (ISA, 2004).

He's spoken at conferences around the world and consulted in over 200 industries, from computer hardware and software to high-end consulting, from health and fitness to corporate finance.

Web Sites

www.perrymarshall.com

Primary Products or Books

The Ultimate Guide to Google AdWords (Entrepreneur Press, 2010)

Industrial Ethernet (ISA, 2004)

Chapter 26

What Makes Things Go Viral

Peggy McColl

Do you want to know how to stand out online and how to create a viral buzz to get people talking about you? Do you want to know the differences between online and offline marketing? Then read on and find out what makes things go viral.

There is a lot of clutter on the Internet right now, but it is possible to stand out.

I believe the Internet provides all of us with a tremendous opportunity, and at the same time, it creates a big challenge (because of the clutter). Yes, it is possible to stand out, but it does take discipline and effort.

To stand out you need to understand two things:

1. Where is your audience going online?
2. What is it they are needing/wanting/interested in online?

If you do not have a presence online you will need to build it by getting help and support from others who are also online. Create an offering; that is, give something of value away to your audience ("audience" is another word for prospective customers) and let others (who do have a following) know that you have something of value. Ask others to let their followers/readers/subscribers know about what you have to offer. Create something so valuable that others will want it *and* they'll want to share it with others.

Do the research to find folks who have a following (small, medium-size, and big). Ask other list owners, bloggers, tweeters, and Facebook friends to tell others about you and your offering. Find a way for people to see you everywhere. I would suggest you reach out to thousands of list owners, bloggers, tweeters, and Facebook friends and not expect that reaching out to a few will make much difference. If you want to be noticed and stand out, you will need to create a presence where people will "see you" everywhere.

To create a viral buzz around your products, you need to understand what makes things go "viral." People make things go viral; therefore, you need to appeal to people's emotions. You can help influence people's emotions and the sharing of a message by creating promotional pieces (e-mails, web site copy, videos, tweets, Facebook posts) utilizing one or a combination of the following in your copy:

1. *Unbelievable:* Your message contains something that is shocking and unexpected in a good or a bad way.

2. *Create curiosity:* It gets people thinking and talking and perhaps even wanting more (curiosity is a big motivator for people—don't underestimate it).

3. *Brilliantly created:* Your message is clever and intelligently presented (it may not be "new," but you've found a way to share something with others in a unique way).

4. *Humor:* It makes people smile or laugh.

5. *Provides a mind-blowing offer:* The offer is so attractive it literally causes people to share it with others. (As a part of my most recent book launch, I gave away 150 other gifts to people who purchased *Viral Explosions* off this web site: http://viralexplosions.com/book.)

6. *Controversial:* It's different from what the masses are saying and/or thinking.

7. *Unusual:* It is unusual, strange, interesting, and creative, and fascinates people.

8. *Deeply needed:* It is something people are hungry for. It solves a very common problem easily, quickly, and better than anyone else (or gives the impression it does).

9. *Adds value:* It is a resource that helps people's lives, and it clearly demonstrates its value.

10. *Important:* Of course, it is imperative that anyone who is marketing online follow the FTC guidelines and communicates ethically, legally, and honestly.

Now, before you begin your marketing efforts, you need to understand that there are a lot of similarities but there are some critical differences between online and offline marketing. For example, when you are attempting to promote or sell anything online, you have only a few seconds to grab people's attention, keep it, and get them to take action. When an e-mail lands in someone's inbox, there is a fraction of a section that occurs between the recipient deciding to either read it or delete it. The subject line in an e-mail is *the* most important line. If the subject line does not get the recipient to open the e-mail, it is ineffective. Online marketing means that you have to communicate your message clearly, quickly, persuasively (appropriately and following the FTC guidelines of course), and be clear on the "call to action" (the call to action is the action you would like the recipient to take—i.e., go to a particular web site or sign up for something or tell a friend).

Online marketing allows us to operate a business without a physical storefront or building. Small businesses are popping up everywhere. Solopreneurs are able to work from the comfort of their own home and, in some cases, build a team and have their team members work from the comfort of their homes, too. You no longer need to employ a large staff when you can outsource certain jobs to experts who live in other parts of the world. I've done business with people I've never met.

It may seem faster and easier than offline marketing, but you have to recognize that it takes just as much effort and dedication.

People need to realize that there is always work involved in anything. Sure, you'll see books and other programs telling you that you can make a fortune in real estate but you need to know the ins and outs of this type of investment strategy; *plus* you need to do the research. I would suggest that if your objective is to make money online to build a business, expand a business, or subsidize an income, you should enter into a business that you are passionate about. If you deeply care about what you are doing, you will more likely have the extra energy to pursue it when you meet challenges or roadblocks. I would suggest you find role models, mentors, teachers, guides . . . people who have created success and are willing to share it with you.

Take a look at results. Results always speak for themselves. For example, one of the things that I do is mentor authors. I teach/guide authors to create best-sellers for their books. I have credibility because, in addition to creating best-seller status for my own books, I've helped *many* other authors create best-seller status for their books, too. I have earned the reputation, but it wasn't an overnight success. It took many months and a lot of work (no blood, but definitely some sweat and a few tears). I learned what to do to effectively market books online, and I've learned what not to do. Each one of those is important (what to do and what not to do). One more thing (and this may seem utterly ridiculous) . . . I also suggest that when you are researching online money-making opportunities, that you let your gut be your guide. Our instincts are a great guide, and I know my instincts have always been right (well, maybe not always but most of the time).

My instincts have also allowed me to follow what I preach. I started out with 3,000 self-published hardcover books sitting in my dining room and a lot of debt. I was unemployed at the time and had exactly *zero* dollars coming in for revenue. I was a single mom and had responsibilities to not only care for my young son, but to provide for my household. I was desperate. I wasn't motivated because I wanted to make money . . . I was motivated because I wanted to get my message out to the world. I knew the money would come. I started marketing online when I had a web site but no subscribers and no followers.

I did my research to find out who was reaching my audience. I made a spreadsheet of hundreds and hundreds of web sites who were in the genre of self-help/inspiration/motivation and any other category that was relevant. I reached out to complete strangers, and I asked them to help me spread my message. I prepared a special offer and gave away some extra value by way of "bonus gifts" for anyone who invested in one copy of my book. Within a 48-hour period I had generated tens of thousands of dollars in revenue. Within a couple of weeks people would e-mail me and say, "What else do you have?". . . I found that fascinating and realized that people are hungry. People are hungry for more. People want to be fed, and I can help them in greater ways online. I created an e-course (a course that was delivered over the Internet), and again it allowed me to stay home with my son and offer my services, generate revenue, and help people in the world. Within a short period of time, my reputation was built. It wasn't built *only* because I was asking others to help me spread the word about my products and/or services.

My reputation was built because I was delivering value. People will talk. Your customers will talk to other prospective customers. My customers started to tell other customers about my products and services. It is like a circle (but not a vicious one) . . . it is a wonderful circle of being of service and receiving great value. When you give out great value, you will receive great value back (that usually comes in the form of remuneration—assuming you are selling something). When I wake up in the morning, I have a question that I ask myself each day, which is: "How may I be of service today? How many I serve the world with something of value?"

And, I created a *personal mission statement* that says: *to make a positive difference in the lives of millions of others.*

This personal mission statement is a part of who I am, and I didn't make it to be arrogant or egotistical. I created this statement because I take my work very seriously and I love helping others help others. Many of the experts in the world have contacted me and asked me to help them . . . to help them create a presence or expand their presence online. I feel blessed to do what I do because every part of it is delivering service that is of value to others.

■ ABOUT THE AUTHOR

Peggy McColl specializes in two areas of expertise. She is a *New York Times* best-selling author and an internationally recognized speaker/author/mentor and an expert in the area of goal achievement. She is also a speaker/author/mentor and an expert in helping authors, entrepreneurs, and experts create valuable products; build their brand worldwide; make money online; and create international best sellers! Her latest book is called *Viral Explosions* (Career Press, 2010). Her innovative and laser-focused work has been endorsed by some of the most renowned experts in the personal development field, including Neale Donald Walsch, Bob Proctor, Jack Canfield, Jim Rohn, Mark Victor Hansen, Caroline Myss, Gregg Braden, Debbie Ford, and many others. Her intensive classes, speaking engagements, goal achievement seminars, and best-selling books have inspired individuals, professional athletes, authors, and organizations to reach their maximum potential. Peggy is the president and founder of Dynamic Destinies, Inc., an organization that trains individuals, authors, entrepreneurs, corporate leaders and employees in some of the most compelling and strategic goal-setting technologies of our times.

Web Sites

www.destinies.com

Primary Products or Books

Viral Explosions!: Proven Techniques to Expand, Explode, or Ignite Your Business or Brand Online (Career Press, 2010)

99 Things You Wish You Knew Before Marketing on the Internet (DocUmeant Publishing, 2010)

The Won Thing: The "One" Secret to a Totally Fulfilling Life (Hay House, 2009)

21 Distinctions of Wealth: Attract the Abundance You Deserve (Hay House, 2008)

Your Destiny Switch: Master Your Key Emotions, and Attract the Life of Your Dreams (Hay House, 2007)

The 8 Proven Secrets to SMART Success (Destinies Publishing, 2002)

On Being: The Creator of Your Destiny (Destinies Publishing, 2002)

Chapter 27

There Is No
Word-of-Mouth "Marketing"

Chuck McKay

Pay close attention to Stephanie's story:

> Roger's feet get cold easily, so I bought him a pair of sheepskin slippers.
> He loved them, but it wasn't long before the wool lining started wearing
> off. So I called Lands' End to see if I could get them replaced under war-
> ranty. The lady I talked to was very nice, but she couldn't find any re-
> cord of my purchase, and she couldn't figure out which slippers I was
> describing. But, she cheerfully told me that she'd be happy to exchange
> them, and gave me a return authorization. I was pretty excited when I
> told Roger that Lands' End had agreed to replace his slippers even
> though I couldn't find the sales receipt. He told me that was because I
> bought those slippers from L.L. Bean.

Stephanie tells her story well. People laugh at it. It's the kind of
story that people tell each other daily. It's the kind of story likely to
be repeated by people who don't know either Stephanie or Roger.

There's a critical lesson, though, in Stephanie's story. Did you
catch it? No problem. We'll come back to it in a minute.

Stephanie's story is an example of word-of-mouth.

It's not, however, an example of word-of-mouth "marketing" (WOMMA).

And apologies to WOMMA aside, I'm not convinced that word-of-
mouth marketing exists.

Why? Because adding the word *marketing* assumes that it's something the business causes to happen. Word-of-mouth may be influenced by business, but by its very nature it can never be controlled.

Go back to Stephanie's story for the critical distinction. Is she
telling a story about customer service at Lands' End? No. She's telling

a story about her own experience as a customer. People love to tell stories about themselves.

Exactly how important is your product or your service in the telling of any customer's story? If the stuff you're selling fits into her narration, it might be included. But whether it is or not, word-of-mouth in any of its forms is always about the experience of the buyer. Only indirectly is the seller even involved.

This makes word-of-mouth "marketing" a misnomer.

Word-of-mouth is not marketing for several reasons.

Marketing becomes cost-effective when there are efficiencies of scale. Word-of-mouth takes place on a one-to-one basis.

In marketing, a company sends its message directly to prospects. Word-of-mouth is farther removed from the company with each iteration of the story. People who know the storyteller will be influenced. People who know those people may be slightly influenced. At three degrees removed there will be minimal effect, if any. (And yes, I'm fully expecting a few e-mails pointing out "viral marketing" as an example to the contrary. Can anyone even predict what goes viral? I thought not.)

Finally, people may get your message wrong, and you can't stop it from happening. In a few more tellings, Stephanie's story could easily mutate into a tale about a lady who had a funny interaction with Sears.

Word-of-mouth is not marketing. It's not advertising.

Word-of-mouth existed long before advertising. When most people lived in smaller communities, walked to the market, talked to their neighbors, and gathered in churches or meeting halls, word-of-mouth was simply conversation. Advertising became important communication when our communities got too big for the people selling stuff to personally know their customers. Mass media carried the message from the manufacturers of goods to the new postwar middle class.

But for the last century, probably due to overexposure, we've all become less susceptible to advertising's claims. Customers now are more likely to believe the opinions of total strangers than the advertising messages of local companies.

Ouch.

Word-of-mouth is now more critical to business success than at any time since the dawn of mass media. And yet, you can't make a customer talk about you. You can't make her not talk about you. You're going to be mentioned when you're part of her story. No more. No less.

Change your role in her story.

Although you may view Ms. Customer as a purchaser of the things you sell, she sees herself as the protagonist in her own story. When you try to make the story about your company, Ms. Customer will dismiss your whole effort as irrelevant.

But if your business is willing to become the secondary character in Ms. Customer's personal narrative, is willing to engage Ms. Customer, and indeed to make her story possible, that's when she'll take you along for the ride. Your business "character" will be portrayed in much the same way as her interaction with you happened in real life.

Treating her well may be the only influence you have in the creation of positive word-of-mouth. Treating her badly adds drama to her story. This not only makes your appearance in her story more likely to be negative, dramatic stories tend to be told more often, and over a longer period of time.

Which leads to what may be the most important question: when she does business with your company, do you treat Ms. Customer as the star she is?

■ ABOUT THE AUTHOR

As an expert at multiplying the market share and profitability of professional practices and owner-operated businesses, Chuck McKay knows most business people don't want to market their companies. They want more highly profitable customers.

That's the knowledge and skill McKay delivers as a marketing consultant, a partner in the Wizard of Ads international marketing organization, and a speaker at meetings of business associations, marketing groups, and civic organizations. Invite him to yours.

His book, *Fishing for Customers and Reeling Them In* (now in its forth printing), and popular free newsletter outlines methods for catching net-loads of new customers. Read about Chuck's common sense marketing approach, and preview excerpts from his soon-to-be-published *How to Boost Your Company's Revenue and Get Top Dollar When You Sell*, at http://FishingForCustomers.com.

Web Sites

www.fishingforcustomers.com

www.chuckmckayonline.com

Primary Products or Books

Fishing for Customers and Reeling Them In (Wizard Academy Press, 2005)

Chapter 28

The Eight Ps of Buying Triggers

Adrian Ott

Time is today's scarcest resource. Everyone is suffering from attention overload—from too many to-dos to overflowing inboxes to constant technology distractions.

As a result, many marketers have resorted to just getting louder (literally and figuratively). But no one wins the attention arms race.

Rather than pushing (and annoying) customers, one must harness the ebbs and flows of customers' time and attention, and work with those forces rather than fight against them.

One way to break through the cacophony is via triggers that redirect customer behavior. There are eight such triggers, or 8Ps, that frequently result in a sale if matched with an appropriate call to action.

1. Prairie-Dog Events

Prairie dogs are animals best known for popping their heads out of their burrows and looking around. Similarly, when certain events occur, customers are triggered to look around at competitive alternatives.

Examples range from major disruptions, such as losing your Internet connection for a few days, to minor issues, such as a rude customer service agent who prompts a desire for a new service. A change in structure, such as a new management regime, regulations, or a life event can also prompt customers to seek alternatives.

Focusing marketing efforts around such events will yield higher product or service adoption, because customers would be willing to devote attention to alternative offerings. Timing is key.

Social media are a new way to find customers experiencing such frustrations, as expressed through their tweets and wall comments about your competitors.

2. Peers and Power

Social triggers are strong drivers of time and attention. People want to be generous and helpful to family and friends. They also want to show off to their peers.

FarmVille, the popular Facebook game played by millions each day, has tapped into this trigger by leveraging social acceptance to increase revenue. Players purchase items, such as virtual cows and goats (online game pieces), to decorate their online farms.

What is interesting is that the virtual cow or goat is not what the customer ultimately values; rather, customers buy virtual items—symbolizing their accomplishments in the game—to be viewed favorably by their peers.

For marketers who use this trigger, it might be more effective to enable Bob to learn through his social network that Frank bought a new BMW, rather than send BMW advertisements directly to Bob.

Social media add a new twist and set of opportunities.

3. Personal Pursuits

Unlike social motivations, personal pursuits are driven by internal motivations. They are enjoyable activities that cause people to lose all track of time while, for example, surfing the Internet, painting, or reading a great book for hours.

Many studies have shown that dwell time (physical or virtual) translates into more revenue. Can you attract and keep customers in your store or engaged with your brand longer via personal pursuits that so entertain or arouse curiosity (e.g., to solve a mystery) that they don't recognize the passage of time?

Scavenger hunts using locations-based services tap into this trigger.

4. Productivity

Everyone likes to save time. In today's hectic world, if you can offer a product or service that saves people time . . . it will generate interest.

Voice2insight, for example, helps busy salespeople update customer records via a voice message. The service acts as a concierge by taking to-dos, assigning action items, and sending thank-yous for sales representatives while they are attending meetings.

In short, a sales rep can spend more time calling on customers and less time sitting in the office updating the customer relations management system.

5. Procrastination

Waiting until the last minute is rarely desirable, but to adapt a popular saying from the eighties, "it happens." And when it happens, people are willing to pay.

Consider how FedEx built an empire on deadline-driven businesspeople who need to get a proposal or contract delivered by the next morning.

6. Physical Need

We all know the danger of grocery shopping when you're hungry: You buy way too much and usually not the things you really need. That is an example of how physical need—hunger—affects attention and decision making. But there are lots of physical needs beyond hunger that can focus the attention of potential customers.

7. Proximity

Have you ever driven to the store to purchase two items and left with a cartful of purchases? Big-box retail stores tap heavily into the proximity trigger by placing complementary products near staples as reminders of other needs.

Effective web sites do that as well. Providing such triggers taps into the notion that people are being efficient with their time and will avoid a return trip.

8. Price

Low prices obviously catch people's attention. When used judiciously with other marketing methods, the price trigger can be very effective.

But a dependency on price is probably the costliest way to grow sales and can lead to long-term erosion of profit margins.

Some companies are caught in a continual loop of discounting for attention and, unfortunately, mistake such attention as customer loyalty.

■ NOT ALL TRIGGERS ARE CREATED EQUAL

Assessing how triggers affect customers is important. Just because a potential customer is experiencing a trigger doesn't mean it will be sufficient to motivate a new customer to invest the time and effort needed to switch.

That's why it's crucial that you consider not only the trigger itself but also how easy it is to switch to your offering, so that you can match switching costs to trigger strength.

Marketers who develop programs that reduce the time to switch and the hassle of switching in effect create a lever for lowering the product- or service-adoption threshold.

For example, bank-switching services, whereby banks offer "concierges" who assist with completing paperwork and manage the transition for the client, make the decision to switch much easier.

Marketers who use techniques that tap into the ebbs and flows of customers' time by focusing on triggers will drive revenue much more effectively than those who merely continue to deploy traditional means of gaining attention and recognition.

■ ABOUT THE AUTHOR

Adrian C. Ott is CEO of Exponential Edge Inc. and the award-winning author of *The 24-Hour Customer: New Rules for Winning in a Time-Starved, Always-Connected Economy* (HarperBusiness, 2010). *Library Journal* said, "Ott is revolutionizing marketing by adding the concept of time," naming it a Best Business Book 2010. She has been interviewed on *Bloomberg TV, The Washington Post,* and other media for her groundbreaking work, and is a regular contributor to *Fast Company.*

Previously, she was an HP executive for 15 years who was recognized in an annual report for "infusing HP with new revenue streams, new technologies, and new business models." She holds an MBA from Harvard Business School and a BS from University of California at Berkeley. Contact her at adrian.ott@exponentialedge.com.

Web Sites

www.exponentialedge.com

www.24HourCustomer.com

Primary Products or Books

The 24-Hour Customer: New Rules for Winning in a Time-Starved, Always-Connected Economy (HarperBusiness, 2010)

Chapter 29

"Robert, They Can't Eat You!"

My Rules for Success in Business and Life in General

Bob Parsons

Late in 2004, I was asked by *bizAZ Magazine* (a local Phoenix magazine) to speak at one of its "Business beneath the Surface" breakfast meetings. As part of the event, participants have the option of submitting questions to the speakers, which are then answered during the breakfast

One of the questions directed toward me was, "What advice do you have for someone who is just starting a business?"

■ I LIKED CLINT EASTWOOD'S RULES

Also at that time, I happened to pick up a copy of *Men's Journal*. Clint Eastwood was on the cover, and an article featured 10 items called "Clint's rules." I found his rules to be interesting. They were things like, "You are what you drive," "avoid extreme makeovers," and so on. As Clint Eastwood is a pretty easy guy to respect, I thought the whole rule thing was pretty cool. And the more I thought about it, I realized that over the years I had accumulated a number of principles (or rules) that I tried very hard to adhere to—and these rules (in many ways) have become the foundation for whatever successes I've had.

So, a few weeks before the meeting, I sat down and started typing— in no particular order—the rules I try to live by. At the breakfast meeting, I read my rules at the end of my presentation. The response was amazing. I was swamped with requests for copies of the rules. An edited list was published in the *Arizona Republic* newspaper a few days later. I was even called and interviewed by a local radio station about the list.

Since then, some of the rules have been edited, some consolidated, and a few new ones added. Despite those changes, the list of rules I presented that morning are pretty much what appears at the end of this chapter.

■ MY RULES COME FROM THE SIGNIFICANT LIFE EVENTS I'VE EXPERIENCED

As I write this, I am now 54 years old, and during my life thus far I suspect that I've encountered more significant life events than most people ever dream about. Here's some information about me: I grew up in a lower-middle-class family in Baltimore's inner city. We were always broke. I've earned everything I ever received. Very little was ever given to me.

I've been working as long as I can remember. Whether it was delivering or selling newspapers, pumping gas, working in construction or in a factory, I've always been making my own money.

■ AND, OF COURSE, NOT ALL LIFE EVENTS ARE HAPPY ONES

I was stood up to be executed during a robbery of a gas station where I was working when I was 16. To my amazement, my would-be executioner could not muster the nerve to pull the trigger. This saved both of us. I lived, and while he went to jail, he did not go there forever. Even though there were other witnesses to the gas station robbery and assault, and other crimes he and a partner committed, I was the only one who testified against them. They both received major jail sentences.

I was with a United States Marine Corps rifle company in Vietnam for a short while in 1969. As a combat rifleman, I learned several key life lessons that resulted in some of the rules I try to live by. I learned firsthand how significant a role "luck" or karma can play in our lives. The rifle company I was assigned to was Delta Company of the 1st Batallion, 26th.

Marines operated in the rice paddies of Quang Nam province. We operated on the squad level (7 to 10 of us, depending on casualties), and most every night we left our command post and went several kilometers out into the rice paddies and set up in ambush. While there are many who saw significantly more combat action than me, I did see my share. After five or six weeks, I was wounded and medevaced to Japan. I returned to Vietnam several times after that, but came back as a courier of classified documents. Although I requested (at least twice) to return to my old rifle company, the transfer was never approved.

After the Marine Corps, I used the GI Bill to attend college, and graduated from the University of Baltimore with a degree in accounting. I attended college mostly at night. After college, I took and passed the CPA exam. I worked only a few years as an accountant. The lion's share of my career has been spent as an entrepreneur.

■ I'VE BEEN VERY LUCKY WHEN IT COMES TO BUSINESS

I started a successful business division for a company called Lease-America. During the four years I was involved with this business, it grew to 84 employees and wrote over $150 million dollars in small office equipment leases. Its success helped redefine how business in that industry is now conducted.

Not long after I started the division for LeaseAmerica, I started a software company in the basement of my house. I started it with the little bit of money I had, and named it Parsons Technology. I owned this business for 10 years, grew it to about 1,000 employees and just shy of $100 million a year in sales. Eventually, we sold Parsons Technology to a company named Intuit. Because my then-wife and I were the only investors, and the company had no debt, we received the entire purchase price.

Shortly after selling Parsons Technology, my wife and I decided to go our separate ways and did the customary "divide everything by two." I then moved to Arizona and retired for a year. This was a requirement of my deal with Intuit.

■ RETIREMENT WAS NOT FOR ME

Retirement wasn't for me, so after the mandatory year passed, and using the money I had from the sale of Parsons Technology, I started a new business. This business eventually became The GoDaddy Group. I started this business from scratch, did it without acquisitions, and developed our own products. In the process, I came spookily close to losing everything I had, and actually made the decision to "lose it all" rather than close GoDaddy. Today, GoDaddy is the world leader in new domain name registrations, and has been cash flow positive since October 2001 (not bad for a dot-com). As of this writing, I continue to be the only investor in GoDaddy.

Throughout all of these life events, I came to accumulate a number of rules that I look to in various situations. Some of them I learned the hard way. Others I learned from the study of history. I know they work because I have applied them in both my business and personal life.

■ AND ONE MORE THING

I've read many times that original ideas are rare indeed. This is particularly true when it comes to the rules herein. I can't imagine that any of my rules represent new ideas.

My contribution is that I've assembled these ideas, put them to work in my life, and can attest—that more often than not—they hold true.

While I put my 16 rules together in response to a business question, I've been told by others that they can be applied to almost any pursuit.

Here are the 16 rules I try to live by:

1. *Get and stay out of your comfort zone.* I believe that not much happens of any significance when we're in our comfort zone. I hear people say, "But I'm concerned about security." My response to that is simple: "Security is for cadavers."

2. *Never give up.* Almost nothing works the first time it's attempted. Just because what you're doing does not seem to be working doesn't mean it won't work. It just means that it might not work the way you're doing it. If it was easy, everyone would be doing it, and you wouldn't have an opportunity.

3. *When you're ready to quit, you're closer than you think.* There's an old Chinese saying that I just love, and I believe it is so true. It goes like this: "The temptation to quit will be greatest just before you are about to succeed."

4. *With regard to whatever worries you, not only accept the worst thing that could happen, but make it a point to quantify what the worst thing could be.* Very seldom will the worst consequence be anywhere near as bad as a cloud of "undefined consequences." My father would tell me early on, when I was struggling and losing my shirt trying to get Parsons Technology going, "Well, Robert, if it doesn't work, they can't eat you."

5. *Focus on what you want to have happen.* Remember that old saying, "As you think, so shall you be."

6. *Take things a day at a time.* No matter how difficult your situation is, you can get through it if you don't look too far into the future, and

focus on the present moment. You can get through anything one day at a time.

7. *Always be moving forward.* Never stop investing. Never stop improving. Never stop doing something new. The moment you stop improving your organization, it starts to die. Make it your goal to be better each and every day, in some small way. Remember the Japanese concept of *kaizen*. Small daily improvements eventually result in huge advantages.

8. *Be quick to decide.* Remember what General George S. Patton said: "A good plan violently executed today is far and away better than a perfect plan tomorrow."

9. *Measure everything of significance.* I swear this is true. Anything that is measured and watched, improves.

10. *Anything that is not managed will deteriorate.* If you want to uncover problems you don't know about, take a few moments and look closely at the areas you haven't examined for a while. I guarantee you problems will be there.

11. *Pay attention to your competitors, but pay more attention to what you're doing.* When you look at your competitors, remember that everything looks perfect at a distance. Even the planet Earth, if you get far enough into space, looks like a peaceful place.

12. *Never let anybody push you around.* In our society, with our laws and even playing field, you have just as much right to what you're doing as anyone else, provided that what you're doing is legal.

13. *Never expect life to be fair.* Life isn't fair. You make your own breaks. You'll be doing good if the only meaning *fair* has to you, is something that you pay when you get on a bus (i.e., fare).

14. *Solve your own problems.* You'll find that by coming up with your own solutions, you'll develop a competitive edge. Masuru Ibuka, the cofounder of SONY, said it best: "You never succeed in technology, business, or anything by following the others." There's also an old Asian saying that I remind myself of frequently. It goes like this: "A wise man keeps his own counsel."

15. *Don't take yourself too seriously.* Lighten up. Often, at least half of what we accomplish is due to luck. None of us are in control as much as we like to think we are.

16. *There's always a reason to smile.* Find it. After all, you're really lucky just to be alive. Life is short. More and more, I agree with my little brother. He always reminds me: "We're not here for a long time; we're here for a good time."

A special word of thanks. I owe a special thanks to Brian Dunn. When I first wrote these rules down and was thinking about compiling them into a book—that book, like most books I suppose, has been half-done for a while—Brian read them and suggested a title. His suggestion was, "They Can't Eat You." I like Brian's suggestion for two reasons:

1. It reminds me of my Dad. I sure miss him.

2. It's true.

No matter how difficult things get, you're going to be okay. It's very important to realize that. Thanks, Brian.

"The above rules for survival is included with the permission of Bob Parsons (www.bobparsons.com) and is copyright © 2004–2006 by Bob Parsons. All rights reserved."

■ ABOUT THE AUTHOR

Bob Parsons is the CEO and founder of The GoDaddy Group, Inc. Parsons joined the U.S. Marine Corps during the Vietnam War and received the Combat Action Ribbon, Vietnamese Cross of Gallantry, and a Purple Heart Medal. Upon his return, Parsons enrolled in the University of Baltimore where he earned a Bachelor of Science degree in accounting. He is a Certified Public Accountant.

A serial entrepreneur, Parsons' first endeavor was Parsons Technology, a software company he started in his basement in 1984, after teaching himself how to write computer programs. After creating the company's initial software, MoneyCounts and Personal Tax Edge, Parsons used direct mail marketing to sell these and subsequent products.

Web Sites

www.bobparsons.me

www.GoDaddy.com

Primary Products or Books

Godaddy.com

Chapter 30

Book Yourself Solid

How to Get Clients Even If You Hate Marketing

Michael Port

Clients often ask me how I built a six-figure income working as an independent professional in less than 10 months. I narrowed it down to seven simple steps. Seven simple internal and intuitive attitude shifts and the exact action items that will kick your business up a notch.

These effective and powerful steps won't come as any mystery to you, but if you take them to heart, they will absolutely and emphatically build your business naturally and authentically.

My advice to you (from someone who has struggled and been exactly where you are now) is to love, embrace, and believe in yourself. Because I know how easy and realistic it is for you to become a successful solo professional.

Combine these simple insights with the gifts you have within yourself to create an abundant, joyful, and prosperous business and life.

■ SEVEN KEYS TO BOOKING YOURSELF SOLID

Key 1: Focus on solutions no matter what you say, think, or do. Take the attention off of yourself, your business, and your services. Every second of every day stay focused on clear, specific, and detailed solutions, benefits, and advantages that appeal to your prospects.

Clearly define the root of your prospects' problems and needs. Then only focus on those solutions. There does seem to be some universal confusion on the definition of a solution these days—or a slip of the mind, perhaps? Solutions are not technical, scientific, mechanical, or procedural. They are simple ideas—profound, deep, and impactful.

If someone wants to lose weight, solutions are not:

➤ Dietary guidelines

➤ Exercises

➤ Nutritional supplements

The core need of losing weight is much deeper. They really want to:

➤ Feel more self-confident

➤ Feel incredibly attractive

➤ Attract their perfect mate

Now you're talking their language. The more benefits you uncover, the quicker you will start to attract new clients. People buy good feelings, news ways of thinking, and solutions to their problems.

Key 2: Seek out ideal clients for maximum joy, prosperity, and abundance. Think about the human you are when you are performing optimally at your peak—when you are with all the people who inspire and energize you.

Make a long list of the characteristics these people have because they are your ideal clients. (ᴘs clients and friends are interchangeable expressions.)

I used to work with anyone who had a pulse and a checkbook. Living the red velvet rope policy of ideal clients increases my productivity—happiness—and more clients than I can handle are being referred to me. I know it's hard to believe, but it's true! Clients are like family to me. Don't get me wrong, I lived through a period of intense and painful negative energy worrying about those challenging client relationships. It exhausted me and took me away from accomplishing the highest good for my clients. It was impossible for me to be productive, effective, or successful in this environment.

Now with your list of inspiring people, I give you permission to release any deadwood in your calendar. If it feels scary, trust the next five steps to energetically fill those spaces.

Key 3: Embrace your authentic self and toss out the societally accepted version of you. Yes! I'm serious. No one likes the IBM stiff blue suit that follows every rule. We're attracted to that perky, authentic, confident soul who says it like it is and filters nothing!

Think about how radiant and attractive you are when you are with your best friends. You are spontaneous, free, and genuine because of the trust within these close relationships.

Our real liberated, confident, empowered self is the true self that only a select few inner circle friends are exposed to. Let me tell you—if you let your quirky, silly side shine—you'll experience far greater self-assurance and an immediate client attraction. Sound easy? It is! Works every time like a charm. Test it for yourself.

Key 4: Branding is not just for Super Bowl advertisers. If you haven't identified your natural skill, talent, interest, or expertise—or if you're not clearly and consistently expressing and defining yourself—chances are your clients can't either.

Most people are afraid of niches or specificity because they think it may limit their success or potential. That couldn't be further from the truth.

Ambiguity and uncertainty translate into insecurity. Personal branding is uniquely you. Own it—love it—express it!

(Oh, and by the way—once you've mastered your niche—then you get to expand and do anything else you want!!!)

Key 5: Articulating what you do is the key that connects your vibrant, branded, and authentic self to the world. Most people are afraid to express themselves in a clear and powerful way.

Speak boldly, clearly, and with purpose. This is the fastest way to eliminate suspicion, guesswork, or speculation. Prospects want to know the exact benefits they will experience and action they should take. Articulate this and you'll have paved the way for a yes.

Remember you won't appeal to everyone. And, that's the beautiful thing!!! What you will do is powerfully impact your ideal clients in a compelling way every time you clearly communicate the vibrant you.

Key 6: The simple selling process is a cinch once you embrace Key 1 (solutions baby!). If you remember this, you'll never have to sell again.

When you think in terms of solutions and problems solved, clients will beg to work with you. You are a consultant—a lifelong advisor. When you have fundamental solutions to help others, it's your moral imperative to show and tell as many people as possible. You are changing lives!

Inquire—What is your goal?

Show—What the benefits will be when they reach their goal.

Ask—Would you like a partner to help you with that?

Gain a commitment. Ask yourself, would this person's life be fuller, happier, and better-off with me in it? Now, let your light shine and give an action plan.

Key 7: Self-promotion is easy and fun. The Internet and modern technology are beautiful things, but too many people get caught up in their web site. Don't waste one more second on any marketing that is ineffective, inefficient, or that you just can't measure.

Master the tried and true techniques that will book you instantly. Network, mastermind, and get synergistic relationships working for you. There's nothing less effective than a solo pro—and a single mind. Collaborate for the benefit of all!

If this seems too vague, open the phone book, look up professionals with similar clients and prospective audiences, make one phone call today, and introduce yourself and the benefits of your services. Now make one five-minute phone call every day. If you're not comfortable calling a stranger, talk to every friend, family member, and colleague you know and ask for names of professionals in the fields you are seeking. Soon you'll have a growing list of warm names to call.

The second easiest way to book yourself solid is to use client referrals. First, ask every client how happy they are with your services. If the answer is positive, then ask who else they know in a similar situation that could benefit from . . . (list those benefits!). If they aren't satisfied, you just bought yourself a second chance. Consider yourself lucky.

With enough time, there are so many more ways to book yourself solid that we could go on for weeks and weeks on end. My recommendation, start with the basics here and write me at Michael@michaelport.com with additional questions, concerns, clarifications, epiphanies, or revelations you have.

Remember you have the ultimate solutions to build an abundant business. Express the brilliance of you and let out the silly one, too. Anything less is criminal.

So let's get down to it and book yourself solid!

■ ABOUT THE AUTHOR

He's been called an "uncommonly honest author" by the *Boston Globe*, and a "marketing guru" by the *Wall Street Journal*.

He's written four best-selling books, including *Book Yourself Solid* (John Wiley & Sons, Inc., 2010), *Beyond Booked Solid* (John Wiley & Sons, Inc., 2008), *The Contrarian Effect*, and the *New York Times* bestseller, *The Think Big Manifesto* (John Wiley & Sons, Inc., 2009). He appears regularly on MSNBC and CNBC and works hard to receive the highest overall speaker ratings at conferences around the world.

His mission to rally big thinkers—prospective, potential, wildly in-motion, and particularly bashful up-and-comers—is officially in motion.

Web Sites

www.michaelport.com

Primary Products or Books

Book Yourself Solid (John Wiley & Sons, Inc., 2010)

The Think Big Manifesto (John Wiley & Sons, Inc., 2009)

Beyond Booked Solid (John Wiley & Sons, Inc., 2008)

chapter 31

Twenty-Three Questions for Prospective Bloggers

Is a Blog Right for You?

Darren Rowse

Before launching further into the Blogging for Beginners series I would like to take a step back from some of the practicalities of setting up a new blog and ask potential bloggers a question. . . .

Is a blog the right type of web site for you?

While I'm a big fan of blogging as a way to get content online— I've seen it built up by some bloggers over the years as being the *ultimate* way of having a web presence.

In my opinion this is just not true.

While blogs are great (in my experience), they are not the *ultimate* type of web site. They do not have all of the answers, and they do not suit every application or situation.

It may be that after analyzing your needs, personality, hopes, experiences, and style that you find blogging does fit well for your purposes—but it may also be that other web applications fit better with where you're at. Don't just rush into blogging and expect the world.

There are probably other people who are much better at selling you some of the other types of web applications out there (look into wikis, static web sites, forums, and so on.) so I'll leave you to do your own research—but here is a list of *23 questions* (written in no particular order except that it is the order they came out of my head in) that you might want to ponder before leaping into blogging. I've put a few brief comments next to each to get you going.

Please note that these questions are in essence a list of qualities of successful bloggers that I've come across over the last few years. If you don't have some of these qualities, it's not the end of your blogging dreams. The list is idealistic, and the questions are there to help potential bloggers enter into blogging with open eyes and making good decisions about whether a blog is right for them. It also might help potential bloggers to think about what type of blog they might start and what type of skills they might need to develop: Without further ado, here are my 23 questions:

1. *Do you enjoy writing?* Blogs are predominantly a written medium. If you do not enjoy writing, then the chances are you might not enjoy blogging.

2. *What's your message?* While there are many applications for blogging, underlying most (if not all) of them is the aim of communicating some sort of message. Do you need/want to communicate something? Do you have a message? Starting a blog just because you want one might be fun, but it might also be a waste of time.

3. *Are you a good communicator?* I don't believe that only good communicators should have blogs (they can be a tool for people learning communication skills to improve), but it can be an advantage to have some basic communication skills.

4. *Are you better at writing or speaking?* Most communicators have a preference (or at least have better skills in one form or another). If speaking is more your thing, you might want to consider podcasting or even a video-based web site.

5. *Do you want to be the central voice on your web site?* While blogs are good at building community, they generally feature one person (or a smaller group of people) as the central voices in a conversation. Other people have to respond to the voice of others. If you're after something where anyone can start a conversation, then a forum might be a better medium.

6. *Are you a self-starter?* Starting a blog takes a little initiative. While blog software these days makes it simple to start them, they don't run themselves and take a motivated person to get them off the ground.

7. *Are you disciplined?* Similarly, blogs require regular attention over time. While daily posting is not essential, it's probably a good level to aim for. Will you be able to motivate yourself to write something new every day?

8. *Do you have time?* Linked to the need for regular updates is the fact that this takes time. Do you have enough time in your schedule to write daily? Not only that, do you have time to moderate comments, respond to reader questions, read other bloggers' posts, network with other bloggers, and so on?

9. *Are you thick-skinned?* If you start a blog, the chances are that it will be found and that others will write about you or some aspect of what you're doing. This is great when the comments of others are positive and in agreement with you—but it's not much fun when you're critiqued (sometimes fairly and sometimes not). Do you have the ability to take criticism well?

10. *Are you willing to be in the public spotlight?* Blogging is a public act. Every day you put yourself into the gaze of others. People will analyze your words and lifestyle. Some will want to know more about you and some might even recognize you in public (it's happened to me a few times). While few bloggers (if any) are celebrities—putting yourself out there every day is a strange thing to live with and can have its consequences. Keep in mind that once you write something online it is very difficult to get it removed. You might be able to delete your blog, but archives services (and other bloggers) pick up a lot of what you write, and so you could be living in the public spotlight for a lot longer than you're a blogger.

11. *Do you have any technical ability?* If this were a requirement of blogging, I'd have never gotten far, but it is an advantage to have the ability to learn and work on a technical level. You'll be working on a computer with Web-based software, and at times you'll need to tweak your blog. Knowing how to do it yourself can be very handy. If you're not this type of person, you might want to make friends with someone who is.

12. *Do you take yourself too seriously?* One of the characteristics I think bloggers should have is a sense of humor—particularly when it comes to looking at themselves. While there are plenty of examples of bloggers who do take themselves too seriously, most successful bloggers seem to have the ability to laugh at themselves also.

13. *Do you have a blend of humility and ego?* Coupled with a sense of humor should be humility. While bigheadedness abounds in the blogosphere, it's often the humble blogger who ends up on top. Having said this, having a healthy ego and view of your own worth as a person is also a good characteristic to have as there is an element of self-promotion that comes into blogging at times. Getting this balance right is not always easy—but it's worth working on.

14. *Are you willing to learn?* I like to look at blogging as a journey where everyone knows something but nobody knows everything. This is the case on any topic you want to blog about, and the best bloggers are willing to share what they know but seek out and promote what others know also. In this way everyone learns—even the experts.

15. *Do you enjoy reading?* Being good at writing is very helpful, but so is the ability to read what others are writing. If I were to videotape myself over a day of blogging, I suspect I'd find that I spend more time

reading each day than writing. For every post I write I would read at least three.

16. *Are you an organized person?* While I'm sure many bloggers are completely chaotic and unorganized, there comes a point in most serious bloggers' lives when they have to get at least a little organized. With incoming e-mails, following lots of feeds, writing perhaps on multiple topics/blogs and moderating comments all going on at once (plus more), it's pretty easy for time to slip away without getting much done.

17. *Are you a social person?* There are many styles of blogging, but when it comes down to it, most bloggers have some sort of a desire to connect with readers. Some bloggers keep readers at arm's length (they might switch off comments and rarely respond to e-mails), but it's probably an advantage to actually engage your readers in some way. If you don't like people, then this might be challenging. You should also consider whether you are an approachable person.

18. *Do you enjoy virtual relationships?* Some of the most social people I know are terrible when it comes to online interactions. They just don't get it and are much better face-to-face than via e-mail, instant messaging, or in a forum or comments thread. Being comfortable with speaking to and working with people you've never met before is an advantage if you're a blogger. Connected to this—it's also important to be what I call "virtually intuitive." One of the dangers of relating to people online is that all cannot be as it seems. Developing the ability to work out whether others are who they say they are and of good character is probably a skill to develop.

19. *Are you a creative person?* Once again this is not a must—just an advantage. The Web is a cluttered place and being able to develop content and community that stands out from the rest and that surprises readers is a big plus.

20. *Do you have stickability?* While some blogs are overnight successes, most are not. In fact many (most) blogs are never as successful as their owners would like. A long-term approach is one of the basic pieces of advice that I'd give most bloggers.

21. *Are you consistent?* One of the common reasons that I see bloggers getting into trouble with their readers or other bloggers is that they change the way they approach their blogging midstream. Bloggers that are constantly changing the topic of their blogs, or who increase their expectations on readers suddenly, or who change the voice that their blog is written in can end up losing the interest, or even respect, of their readers. While no one likes a boring blog, people do like to know what to expect to some extent.

22. *Are you honest and transparent?* If you answer no to this one, then you can expect to eventually be found out. While in real life it can

be reasonably easy to keep secrets or be two-faced, the blogosphere has a culture of people keeping an eye upon each other and digging where you don't want them to dig. While you'll want to develop boundaries around what you do and don't blog about, you will need to be willing to disclose conflicts of interest and be willing to be held accountable for the things that you say.

23. *Are you willing to work hard?* The level that you need to work on a blog will be dependent upon your goals and objectives for it—but if you have goals of being the next big thing, then you'll be guaranteed of a lot of hard work. Of course, this is the case with any thing in life and not just blogs.

I'm sure there are plenty of other questions worth asking before deciding on whether a blog is right for you (feel free to suggest more on my web site) but these are what come to mind for me. In reading them back they almost read like a job interview for prospective bloggers!

Keep in mind that I'm coming from a background of blogging as a job, and this is reflected in my advice. As a result the above list might be more aimed at your serious blogger who is getting into blogging either as an entrepreneurial activity or with some sort of business application.

■ ABOUT THE AUTHOR

Darren has been blogging since 2002 and has been doing it professionally (or at least earning a full-time living from the medium) since 2004–2005.

Before he was a blogger he worked in quite a few jobs but had mainly been working in churches as a minister (mainly with youth and young adults) for around 10 years. He was also the team leader for the planting of a new emerging church LivingRoom in Melbourne in 2002.

He has a degree in theology.

Darren Rowse is a blogger, speaker, consultant, and founder of several blogs including ProBlogger.net, Digital-Photography-School.com, and FeelGooder.com. You can find him on Twitter at @ProBlogger.

Web Sites

www.darrenrowse.com

www.ProBlogger.net

Primary Products or Books

ProBlogger: Secrets for Blogging Your Way to a Six Figure Income (John Wiley & Sons, Inc., 2010)

Chapter 32

Ten Ways to Surf for Buried Treasure in Your Market

Rich Schefren

There are 10 steps I take to find out everything I need about a prospect. You probably haven't heard of most of these strategies. But this is some of the most important work you'll do for your business. The better the information you gather here, the more likely you will achieve the success you dream of.

■ BURIED TREASURE FINDER 1: BUILD A BETTER KEYWORD LIST

If you don't know which keywords represent 80 percent of your market, you need to figure it out. Your keywords are what bring your prospective customers to your site.

You need two resources: Google's keyword research tool https://adwords.google.com/select/KeywordToolExternal and KeyCompete (www.keycompete.com).

First go to Google's tool and type in your most popular keyword to see what Google recommends and the amount of traffic it receives. Choose the 10 most popular, relevant keywords.

Next, head to KeyCompete.com.

1. Type the first keyword you got from Google into the search box.

2. You'll see all the domains bidding for that keyword, so click on one of the top sites listed to see all the keywords that site is bidding on.

3. Write down any interesting keyword phrases—those you've never thought of—and click on them to see which companies are advertising with those terms.

4. Repeat with all 10 keywords.

At the end, you'll have a killer keyword list based on the efforts of your competitors.

■ BURIED TREASURE FINDER 2: STAND ON THE SHOULDERS OF YOUR COMPETITORS

You can learn a lot about your prospects right from your competitors' web sites.

Go to Google and type in your primary keywords one at a time. Check out the pay-per-click ads (the sponsored listings) that appear when you search for each keyword. Are there any common themes? You should certainly pick up some clues on this page; it's a goldmine once you've done it a few times.

Scan the ads until the ideas and insights start percolating. Then record all your thoughts.

Next, click through to your competitors' web sites.

If your competitor happens to have sales letters on his site, you've just hit a jackpot. If he happens to have great copywriters writing those sales letters . . . then you've just hit the motherload. You see, if you read a sales letter through a few times, you can easily tease out the beliefs, feelings, and desires the writer was trying to target. When first starting out, you might have to read each sentence and think about it for a second. Do it anyway, because with a little practice, you'll eventually be able to read the sales letter faster and still get what you're looking for.

Spend some time on the site. Read the ads, skim any articles or blog entries, and look for anything that may be a clue to what your competitor believes about his visitors. Sign up for any free offers or newsletters so you can study your competitor's marketing strategies.

When you are done, head over to compete.com, do a site profile, and pay careful attention to their search analytics. Then head over to quantcast.com and check out the site's demographics. The site demographics may not be 100 percent accurate, but I do believe they're right more often than they're wrong. And if you look at the demographic data from each of your big competitors, you should get a very accurate representation of who your competitors' prospects are.

■ BURIED TREASURE FINDER 3: USE AMAZON TO REVEAL YOUR BUYERS' THOUGHTS

You can learn a lot about your prospects at Amazon.com. Simply use your keywords to search for the best-selling books associated with your market. Read all of the customer reviews (both positive and negative) of the books. Pay careful attention to the words the readers choose—and to the reasons they either liked or hated the book. Write down any observations or insights you have.

■ BURIED TREASURE FINDER 4: LEVERAGE YOUR OWN SITE'S ANALYTICS

Do you already have a web site? Does it get any traffic? If so, you're sitting on heaps of highly prized data that's guaranteed to grow your business. (If you aren't running analytics on your site, you should be!)

Look at your keywords report. This will show which queries brought visitors to your site. When you look at each keyword phrase, ask yourself, *What are my visitors looking for? What type of language brings them to my site? What does this tell me about my visitors' motivation and goals?*

After that, look at your referring site report. This will answer questions like, *Do my visitors come from search engines or other sites, or do they arrive directly with no referrer? What do these answers tell me about their online habits? And, what does that tell me about who they really are?*

You'll also want to segment between new visitors and returning visitors to discover:

➤ Which content repels first-time visitors and which content sucks first-time visitors into your circle of influence. Just look at your new visitor segment, then look at the most popular pages in order of their bounce rate. Those with the highest bounce rate aren't working—since more people are bailing off this page than any other (by the way you should fix these as soon as possible). At the bottom of the list (the lowest bounce rate) are the pages that are resonating the most with your visitors.

➤ Which pages are most popular with visitors who've been to your site before. In other words, why do visitors return to your site? Your analytics program tells you the answer, which gives you a glimpse into their core complex.

➤ The keywords that bring visitors who stick around or return to your site. Just sort the most popular keywords drawing return visitors to your site and compare them to the most popular keywords drawing single visitors to your site.

And that's just the beginning. Analyze the differences between these two groups on every metric you study. You'll be amazed at how much insight you'll gain in a short time.

■ BURIED TREASURE FINDER 5: FIND AND MINE THE FORUMS

There's a goldmine of useful information to be mined from forums. To extract some really juicy information at breakneck speed, you need to find the popular forums in your niche. The easiest way to find them is to go to Google and search "(your primary keyword) and forum."

A totally overlooked, fast, and easy way to get some overall market knowledge is to get the visitor profile on each of those forum sites. This is priceless information every marketer wants to know, and this is how you get it: Just go to www.quantcast.com and get a profile of each forum you identified by typing in the URL of the forum. Go through the forum's demographics by clicking the demographics tab. Make sure you print out the demographics and cut and paste it into a Word document.

Before diving into each forum, summarize the visitor base on the profile from quantcast. Then put everything you uncover on that forum into a list below your summary.

Now you have to drill down deep into the forum. Pay close attention to the threads that get the most action in views and posts. There's a lot to be found by sniffing around. Remember, you're looking for clues, not answers. You should be able to find clues about:

➤ *Their purchasing hot buttons:* Identify the most common questions, what they consistently ask for advice on, and the words they use to describe themselves.

➤ *The real reason they are buying what they are buying:* It's easy—just uncover the posts that mention their goals. Pay careful attention to how they describe their goals. What do you think they'll get out of achieving their goal—how would their lives be different afterward? How would they feel after each accomplishment?

➤ *How best to communicate with your prospective customers:* Record the words and phrases they use. Identify what gets them excited (most active posts). This will help you form a bond with them and get them to like, trust, and most importantly, buy from you.

There are many other profit-multiplying insights you can glean from a forum. Keep going and explore.

■ BURIED TREASURE FINDER 6: USE THE MOST POPULAR BLOGS

Blogs are another amazing resource. And once again, they are overlooked by almost everyone. If you want to know the topics your prospects get excited about, and the words they use when they are excited, you can easily get it all from blogs.

1. Locate the most popular blogs on your topic by going to www.technorati .com. First type in your main keyword in the search box. Then filter your results (it'll show up in a green box right there on top of your results) by changing the first drop-down menu from "search posts" to "search blogs."

2. Next, run their visitors' profiles by going to www.quantcast .com again. (If you're game, the same summary and list method I described in the forum section applies here, and it is just as powerful.)

3. Scan old posts and approximate the average number of comments. Any post with significantly more comments tells you a lot about what turns these visitors on. Read those comments, and you'll know the words they use to describe what gets them excited. For example, if you were to study StrategicProfits.com, you'd find that any time I write about procrastination we get lots of comments. In other words, procrastination is a hot topic for our readers. Don't dismiss the posts that have far fewer comments than average. They'll give you a clear direction on which topics to avoid.

■ BURIED TREASURE FINDER 7: MAGAZINE STAND MAGAZINES

If there are magazines in your niche, you should be analyzing the covers every month.

You'll also be able to spot areas of interest to your ideal customers, and gain insight into the ultimate benefits they are looking for. Some sophisticated magazines have different cover copy for different groups of subscribers. If you can identify any of these advanced marketers in your niche, pay very careful attention to both covers. What's the same and what's different? From this, you can identify the different bait that attracts your prospects and retains your customers.

■ BURIED TREASURE FINDER 8: DELICIOUS SEARCH

Delicious is a great resource. Simply type in your top keywords and read through the content that's been bookmarked the most (you can find that information in a blue box to the right of each result). Read the top bookmarked content carefully to identify what about it got it bookmarked so much. Just go to delicious.com and search under your main keywords—it's that simple.

■ BURIED TREASURE FINDER 9: Q & A SITES

Question and Answer sites are great resources for learning the problems and issues your prospects want advice on. There are tons of these sites: answers.yahoo.com, wiki.answers.com, answers.google .com, pointask.com, and many more. Just search for your keywords and see what you discover. The information you find here can easily boost your profits.

■ BURIED TREASURE FINDER 10: CLICKTALE

How would you like to peer over the shoulder of each and every visitor to your web site? Watching what they read and what they skip over? What gets them to do a double-take, and what triggers them to start scrolling? Clicktale offers a free service to get started with, and you'll love it for everything you discover. This is such a valuable tool—it's the closest you can (legally) get to being Big Brother. You can learn all about it here . . . ClickTale.com.

■ WHO'S YOUR IDEAL CUSTOMER?

Once you've used the 10 Buried Treasure tools, you'll be closer than ever to answering the question, "Who is my customer?"

You really can never know too much. Knowing your customer is the central leverage point of all marketing, product development and improvements, sales, and profitability. It really is the primary determinant of your business success.

Consistently be on the lookout for clues that define your customers as accurately and precisely as you can. Try your best to know their age, education, income, position, background, and so on. . . . What do they value? What are they willing to pay for? How much are they willing to spend? What does your customer want or need that they feel they're not getting from anyone in your industry? Why do they buy from your competitors? And what would you have to do to get them to switch to your products and services?

The big challenge for you is to do this research now.

Remember, your ideal customers are the people who are going to pay for you to live your ideal life. You owe it to yourself to know as much about them as possible before you design your profit model and build out your business blueprint.

The choice is yours. What's it going to be? Greatness or mediocrity? Only you can choose!

■ ABOUT THE AUTHOR

After graduating in accountancy at Case Western Reserve University, Rich went to work for Arthur Anderson's Strategic Planning division.

Rich left to rescue the family business, which he turned into Soho's hottest eclectic clothing boutique, with loyal customers like Prince and Uma Thurman and increasing revenue from $1.5 million to $6.5 million in three years.

Next he created a hypnosis center, which he built up to $13 million in four years before taking his business building ideas and selling them to other hypnosis businesses.

He then started working on the Internet building joint ventures with some of the best-known Internet marketers.

In 2004 Rich Schefren formed Strategic Profits to coach online entrepreneurs to build their businesses and to get free of the daily grind. Behind the Scenes, he has coached practically every single Internet marketing guru online today to grow their business while working less and making more. He is also a secret marketing weapon to companies such as Google, Microsoft, Yahoo!, Agora Publishing, and so on. . . . He now spends the majority of his time coaching entrepreneurs to grow their businesses online.

Web Sites

www.squidoo.com/richschefren1

www.strategicprofits.com/blog

Primary Products or Books

Internet Business Manifesto (CreateSpace, 2009)

Business Growth System

Chapter 33

Avoiding Dreadful Marketing Ideas

Barbara Findlay Schenck

The following marketing landmines masquerade as quick fixes. When the business chips are down, each of these worst ideas pops up to look like a good solution. Don't be fooled. Make sure every new idea soars above every single idea on this list.

■ FIGHT BAD BUSINESS WITH GOOD ADVERTISING

Here's the scenario: Business is down, so the owner points fingers at the economy and the competition, and decides to run ads to overcome the problem. But the economy and the competition likely aren't the culprits. Business is down because customers have defected—and new prospects haven't been converted—because the company's product or service is lacking.

Running ads before improving the offering will only put a spotlight on the problem. In the words of advertising legend Bill Bernbach, "Nothing kills a bad product like a good ad." Instead, fix the product, polish the service, then run the ad.

■ RUN KITCHEN SINK ADS

A kitchen sink ad is like a kitchen sink argument in that every point—every feature, every idea, every department's viewpoint—is tossed into the mix in an effort to get more bang for the buck (a truly awful phrase that deserves its own place on the list of worst ideas). The result is a jam-packed ad featuring a long list of product bells and whistles but no clear focus and no attention-grabbing consumer benefit to seize and hold the prospect's mind.

142

Take aim instead: Know your best prospect and what need that person seeks to address. Then stop that person with a headline that highlights the promise of your most compelling benefit, backed by copy that proves your claim with facts.

■ PORTRAY THE CUSTOMER AS A FOOL

Trying to be funny or grabbing attention by showing the customer as an inept bumbler wandering through life in search of your solution is hardly the way to win customers and influence buying decisions.

Form a sincere relationship with your prospect instead of poking fun at the very person you're trying to influence.

■ SAVE THE BEST FOR LAST

It happens in presentations, sales letters, and ads. Businesses wait to divulge the greatest benefits of their product until the last minute, thinking that prospects will be sitting on the edges of chairs in rapt anticipation.

Not so. If your opening doesn't grab them, they won't wait around. Four out of five people read only the headline, they listen to only the first few seconds of a radio ad, and if the first impression of a personal presentation is weak, they tune out for the rest. Eliminate slow starts and lead with your strengths.

■ CHANGE YOUR LOGO OFTEN AND DRAMATICALLY

And while you're at it, change your web site constantly. And your advertising tagline, too. It sounds ridiculous, but it's what happens when businesses let media departments, freelance artists, employees, and others create materials without the strong parameters of image guidelines to ensure a consistent company image.

If you want prospects to trust that yours is a strong, steady business (and you do!), show them a strong, steady business image.

■ BUILD IT AND TRUST THEY WILL COME

Sorry, but consumers aren't just sitting around waiting for the next new business, new web site, new branch outlet, or new event to come into existence. They need to be told, reminded, inspired, and given reasons and incentives to take new buying actions. When you build it, build a plan to market it.

■ MOVE FAST: IF YOU SNOOZE, YOU MIGHT LOSE

This is irresistible bait for businesses that operate without a marketing plan. They don't know their own objectives and strategies, and so any tactic sounds like a fine idea.

As a result, when a proposal comes in from an ad salesperson, an Internet business opportunity promoter, or even from a company that wants to merge or partner, the business owner is all ears, fearful that this might be an opportunity too good to pass on. Often, the idea comes with a quick deadline or the threat of involving a competitor instead, leading straight to a hasty decision.

Remember what they say about the correlation between haste and waste.

■ THINK PEOPLE WILL CARE THAT YOU'RE UNDER NEW MANAGEMENT

Or think that they'll care that we've doubled our floor space, we've added a new drive-up window, or any other self-congratulatory announcement that produces similarly low market enthusiasm. To move the spotlight off yourself, add a customer benefit. Turn WE'RE CELEBRATING OUR FIFTH ANNIVERSARY into WE'RE CELEBRATING OUR FIFTH ANNIVERSARY WITH FIVE FREE EVENTS YOU WON'T WANT TO MISS.

Remember, prospects care most about what's in it for them.

■ BELIEVE THERE'S A PIE IN THE ONLINE SKY

Contrary to rampant belief, the opportunities of the cyber world aren't just ripe for the picking. The chance of opening a web site and instantly winning business from distant new prospects is as likely as opening a toll-free line and immediately having it ring off the hook with orders.

To win your slice of online opportunity, invest time and money to drive people to your site.

■ BELIEVE YOUR CUSTOMER IS CAPTIVE

Reality is, your customers know they have other options.

"If they're standing in front of you, and you turn your attention to answer a phone, they notice. If you offer new customers a better deal than current customers enjoy, they notice. If you spend more time and money courting new prospects than rewarding business from current clientele, they most certainly notice and in time will begin to disengage from your business as a result.

Realize that customer loyalty is the key to profitability, and that earning it is a never-ending process."[1]

■ ABOUT THE AUTHOR

A marketing strategist and small business advocate, Barbara is the author of *Small Business Marketing For Dummies* and *Selling Your Business For Dummies* (John Wiley & Sons, Inc., 2005), and coauthor of *Branding For Dummies* and *Business Plans Kit For Dummies, Second Edition* (John Wiley & Sons, Inc., 2009). She is also a business columnist for MSN.

A native Oregonian, she began her career as admissions director and writing instructor at Hawaii Loa College (now part of Hawaii Pacific University) before joining the staff of Hawaii's largest public relations firm. After seven years in Honolulu, she moved with her husband, Peter, to Southeast Asia to manage a community development program for the Peace Corps in Malaysia. On return to the United States, they founded a marketing agency in Oregon, which was one of the Northwest's Top 15 at the time of its sale in 1995.

Today, through her business, Bizstrong (www.bizstrong.com), Barbara focuses her efforts on small business success, helping entrepreneurs and business owners achieve their goals through good planning, branding, marketing, and exit planning.

Web Sites

www.bizstrong.com

Primary Products or Books

Branding For Dummies (John Wiley & Sons, Inc., 2009)

Small Business Marketing For Dummies (John Wiley & Sons, Inc., 2005)

Selling Your Business For Dummies (John Wiley & Sons, Inc., 2005)

---

[1] © *Small Business Marketing For Dummies* by Barbara Findlay Schenck. All rights reserved. Reprinted with permission.

Chapter 34

Ten Web Landing Page Tips to Drive Action

David Meerman Scott

I love marketing with Web landing pages. It's one of the easiest and most cost-effective ways to get a message read by a target market and a terrific tool to move prospects through the sales cycle. Landing pages, done well, can generate high response rates and marketing programs using landing pages with effective calls to action will generate results: e-commerce sales and valuable sales leads.

A landing page is simply a place for a targeted message to a particular demographic and can either be linked from a home page or as part of a marketing campaign. Landing pages work well to tell an organization's story to a particular target market, to promote a new product offering, as a way to capture leads from an e-mail marketing program, or as part of an advertising campaign, PR program, or tradeshow initiative. In the classic sales cycle definition, marketing programs such as advertising, PR, tradeshows, and search engine optimization are designed to attract the prospect's attention (get them to your landing page). The landing page is where you generate interest and develop conviction. In an e-commerce sale you drive people to the "buy" button and in a B2B company the sales team gets a warm suspect ready to be worked to a closed sale.

Effective landing page copy is written from the buyer's perspective, not the company's. Too often, companies invest time and money creating web pages that describe their wonderful products, but don't provide information from the prospective customer's point of view. Buyers don't care about your products, they care about themselves and their problems. Write for them, not for you. On your home page, create a series of "personas" or "self-select paths" that people new to your company can click. Examples might be: "Learn about products for mid-sized companies" or "Services for Competitive Intelligence Professionals."

As your buyers self-select based on the path that is best for them, the landing page they reach is written with appropriate copy to generate the interest of that target market. Landing pages typically make use of multiple links to appropriate offers, additional information, and in the B2B world materials like white papers, webinars, and the like, each with a short form to fill out so the buyer becomes a lead or a sale.

A mistake many companies make is investing tons of money in online advertising (say a search engine advertising program) and then sending all the traffic to the company home page. Because the home page needs to serve many audiences, there's never enough information for each demographic. And research shows that people give a home page only a few seconds before they leave. Landing pages tied to campaigns are highly effective to solve these problems. A specific landing page should be set up for each and every campaign. If prospects find your company by clicking an e-mail campaign or searching on a specific term in a Google AdWords program, your marketing should include landing pages to expand on the prospects' interest with appropriate copy and links.

It's simple really: A campaign with a great landing page can generate double digit response rates while a generic campaign throws money away.

Here are 10 tips on creating effective landing pages:

Tip 1 Keep the landing page copy short and the graphics simple.

The landing page is a place to deliver a simple message and drive your buyer to respond to your offer. Don't try to do too much.

Tip 2 Create the page in your company's look, feel, and tone.

A landing page is an extension of your company's image. While different from the web site, it still must adopt the same voice, tone, and style as your main site.

Tip 3 Write from the buyer's point of view.

Think carefully of who will be visiting the landing page and write copy for that demographic. You want visitors to feel the page speaks to their problems and concerns and that you have a solution just for them.

Tip 4 A landing page is communications, not advertising.

Landing pages are where you communicate valuable information about your product and make sales or generate the names of interested potential customers. Advertising is great to get people to click to your landing page. But once a prospect is there, the landing page should focus on communicating the value of your offering to the potential customer, not more advertising.

Tip 5 Provide a quote from a happy customer.

A simple testimonial on a landing page works brilliantly to show people that others are happy with your product. A sentence or two with the customer's name (and affiliation) is all you need.

Tip 6 Make the landing page a self-contained unit.

The goal of a landing page is to get a prospect to respond to your offer so you can sell to them. If you lose traffic from your landing page, you may never get a person to respond to the offer so it is often better not to provide links to your main web site.

Tip 7 Make the call to action clear and easy to respond to.

Make certain you provide a clear response mechanism for those people who want to go further. Make it easy to sign up or express interest.

Tip 8 Use multiple calls to action.

You never know what offer will appeal to a specific person, so consider using more than one. In the B2B world, you might offer a white paper, a free trial, and a price quote all on the same landing page. An e-commerce company might offer options such as color or size.

Tip 9 Only ask for necessary information.

Don't use a sign-up form requiring lots of data to be entered. People will abandon the form and you won't get a lead or a sale. Ask for the basics—name, e-mail address, company, and phone number.

Any additional information you ask for will reduce response rates. Never ask for people's income level, budget, or if they are planning on purchasing the product you offer.

Tip 10 Don't forget to follow up!

Okay, you've got a great landing page with an effective call to action and the sales or leads are coming in. Great! Don't drop the ball now. Make certain to follow up with each buyer as quickly as possible. Follow up the same day—or better yet, the same hour.

■ ABOUT THE AUTHOR

David Meerman Scott, best-selling author of *The New Rules of Marketing & PR* and *Real-Time Marketing & PR,* opened people's eyes to the new realities of marketing and public relations on the Web. Six months on the *BusinessWeek* best-seller list and published in 26 languages, *New Rules* is a modern business classic.

His newest book *Real-Time Marketing & PR: How to Instantly Engage Your Market, Connect with Customers, and Create Products that Grow Your Business Now* was released in November 2010.

He is also the coauthor (with Brian Halligan) of *Marketing Lessons from the Grateful Dead: What Every Business Can Learn from the Most Iconic Band in History* and wrote three other books, including *World Wide Rave.*

His Web Ink Now blog is ranked by *AdAge* Power 150 as a top worldwide marketing blog.

He is a recovering VP of marketing for two publicly traded technology companies and was also Asia marketing director for Knight-Ridder.

Web Sites

www.davidmeermanscott.com

Primary Products or Books

Marketing Lessons from the Grateful Dead: What Every Business Can Learn from the Most Iconic Band in History (John Wiley & Sons, Inc., 2010)

Real-Time Marketing & PR: How to Instantly Engage Your Market, Connect with Customers, and Create Products that Grow Your Business Now (John Wiley & Sons, Inc., 2010)

The New Rules of Marketing & PR (John Wiley & Sons, Inc., 2007)

Chapter 35

Everything You Need to Know about Word-of-Mouth Marketing

Andy Sernovitz

Okay. Here's the quick version. Everything you wanted to know about word-of-mouth marketing but were afraid to ask. It all comes down to this:

Happy customers are your best advertisers.

If people like you and like what you do, they will tell their friends.

■ LESSON 1: THE DEFINITION OF WORD-OF-MOUTH MARKETING

Word-of-Mouth Marketing is (a) giving people a reason to talk about you and (b) making it easier for the conversation to take place.

It's C to C Marketing—when a consumer tells a consumer about you. Actually, it's B to C to C. When it comes out of the mouth of a marketer, it's marketing. When a real person repeats it, it's word-of-mouth.

It's more than just marketing—it's also product design and customer service. People talk about fantastic stuff and great treatment from companies they like.

■ LESSON 2: THE FOUR RULES OF WORD-OF-MOUTH

➤ Rule 1: Be Interesting

Nobody talks about boring companies, boring products, boring ads. Everyone can be interesting. Before you run an ad, before you launch a product, ask your spouse about it. Trust me . . . if a spouse finds it interesting, you've got a winner.

➤ Rule 2: Make People Happy

Create amazing products. Provide excellent service. Go the extra mile. Make sure the work you do gets people energized, excited, and eager to tell a friend.

➤ Rule 3: Earn Trust and Respect

Nobody talks positively about a company that they don't trust or don't like. Earn the respect of your customers. Be good to them. Talk to them. Honor their intelligence. Fulfill their needs. Stay honest. Every company can be nicer, and every one of us can work to make our company a little better to its customers.

➤ Rule 4: Make It Easy

Find a simple topic that is easy to repeat. Not your formal brand statement, not your product description. Forget elevator pitch . . . it's the pass-in-the-hall test. What can people tell a friend about you in one sentence?

Then do everything you can to make it easy to share that topic. Use tell-a-friend forms on your web site. Put it in an e-mail. Pass out flyers. Blog it. Stick it on a T-shirt.

■ LESSON 3: THE THREE REASONS PEOPLE TALK ABOUT YOU

➤ Reason 1: You. They Like You and Your Stuff

They like you. They feel a connection to your company, they respect what you do, and they want to support you. So they bring their friends. People feel driven to share things they like with their friends, so their friends can enjoy them, too. Create great products and services that inspire them. (Think about TiVo, the best album ever, the best cookie you ever ate, or the spot remover that actually works.)

Be likeable. Make great stuff. Provide great service.

➤ Reason 2: Them. Talking Makes Them Feel Good

People talk because it makes them feel special, smart, connected, in the know, and important. (Think about the restaurant guy, the what's-on-sale maven, the computer guru.) People also feel good when they can help others find what they need or solve problems. (Think about the guy who always knows which contractor to call or which car to buy.)

Provide reasons to talk that make your talkers feel smart and special.

➤ Reason 3: Us. They Feel Connected to the Group

Talking about a company and being passionate about it makes us feel like part of a family. We talk about it because it makes us feel included on the team. (Think about Harley owners, Apple junkies, sports fans, and anyone who loves a great band.)

Rally the team. Give them shirts, private discussion groups, special events, and public recognition.

➤ Lesson 4: Making It Happen — The Five Ts of Word-of-Mouth Marketing

Talkers: Find the People Who Like to Talk
Are they your customers? Neighborhood moms? Doctors? Bloggers? Think about the people who are most likely to tell a friend about what you are doing. Make sure they know about your new topic of conversation.

Topics: Give Them a Reason to Talk
Give people a reason to talk about you. It doesn't need to be fancy. A special sale, good service, a neat new feature, a better flavor, a funny package. (Remember the Gateway computers that came in cow-patterned boxes?)

Tools: Help the Message Spread Faster and Farther
Do everything you can to make it easy for talkers to pass along your topic. Include postcards and stickers in the box when you ship a package. Put up a chat room so people can talk to each other. Join a blog conversation. Hand out samples. (Did you ever get one of those e-mails with a "secret" coupon that was supposedly for employees only? Did you forward it?)

Taking Part: Join the Conversation
Conversations die out when there's only one person talking. When people are talking about you, answer them. Reply to their e-mail.

Comment on blogs that write about you. Send a lot of thank-you notes.

Tracking: Measure and Understand What People Are Saying
The word-of-mouth conversation is the best feedback you're ever going to get. It's far better than any other kind of market research, because it is the authentic voice of the consumer. Hear what people are saying, learn from it, and use it to be a better company.

Your Homework

1. Ask yourself why anyone would talk about your stuff.
2. Do something worth talking about.
3. Search the blogs to find out who is talking about you.
4. Join the conversation.

■ ABOUT THE AUTHOR

Andy Sernovitz teaches word-of-mouth marketing and social media, and is the author of *Word of Mouth Marketing: How Smart Companies Get People Talking*. He is CEO of SocialMedia.org, the community for heads of social media at the world's greatest brands, and GasPedal, a word-of-mouth consulting company. He taught Word-of-Mouth Marketing at Northwestern University and Internet Entrepreneurship at the Wharton School of Business, ran a business incubator, and started half a dozen companies. He created the Word-of-Mouth Marketing Association and the Association for Interactive Marketing. His fantastic blog is called Damn, I Wish I'd Thought of That (http://damniwish.com).

Web Sites

www.damniwish.com

www.socialmedia.org

www.wordofmouthbook.com

Primary Products or Books

Word of Mouth Marketing: How Smart Companies Get People Talking (Kaplan Business, 2006)

Chapter 36

Five Ways to Not Screw Up Your Networking Attempts

Peter Shankman

I was at a conference this weekend in Las Vegas—it's bad enough to fight with the recycled air, the perfumed-at-50-degrees conference rooms, and the endless fried foods that pass for "healthy," but you add in 200 people who have absolutely no clue how to network, and it's enough to make you pull an *Ocean's Eleven* and sneak out of the hotel in an ambulance.

Here are the top five ways to not screw up your next networking opportunity.

1. Networking doesn't begin when you get to the conference; it begins the second you leave your house.

   Anyone is a potential hiring manager, client, or customer. True story: I was behind a real jackass at a ticket counter for an international flight last year. At one point, he actually had the nerve to say, "Well, I work for company XYZ (a big global company), and I can make *sure* that we never give you any business again if you don't fix my problem," or something just as arrogant. At that point, the person behind me walked up to him, and said quietly, "What's your name?" The arrogant slob said, "Why do you care, pal?" To which the first gentleman said, "Because I'm senior executive vice president at [said big global company], and I won't have anyone sullying our good name with their petty bullshit."

   I'm pretty sure the arrogant guy doesn't work for the company anymore. In today's world, you've simply got to be on your best behavior. I can promise you, if you're a screaming jerk at check-in, or on the rental car bus, or virtually anywhere, and I happen to be there, I'll be the guy with the FlipCam, posting your idiot rant onto

YouTube. Why? Because I can. You don't want to be the guy in the video. Besides—I know a lot of people—what if I know your boss? Or what if you find me one day as the guy doing the hiring?

2. Turns out, "It doesn't always have to be about you!" is actually a good comment.

    As we sit down at the conference lunch, I don't need to know what you do, how well you do it, how many awards you've received for doing it, and how you're pretty sure you can do it for me if I'd simply pay you to, all before I've had sip one of my watered-down iced tea.

    Here's a thought. Try making it about someone else for a change. Instead of sitting down and launching into your prerehearsed litany of how great you are, what about shutting up and listening once in a while? Put the business-card-Uzi away, and don't rapid fire them to anyone within range. You know how it seems how some people are only listening to find a break in the conversation so they can talk? Don't be that person. Ask questions! It's the ultimate way to learn, and allows you the opportunity to actually contribute something of value to the conversation, as opposed to the spiel of your latest victory. Remember: Value gets remembered, verbal diarrhea simply gets recalled—and not in a good way.

3. Going up to the speaker at the end of her speech ensures only one thing: You'll be one of a hundred people going up to the speaker at the end of her speech.

    So rather than giving yourself the opportunity to not get noticed in the slightest, why not buck the crowd? Find the speaker 20 minutes *before* she goes on stage, and introduce yourself. On your business card, write "I'm the one who met you before your speech." You'll be remembered.

4. Do something different.

    My business card is a poker chip. You can't scan it in, you don't want to throw it out. You keep it on your desk and play with it. I've seen other business cards that were actual credit cards, bottle openers—anything but a boring piece of cardboard. Try and be original. If you're creative enough to give me something I'll remember, chances are I'll want to do some business with you.

5. Finally

    Be wary of making the leap from "Met you at the conference" to "Friending you on Facebook so you can see photos of me in my Speedo." Until Facebook becomes the norm and networking is ubiquitous with it, (probably 24 months), there are still people wary of it. And until you learn what to post online and what not to post, remember that not everyone is going to assume that a FB connection request is either (a) acceptable or (b) worth their time. We'll get there, but we're not there yet. We'll eventually learn what's acceptable and what's not—because in the end, we'll only have one network—it'll have everyone in our lives, both business and professional, and we'll have to be smart enough to know that what we post can be seen by everyone, forever. Until we are, asking a potential business contact who doesn't know you that well to till your crops on Farmville is just asking for trouble. (And massive ridicule.)

6. Bonus rule

It's no one's fault but your own if your personal or professional brand isn't seen as you want it. It's not Facebook's fault, it's not Twitter's fault, it's not LinkedIn's fault. It's your fault. Make sure to keep up appearances as you want them to be. Otherwise, you've got no one to blame but yourself.

■ ABOUT THE AUTHOR

An entrepreneur, author, speaker, and worldwide connector, Peter is recognized worldwide for radically new ways of thinking about social media, PR, marketing, advertising, creativity, and customer service.

Peter is perhaps best known for founding Help A Reporter Out (HARO), which in under a year has become the de facto standard for thousands of journalists looking for sources on deadline, offering them more than 125,000 sources around the world looking to be quoted in the media. HARO is currently the largest free source repository in the world, sending out over 1,200 queries from worldwide media each week.

Peter is the founder and CEO of The Geek Factory, Inc., a boutique marketing and PR strategy firm located in New York City, with clients worldwide. His blog, which he launched as a web site in 1995 at http://shankman.com, both comments on and generates news and conversation.

Web Sites

http://shankman.com

www.helpareporter.com

Primary Products or Books

Customer Service: New Rules for a Social-Enabled World (Que, 2010)

Can We Do That?! Outrageous PR Stunts That Work and Why Your Company Needs Them (John Wiley & Sons, Inc., 2006)

Chapter 37

Seven Direct Mail Secrets Guaranteed to Create a Stampede of New Business

Yanik Silver

If you think junk mail doesn't work . . . you're absolutely right! However, using highly targeted direct mail will almost always work. Maybe you've heard that 1 percent or 2 percent is the industry standard—well, I'll show you how you can multiply that figure many times over.

A common story I hear from my clients is how they mail out thousands of glossy, beautiful brochures with pretty pictures, flowery text, and everything looking absolutely gorgeous, but they get *zero* response. So they mistakenly believe direct mail does not work.

What could be the problem?

You see direct mail when done wrong is almost always a huge waste of money. But when it's done right you can expect tremendous results and profits. That's why doing right only means only one thing in my book—getting *results*!

Direct mail can become the most predictable and consistent way to generate more customers, yet most businesses are guilty of doing it wrong simply because they've never been taught these jealously guarded secrets. With these seven secrets your next mailing campaign will be a massive success.

■ SECRET 1: YOUR LIST IS THE FIRST AND FOREMOST

Your mailing list is essential to your success. Let's say you were selling snow tires—you wouldn't want to send out your offer to people in

Phoenix, right? Well, as silly as this sounds, many people will make this same mistake. You cannot just pick a random resident list of nearby zip codes to your office. What you need to do is consider who your ideal customers would be and then find a way to target your message directly to them.

With direct mail, you're given the opportunity to use laser-beam, pinpoint accuracy to specifically target your message. And thanks to the growing direct marketing industry, privacy is dead in America.

So if you told me your ideal customer is a man age 45 to 55, who drives a Chevy Chevette, who lives with his parents, who watches Pro Wrestling, and who goes bowling once a week—I can get you that list. It might not be that big of a list, but it is available.

Now you probably don't need to be as specific as this but you can. There are two major types of lists available.

1. The first kind of list is simply compiled information, taken from directories, phone books, motor vehicle records, and so on.

Probably the most common way of using a compiled list is to buy a geographic list, like all the residents around a five-mile radius of your office. Usually this will not yield the greatest results.

Another way is to segment a compiled list by demographics (that's the fancy term for age, sex, income, whatever). This is a little better way to target. For example you could specify you only want females, age 50 to 65, who earn $75,000 and above.

But there is an even better way to combine them using "Geo/Demo" characteristics.

You can pick certain geographic areas and certain demographic characteristics that you desire. Think of your ideal prospect; the more you know about them the better targeted lists you can purchase.

For most people a good starting point is to comb through your customer records to find common characteristics, like region, age, and so on. Or if you sell business to business then you should try to look for common industries or SIC (Standard Industrial Classification) codes that a majority of your business comes from. Your goal is to try to *clone* your best customers!

2. The second type (and much more valuable) is called a "direct response list." These are lists of people who have bought or responded to direct marketing.

In some cases it will make more sense for you to buy a mail order list. The people on this list have bought something from direct response methods (mail, print ads, infomercials, etc.).

This kind of list is the most specific you can get. To get an idea of what I'm talking about go down to your local library and ask the librarian for the SRDS (the Standard Rate and Data Services) Direct Mail List Source Directory, usually in the reference section. Or you can get more information on www.srds.com.

The SRDS is a huge, four-inch-thick reference book with nearly every public list available for rental—it's the bible for direct mailers.

Just glancing through this book you can find lists of buyers of almost anything that has some affinity to what you're selling. The best part about these lists is that you know these people have a high interest in whatever they bought. So if you're an accountant, you could rent a list of people who bought tax planning information by mail.

Or maybe you're a dentist. What better list could you find for a teeth whitening offer than someone who just bought a tooth whitening product from an infomercial?

What you want is a "starving crowd," somebody who has expressed an interest in looking better. Somebody who has paid money. And that's exactly who you can find using direct response lists.

But there's one more list that almost everyone forgets. It's literally a gold mine lying at your feet. And that's your *own* list!

If you have not put all your customer's names and addresses into a database you're overlooking an incredible source of added business. This list will be the most powerful list and responsive list you can use for any offers because these people already trust you and like doing business with you.

This is critically important. Especially if you're in a business that typically doesn't keep their customer names and addresses because you're missing an incredible amount of money. Maybe you're a retailer or a restaurant owner—make it a habit for your staff to collect customer names! It is absolutely critical! I cannot stress this enough.

■ SECRET 2: HOW TO GET YOUR LETTER OPENED AND MOST IMPORTANTLY, READ

The first thing you need to do is to get your letter delivered. I know this sounds silly, but it's more difficult than you think. Many consultants will tell you to save money by using bulk-mail postage or, as it's now called, standard rate. Bulk rate is the dumpster rate. After taking the proper steps to get the best list, don't blow it by being cheap on the postage.

In fact, the Post Office freely admits that 20 to 30 percent of all bulk mail gets thrown out for various reasons. The reason is simple; when your mailman's sack gets heavy, which letters do you think he would dare not deliver? That's right—bulk mail. So if something looks like it's junk mail it is more likely to get tossed.

So in order to get your mailings respected (by the post office and your recipient) all your mailings should go out first class and use a real "live" stamp. That also means don't use mailing labels, or even worse than that, a "postage indicia."

All these smack of junk mail. The closer you can make your envelope look like personal correspondence the better since people sort their mail over the trash can. That means you only have a split second for them to decide if they'll open your letter or not.

■ SECRET 3: A LETTER MEANS ACTION

Brochures and self-mailers do not work. What do you do when you get a brochure in the mail? Most people will either toss it out or file it away. Hardly anyone gives it more than just a casual glance on the way to the circular file.

What you need is an action device, and that's what a letter will give you. You need to take advantage of the greatest benefit direct mail has for you—personalized, intimate conversations. A letter allows you to "talk" one-on-one to your prospect. That means you should use "I" and "me" and "you" freely in your letter.

Don't use the corporate sounding "we."

Remember just one person is reading your letter at once. So don't write in the plural, even if your mailing is going out to thousands and thousands of people. Just sit down and write the same way you'd talk to a friend over dinner explaining the advantages and benefits of the product or service you're offering.

Start your letter with a compelling, benefit-driven headline. Prospects will decide to continue reading by the headline. If your headline fails to capture their attention and keep them engaged, your letter will quickly end up in the trash.

The most common mistake you can make is to put your company name, big and bold, on top of the letter. This is the worst thing you can possibly do. You see, every person is concerned with one thing:

What's in it for me?

Your company name does not show what, if any, benefits the prospect will get from your letter. So put your company name at the bottom of the page where it belongs.

■ SECRET 4: NO OFFER = NO RESPONSE

Without an offer, your letter is doomed. It is not enough just to send out a mailing hoping people will call if they're interested. You've got to tell people exactly what next step they should take, and if you don't, your mailing has failed.

The best type of offer is something that is nonthreatening and completely irresistible. If you can offer anything for free this works best. Such as a free educational report, tape, seminar, consultation, service, and so on. Try to come up with such an irresistible offer that anyone would be foolish not to take advantage of it.

Plus, by making a compelling offer you can then keep track of how many people responded to your mailing.

■ SECRET 5: CONTINUOUS MAILINGS

Why do people believe they can send out one mailing, one time, and all of a sudden become bombarded with new customers?

It's ridiculous to believe any one-shot mailing is going to uncover *everybody* interested in your service or product.

Think about your own life. You've probably received some offers that you were interested in but you never acted on. Perhaps you put it aside for a phone call or maybe one of your kids came running in and distracted you, or any number of other reasons. Your prospects are the same way.

To overcome this, you've got to create a plan for multiple contacts. Also, this way you can take advantage of the "moving parade of life." You are not selling to a standing army, but rather a moving parade of prospects. People will move in and out of different needs and wants as they go through changes in their life.

Here's an example: Let's say you're an owner of a furniture store and you sent me an offer for deeply discounted furniture. Well, you probably wouldn't have much luck with me because my house is full of furniture. But what if when your second (or third or fourth) offer came, my fiancée had left me and taken all our furniture.

Now, all of a sudden, I'm a *very* eager customer.

That's why using multiple mailings often leads to double-digit returns.

■ SECRET 6: TESTING

With direct mail you have the precision to test any offer on a small group before mailing on a massive scale. Even if you think you have the greatest idea in the world for a letter, you can still test it to a few names, instead of mailing to 50,000 people.

Then if you get a good response you can move on to mail a higher number of pieces because with a high probability you know it will work again. A reasonable test is about 2,000 to 3,000 names, depending on how many names you have on your list. You can even test with as little as a few hundred—but you won't get a statistically valid response. However, you will get an indication of the letter's success.

But don't make the crippling mistake of mailing out tens of thousands of pieces unless you can afford to lose everything.

Once you've created a letter that works well, this is called your "control" and now you can use testing to see if you can do better.

Here's how:

On your next mailing you change only one element like the headline, offer, pricing, and so on and then you split your list in half. One half gets letter number one (your control) and the other half gets letter number two (the test); then see which one does better.

And I guarantee you will see changes in results once you start testing. However, in order to accurately measure your test you've got to follow secret number seven. . . .

■ SECRET 7: TRACKING

John Wannamaker (and then later P.T. Barnum and William Wrigley), said that 50 percent of their advertising was being wasted—but they didn't know which 50 percent.

But now each letter campaign you send out gives you the ability to precisely track what your return on investment is. This way you know to the penny if your marketing is working or not.

Unlike many other forms of advertising you do to just get your name out, direct mail gives you an easy way to track your returns.

Subtracting your expenses (cost of postage, printing, and list rental) from how much business your direct mail campaign brought you gives you your profits. You must keep track of each and every prospect calling from your letter and responding to your specific offer (secret number four).

That's why you'll want to assign unique priority codes, extension numbers, or fake employee names for each promotion. Each letter you send should have a unique code. Then you will be able to credit that letter with the inquiry or sale. So you know what works and what does not.

Many times I'll use a priority code at the top of the letter. When prospects call in your staff should be trained to ask for the priority code. Or you can use extension numbers like this:

Call 301–555–1234 xF00. This way you know this code (the extension #) stands for an offer you made F (February) 00 (2000).

Or if you do face-to-face business, an easy way is to require people to bring the letter with them and/or present it to your staff in order to get the special offer. Tracking is critical, or else you'll still be flying blind.

Now you can track your revenues and results from each mailing. Plus, you get a clear handle on where your business is coming from and which promotions are working.

Adding direct mail to your marketing is a surefire way to produce immediate results for your business. And by applying these seven little-known secrets, your next mailing can't help but be more profitable and successful.

■ ABOUT THE AUTHOR

Yanik Silver is a serial entrepreneur, although he still considers himself a techno dunce. Starting from his one-bedroom apartment and with just a few hundred dollars, Yanik has built multiple seven-figure businesses.

He is the author, coauthor, or publisher of several best-selling marketing books and tools, including *Moonlighting on the Internet* (Entrepreneur Press, 2008), *Instant Sales Letters* (Surefire Marketing, 2002), and *34 Rules for Maverick Entrepreneurs* (Maverick Business, 2008). Yanik is a highly sought-after speaker, addressing groups ranging from the prestigious Wharton Business School to international audiences of 3,000-plus.

As a self-described adventure junkie, Yanik has found that his own life-changing experiences such as running with the bulls, bungee jumping, sky diving, exotic car road rallies, and zero-gravity flights have not only brought a profound sense of accomplishment but also led to breakthroughs in ideas, focus, and business thinking. That's why he combined both his passions to found Maverick Business Adventures creating the kind of "club" he'd want to be part of.

Web Sites

www.surefiremarketing.com

Primary Products or Books

34 Rules for Maverick Entrepreneurs (Maverick Business, 2008)

Moonlighting on the Internet (Entrepreneur Press, 2008)

Instant Sales Letters (Surefire Marketing, 2002)

Twenty-One Creative Ways to Increase Your Facebook Fanbase

Mari Smith

A compelling, *active Facebook fan page* should be an integral part of your marketing plans. With its hundreds of millions of users and an average daily session time of 55 minutes, *Facebook provides an exceptional opportunity for visibility, Google indexing, live search ability,* and *fan engagement*—whether you're a solopreneur, a large brand, or anywhere in between.

But, if you build a Facebook page, will fans come? This is the great hope for many businesses. However, fans do not magically appear from the Facebook mist.

People must be lured to your fan page. And there are some good and bad ways to go about doing this. In this chapter, I'll share a big myth and 21 ways to drive more fans to your Facebook fan page. (Facebook changed the "Become a Fan" button to the omnipresent "Like" button—and a fan page is called a "Business Page" or "Facebook Page." However, we can still call them fan pages and people who join are fans!)

■ THE BIG MYTH

There's a great myth that once you create a Facebook fan page for your business, the first thing you should do to get fans is invite ALL your friends from your personal profile using the "Suggest to Friends" feature (see Figure 38.1).

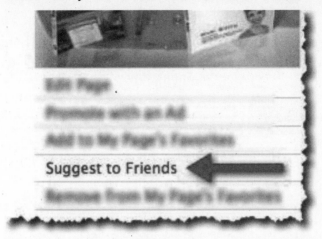

Figure 38.1

This strategy may not be that effective. I have seen many industry gurus complain that when they decline a fan page request, it's frustrating to continue to be asked again and again.

There are several *reasons not to use the Suggest to Friends* feature:

➤ *Facebook users can only like up to 500 pages* and may wish to be selective (though I have seen it's possible to go over this limit).

➤ *Fan page suggestions may often build up, unnoticed.* (At last count, I have 593 overlooked fan page suggestions and am already a fan of well over 600!)

➤ You already have visibility with your friends in their News Feed, so it's best to proactively reach out to a fresh audience. Besides, to aggressively pursue all your friends to join your fan page is *counterintuitive to the nature of social media.*

The good news is there are many ways to promote your fan page and proactively increase your fanbase without bugging all your current Facebook friends, and also by thinking wider than just Facebook.

➤ **Twenty-One Ways to Increase Your Facebook Fans**

1. Install Social Plugging on Your Web Site/Blog
Select from a number of the new Facebook Social Plugging and place them on your web site and blog. The Like Box Social Plugin (formerly "Fan Box widget") works well to *display your current fan page stream and a selection of fans*—see Figure 38.2 with Whole Foods

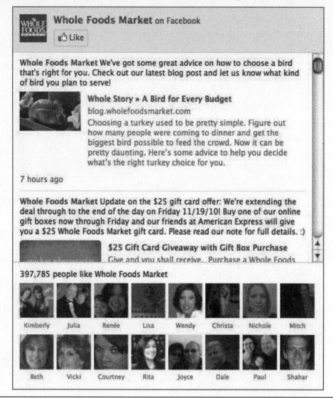

Figure 38.2   Whole Foods Market Facebook Like Box

Market Facebook Like Box. I would recommend adding a title above the box encouraging visitors to your site/blog to click the "Like" button (which makes them a Facebook fan).

You might also consider the Live Stream widget for more advanced uses, particularly on an FBML custom tab of your fan page itself. The Live Stream widget allows Facebook users to *add their comments to a live event*, for example, and that activity pushes out into their stream.

2. Invite Your E-Mail and Ezine Subscribers

Assuming you have an opt-in e-mail list, *send out an invitation to your subscribers via e-mail* (several times, over time) letting them know about your fan page and encouraging them to join. Ideally, provide them with a description of the page and an incentive to join.

Be sure to have the *Facebook logo/badge appear in your HTML newsletters*. Instead of the usual "Join our Fan Page," *say something creative like "Write on our Facebook wall,"* or "Join our Facebook community," or "Come add your photo to our Facebook group" (where "group" is actually your fan page). Users have to be a fan in order to interact with your fan page in this way.

3. Add to Your E-Mail Signature Block

Instead of promoting your Facebook personal profile (if you do), *include a link to your fan page in every e-mail* you send out. If you use Web-based e-mail, check out the Wisestamp signature add-on at www.wisestamp.com.

4. Make a Compelling Welcome Video

Create an attractive landing tab (canvas page) with a video that explains exactly (a) what your fan page is about, (b) who it's for, and (c) why they should become members. The result? You'll increase your conversion rate from visitors to fans.

One of my favorite fan page welcome videos is by Steve Spangler, the Science Guy (see Figure 38.3). After watching his video, you can't help but want to join!

Figure 38.3

5. Use Facebook Apps

I enjoy using the *live video-streaming app called Vpype.* The app adds a tab to your fan page called "Shows" and when you broadcast as your fan page, everyone can view by default. (You can also broadcast as your personal profile and selectively invite friends/friend lists.)

I wrote up a review of this app here. By announcing via Twitter, your personal Facebook profile, your blog, and your e-mail list, *you can broadcast regular live Internet TV shows from your fan page and create much buzz.*

Another example of app integration is Target's "Bullseye Gives" campaign (created by Context Optional). *Target had their fans vote on which of 10 charities they most wanted to see the company donate to.* By voting, a post goes out onto your Facebook wall and into the News Feeds of all your friends, thus providing Target with valuable exposure (see Figure 38.4).

(For custom apps, see companies like Buddy Media, Fan Appz, Wildfire Apps, Involver, Virtue, Context Optional.)

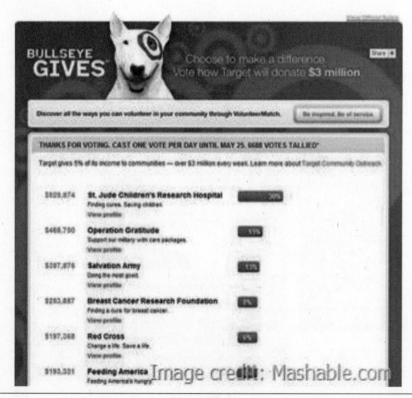

Figure 38.4

Figure 38.5

Source: Threadless Facebook Fan Page landing tab.

6. Integrate the Facebook Comment Feature

My favorite example of this is the T-shirt company Threadless. On their landing tab (canvas page), you can view and purchase t-shirts as well as *Like and comment on any item and choose to have that comment posted to your Facebook profile*, as shown in Figure 38.5.

Threadless actually has their landing tab set up so visitors don't have to become a fan to purchase/comment/interact. Yet they have organically built over 200,000 fans.

As users comment on items, *that activity is pushed out into their stream* (profile wall and their friends' News Feeds), which creates *valuable viral visibility* for your fan page.

For further information on adding the comment box to your FBML page/app, see these pages.

7. Get Fans to Tag Photos

If you host live events, be sure to take plenty of photos (or even hire a professional photographer), load the photos to your fan page, and encourage fans to tag themselves. This, again, pushes out into their wall and friends' News Feeds, providing valuable (free!) exposure. And a picture says a thousand words—we notice the thumbnails in our feed more than text. *(Props to Nick O'Neil of AllFacebook.com for this tip.)*

8. Load Videos and Embed on Your Site

Facebook's Video feature is extremely powerful. You can load video content to your Facebook fan page, then take the source code and

Figure 38.6

(Screenshot shows example of an embedded Facebook video on an external site.)

embed on your blog/web site. There is a hot-linked "Facebook" watermark right in the video itself in the top left corner. For an excellent tutorial, see Nick O'Neil's post: "How To Get Thousands of Facebook Fans With a Single Video."

When viewers click the watermark, it takes them to the original video page on your fan page (see Figure 38.6).

Once on Facebook, viewers will see a Like button at the top left corner of the video player—see second screenshot in Figure 38.7.

9. Place Facebook Ads

Even with a nominal weekly/monthly budget, you should be able to *boost your fan count* using Facebook's own social ad feature. It's the most targeted traffic your money can buy. To buy an ad, scroll to the foot of any page inside Facebook and click the link at the very bottom that says "Advertising." From there, you can walk through the wizard and get an excellent sense of how many Facebook users are in your *exact* target market.

Then, *when you advertise your fan page, Facebook users can become a fan (click the Like button) right from the ad* as shown in the screenshot (Figure 38.8). Additionally, *Facebook displays several of your friends who have already liked you, thus creating social proof.*

My book with Chris Treadaway, *Facebook Marketing: An Hour a Day* (Sybex, 2010) contains comprehensive instructions on maximizing your marketing through Facebook social ads.

Figure 38.7

(Screenshot shows the same video on the original page of the fan page with the Like button.)

10. Run a Contest

Facebook has rigorous promotional guidelines. Essentially, in order to administer a contest, competition, drawing, or sweepstakes, you need to meet these three criteria: (1) obtain prior written permission from Facebook; (2) administer the promotion via a third-party app, not directly on your Facebook Page wall; and/or (3) meet the minimum monthly ad spend (which is significant!).

Running a contest on your fan page can build tremendous buzz and grow your fanbase. It's best not to start with a contest though; wait until you have achieved a reasonable number (could be 500 to 1,000+). Then choose from one of the following third-party app providers: WildfireApp.com, Votigo.com, or FanAppz.com.

11. Link to Twitter

Link your Twitter account to your Facebook fan page and automatically post your Facebook content to Twitter. You can edit what gets posted, choosing from Status Updates, Photos, Links, Notes, and Events.

You have 420 characters on the Facebook publisher and 140 on Twitter. In the tweet that goes out, Facebook truncates your post and inserts a link back to your fan page. This then provides your Twitter followers an opportunity to come over to your fan page.

Create an Ad

Dancing with the ✕
Stars
(DWTSshow.com)

Come check out why Kate
Gosselin says she needs
to be famous at the fan
page with the best DWTS
content on Facebook! Oh,
and Fan us!

Mei Yu, Mary Jo Finn and
Lynn Rose like Dancing
with the Stars
(DWTSshow.com).

 Like

Want Some Free ✕
Publicity?

Reporter Connection is
free service that gets you
publicity in magazines,
newspapers and radio/TV
shows for your book, biz
or website.

Jennifer Schaecher
Scherlizin and Faith
Barnard like this ad.

 Like

Figure 38.8

I also recommend you promote your Facebook fan page on your Twitter background and possibly in your Twitter bio/URL field too.

12. Get Fans to Join Via SMS

Your fans can join your fan page via text message! You'll need to get your first 25 fans and secure your username.

Then, to join your fan page, Facebook users just *send a text message to 32665 (FBOOK) with the words "fan yourusername" OR "like yourusername"* (without the quotes).

This feature is ideal when you're addressing a live audience, say. Have everyone pull out their mobile phones and join your fan page on the spot! This would also work well for radio or TV. (Note that this only works for Facebook users with a verified mobile device in their accounts—don't worry, it's in the hundreds of millions!)

13. Use Print Media

Look at every piece of print media you use in your business. Your Facebook fan page (as well as Twitter and any other social sites you're active on), should be clearly displayed. *Put your Facebook fan page link (and the logo) on your business cards, letterhead, brochure, print newsletter, magazine ads, products*, and so on.

14. Display at Your Store/Business

If your business is run from physical premises, *put a placard on the front desk* letting your customers know you're on Facebook. Ideally, you have a simple, memorable username. *Incentivize customers to join right away via their mobile device and show you/your staff the confirmation for some kind of instant reward!*

You might *give out physical coupons promoting your fan page*. For restaurants, put the Facebook logo, your username, and a call to action on your *menus*.

I was at a hotel in San Francisco last fall and they had *a placard in the elevators promoting their presence on Facebook and Twitter*. The sign was very noticeable because of those ubiquitous Facebook and Twitter logos/colors!

15. Add a Link on Your Personal Profile

If you'd like to *promote your fan page to your Facebook friends*, just under your photo on your personal profile there is a section to write something about yourself. I call this the "mini bio" field and strongly suggest adding a link to your fan page as shown in Figure 38.9.

You have a limited number of characters, so keep it succinct. You can put in hard line breaks though to make the content easier to read.

View Photos of Me (1,043)

View Videos of Me (201)

Edit My Profile

Hello Friend! ♫♥♫

I'm passionate about making a positive difference on the planet by sharing light, love & truth via Facebook and social media.

Join my fab Fan Page & I'll happily answer your questions there ⇩
www.facebook.com/marismith

Figure 38.9

16. Add a Badge/Button to Your Profile
Using an app like Profile HTML or Extended Info, you can *create your own custom HTML*, including a Facebook badge and/or graphic embedded, as shown in the screenshot in Figure 38.10.

17. Use the Share Button
The *Share button* is all over Facebook and is a very handy feature. It only works for sharing on your personal profile. So periodically go to your fan page, scroll toward the bottom left column and click the "Share+" button.

Add a compelling comment along the lines of exciting news, recent changes, special incentives, and so on, happening on your fan page and invite your friends to join if they haven't already.

I find the Share button (see Figure 38.11) far more effective than the Suggest to Friends approach. (And, if you'd like to Share content from the Web on to your *fan page* vs. profile, I highly recommend using the *Hootlet bookmarklet tool* at HootSuite.com).

Figure 38.10

Figure 38.11

18. Use the @ Tag

As long as you're a fan of your own fan page, you can "@ tag" it on your own personal profile wall. From time to time, you can let your friends know about something happening on your fan page by writing a personal status update that includes tagging your fan page with an @ tag.

Simply start typing the "@" symbol and the first few letters of your fan page name (this works whether you have your username registered or not), and it will appear from a drop-down menu to select (see Figure 38.12). This then makes it a nice, subtle hyperlink that your friends can choose to click on.

19. Autograph Posts on Other Walls

A subtle way to gain more visibility for your fan page is to add an @ tag for your fan page when writing on your friends' walls as a way to sign off.

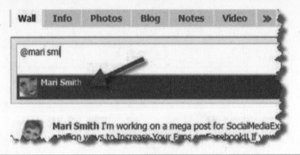

Figure 38.12

I would use this one sparingly and, again, monitor the response from your friends. I have never been a fan of adding a signature block on Facebook wall posts because our name and profile picture thumbnail are always hyperlinked right back to our profile anyway. But the simple @ tag could be effective.

20. Autograph Other Fan Pages
As with adding your fan page @ tag to posts you make on your friends' walls, you could equally *use the same technique when posting on other fan pages* (see Figure 38.13). This *needs to be used with discretion*, and I would advise against doing this on any potentially competing fan page!

21. Maybe *Use "Suggest to Friends"*
I won't rule this one out completely as it does *depend on how many friends you have*, your relationship with your friends, how often you

Figure 38.13

Figure 38.14

suggest fan pages/friends to your friends, and so on (see "The Big Myth" above). But I do recommend *monitoring the response to this technique*—perhaps simply by asking for feedback in your status update (see Figure 38.14).

So, these are just 21 ways to create strategic visibility and promote your Facebook fan page.

Come and write on my Facebook fan page wall—let me know which of these strategies you implement with success! http://facebook.com/marismith.

■ ABOUT THE AUTHOR

Mari Smith is one of the world's foremost experts on using Facebook as a marketing channel. She is coauthor of *Facebook Marketing: An Hour A Day* (Sybex, 2010) and her new book on the topic of relationship marketing is due out in August 2011. *Fast Company* dubbed Mari, "the Pied Piper of the Online World." With her popular blog MariSmith.com, and her large loyal following on both Facebook and Twitter, Mari is considered one of the top resources and thought leaders in the world of online marketing. She frequently appears in media locally and nationally. Mari is also a popular Social Media Keynote Speaker and Trainer. She travels the United States and internationally to share her wisdom and provide social media keynotes and in-depth training. She has shared the stage with the likes of Sir Richard Branson, the Dalai Lama, President F.W. de Klerk, Tony Robbins, Dr. Stephen R. Covey, and Paula Abdul. A self-described "bubbly Scottish-Canadian," Mari currently lives in San Diego, California, and has a penchant for turquoise and bling!

Web Sites

www.marismith.com

www.twitter.com/marismith

www.facebook.com/marismith

www.youtube.com/facebookmari

Primary Products or Books

Facebook Marketing: An Hour A Day (Sybex, 2010)

Chapter 39

The Great Brand Dilution

Brian Solis

For decades brands basked in the glory of control—control over consumers' perceptions, impressions, and ultimately decisions and ensuing experiences. Or better said, business leaders enjoyed a semblance of control. While businesses concentrated resources on distancing the connections between customers, influencers, and representatives, a new democracy was materializing. This movement would inevitably render these faceless actions not only defunct, but also perilous.

Fueled by the socialization of media, content and connections served as the foundation for this new democracy and "we the people" ensured that our voices were heard. Social media would forever change the balance of power within markets, placing the fate and stature of brands in the words and actions of consumers and the people and groups that influence their decisions. Brands didn't just "lose" control of defining impressions; businesses lost the ability to govern shared experiences.

Suddenly people enjoyed the freedom to publish their thoughts and the capacity to earn prominence in these fledgling social ecosystems. No longer was it an era of brands saying what they wished us to think; it was now clear that people were in control of their impressions and more importantly, how, where, and when they shared them.

It's no longer about what we say, it's what they say about us now that counts.

Sometimes truth and reality awaken us to a new reality. And in this case, everything changes . . . for the better.

Contrary to popular belief, social media didn't invent conversations; they just allowed us to organize and surface them. But when we look at the importance of branding, the mechanics and methodologies for defining, protecting, and growing the brand profoundly change. As such, the value of brands is at risk of dilution based on the aggregate of shared experiences by the new social consumer. And, perhaps the greatest challenge that faces brands in addition to dilution, is the inability to right their course in real-time. As media democratized, the meter for establishing prominence started to accrue varying levels of influence for its participants while many businesses missed their calling. It's not too late for brands to *engage*; however, the difference is that everyday people have earned greater reach than some businesses within these social channels.

■ THE EVOLUTION OF BRAND MARKETING

The medium is no longer just the message. In social media, the medium is the platform, and as such people now represent both the medium and the message where *reach* is defined by a blending of the social graph, the context of the story and ensuing connections, and also by the state of the *attention aperture* of those to whom we're connected.

Simply stated, social media is changing brand marketing and forcing a (r)evolution that will unfold differently within each organization.

MiresBall and KRC Research recently conducted a study that found 4 out of 10 brand marketers believe that social media create challenges to maintaining brand integrity. In addition, more than a third believed that social networking affected brands to the point where marketing strategies would require new thinking. This new direction, however, is rife with new challenges as well as opportunities.

■ BELIEF THAT SOCIAL MEDIA CREATES NEW CHALLENGES FOR PROTECTING BRAND INTEGRITY, 2010

➤ Belief that Social Media Provides an Opportunity to Reach New Customers

Brand marketers realize the importance of social media, but they're unclear as to how it can specifically help with engendering loyalty. Thirty-five percent believed social media lend to loyalty, but 30 percent disagreed, and another 35 percent were neutral on the subject. While marketers were split on loyalty, over one-half agreed that social media serve as bridges to reaching customers and prospects.

■ UPDATE THE BRAND STYLE GUIDE

The study also revealed a growing concern among brand marketers on how they engaged with consumers today. The consensus was that in order to successfully connect with consumers in a way that reinforces brand attributes, representatives require training, messages, and empowerment.

When it comes to brand dilution, consumers aren't alone in their endeavors. Brand representatives and the lack of a prevailing strategy, mission, or purpose in social media cause the breakdown of branding and messages directly from the source. At the moment, a disconnect exists between the brand, its representatives, and its consumers in social media. This disconnect starts with understanding the brand's voice, presence, and personality, and what it is the brand needs to say to the varying roles of the social consumer.

I refer to this series of fragmented touchpoints as The Last Mile. And in order to establish connections with individuals in their domains where they are in control of their experiences, it takes empathy combined with value, reinforced by branding elements that strengthen the story, the engagement, and the resulting activity. Without first defining the brand in these prominent social networks, how can we expect it to thrive and flourish let alone inspire consumers?

To prevent the dilution of our brands in social media, everything must begin with revisiting and revising the brand style guide. This style guide must be embodied by brand representatives where engagement is clearly led not by the "brand you," but instead the brand "you represent."

In an era where brands are both created and cocreated, defining our brand, its meaning, and its value, and then humanizing it, will set the stage for collaboration and brand concentration.

Losing control in an era of socialized media and equalized influence, actually gives birth to an important form of empowerment. With a new-found ability to listen to conversations tied to brands, products, and experiences and also to analyze associated sentiment in real-time is stirring and enlightening. If ignorance is bliss, awareness is awakening. We now have the ability to understand impressions and perceptions and through engagement, we can contribute to their accuracy as well as define our brand relevance and legacy through every profile, conversation, and social object we introduce.

■ ABOUT THE AUTHOR

Author of the acclaimed new book on social media and business, *Engage!*, Brian Solis is globally recognized as one of the most prominent thought leaders and published authors in new media. A digital analyst, sociologist, and futurist, Solis has influenced the effects of emerging media on the convergence of marketing, communications, and publishing. He is principal of FutureWorks, an award-winning New Media and business strategy consultancy in Silicon Valley, and has led interactive and social programs for Fortune 500 companies, notable celebrities, and Web 2.0 startups. BrianSolis.com is among the world's leading business and marketing online resources.

Web Sites

www.briansolis.com

www.bub.blicio.us

Primary Products or Books

Engage! (John Wiley & Sons, Inc., 2010)

Chapter 40

How to Write a Great Press Release

A Sample Press Release Template

Bill Stoller

■ **WHAT IS A PRESS RELEASE?**

A press release is pseudo-news story, written in the third person, that seeks to demonstrate to an editor or reporter the newsworthiness of a particular person, event, service, or product.

■ **HOW IS A PRESS RELEASE USED?**

Press releases are often sent alone, by e-mail, fax, or snail mail. They can also be part of a full press kit, or may be accompanied by a pitch letter.

■ **WHAT IS THE PROPER PRESS RELEASE FORMAT?**

Here's a sample press release template you can use to format your press release correctly:

■ **WHAT SHOULD I PUT IN MY PRESS RELEASE?**

Stop right now and click here to read our in-depth advice about packaging yourself as newsworthy. This is an important step—so don't skip it!

[COMPANY LOGO]

Contact: John Smith   FOR IMMEDIATE RELEASE
Tel. 555/555-2222
Cell Phone: 555/555-2222
Email: johnsmith@anywhere.com

MAIN TITLE OF PRESS RELEASE GOES HERE IN ALL UPPER CASE
Subtitle Goes Here in Title Case (Upper and Lower)

body of press release body of press release body of press release body of press release body of press release body of press release body of press release body of press release body of press release.

body of press release body of press release body of press release body of press release body of press release body of press release body of press release body of press release body of press release body of press release body of press release body of press release body of release body of press release.

body of press release body of press release.

body of press release body of press release body of press release body of press release body of press release.

boilerplate boilerplate boilerplate boilerplate boilerplate boilerplate boilerplate boilerplate boilerplate boilerplate boilerplate boilerplate boilerplate boilerplate boilerplate boilerplate boilerplate.

# # #

If you'd like more information about this topic, or to schedule an interview with John Smith, please call Pat Brown at 555/555-2222 or e-mail Pat at pr@theplace4vitamins.com

Figure 40.1

Note: The three #'s mark the end of the press release.

Let's stick with the theme presented in that report: You run a vitamin web site specializing in weight-loss products. Through the process described in the report, you've nailed down a nice, newsworthy topic—teenagers and how they deal with issues of weight. But that's a broad topic, not a story.

In the report, we provided a number of ideas for potential stories. Let's pick the first one and craft a press release.

The story: What do kids think about a "thin is in" society?

As you sift through your message boards looking for quotes, you see a trend appearing. There are lots of messages criticizing Hollywood actresses and pop singers for being too thin. Many girls are saying that seeing these women makes them feel bad about their own bodies. A number of the boys are pointing out that they don't find ultrathin women appealing.

Now you've got your angle—your hook that will grab a reporter's attention:

Teenagers think that a "thin is in" society pretty much stinks.

Now let's get writing.

■ PRESS RELEASE HEADLINE

Before you write a word, remember this:

The reporter isn't interested in helping you make money or driving visitors to your site. He's looking for a story that will be interesting to his readers and pleasing to his editor. He could care less about your great selection, super customer service, and commitment to quality. He wants to know only the info that will help him craft a good story about teens and their weight.

Take your ego out of it. Take your natural inclination to sell, sell, sell out of it. Look at your story with a cold, objective eye.

Okay, let's get to our press release headline.

State your most exciting news, finding, or announcement in as few words as possible. Emulate the headlines you see in the newspaper every day.

Bad press release headline:

NEW WEB SITE THAT OFFERS HERBAL WEIGHT LOSS PROGRAMS LETS TEENS SPEAK OUT ABOUT WEIGHT ISSUES

Good press release headline:

TEENS: ULTRA-THIN MOVIE, POP STARS SET BAD EXAMPLE

Don't worry, you'll get to plug your web site soon enough. In the meantime, you've just thrown a meaty hook at the reporter.

■ THE PRESS RELEASE SUBHEAD

Subheads are remarkably useful tools, yet usually overlooked by press release writers. Basically, the press release subhead gives you the opportunity to flesh out your angle and further hook the reporter, without stepping on the drama of the press release headline.

Here's a headline/subhead combo I might use for this press release:

TEENS: ULTRA-THIN MOVIE, POP STARS SET BAD EXAMPLE
WEB SITE FORUMGOERS WEIGH IN: TEENS DON'T FIND
ULTRA-THIN CELEBS ATTRACTIVE; GIRLS SAY NEGATIVE
SELF-IMAGES REINFORCED BY HOLLYWOOD'S SUPER-SKINNY

■ THE PRESS RELEASE LEAD

It's Journalism 101—the lead paragraph includes the who, what, when, where, and how of the story. If the reporter were only to read the lead of a good press release, she'd have everything she needed to get started.

There's no room for BS, hype, or sell. Just the facts.

Bad Press Release Lead

Recently on theplace4vitamins.com, an online store dedicated to selling the best herbal products, teenagers had the chance to say what they thought about weight loss and whether a society that pressures young people to be thin is a good thing or a bad thing.

Good Press Release Lead

America's teenagers are angry at Hollywood for glamorizing ultra-thin bodies, and many girls say they feel too self-conscious about their bodies as a result of watching TV, movies, and music videos. The findings are gleaned from more than six months of ongoing discussion and debate at the web site theplace4vitamins.com. According to theplace4vitamins.com President John Smith, anger and resentment toward the Hollywood ultra-thin runs deep, particularly among teenage girls.

■ THE REST OF THE PRESS RELEASE

The balance of the press release serves to back up whatever claims were made in the lead and headline. In this case, you'd pull some quotes from the message boards (an aside here: If you really were to pull quotes in this fashion, you should only use the poster's name or identifying information with his permission; otherwise, simply say "a 14-year-old boy said . . ." or "a 16-year-old Midwestern girl added. . ."; also, if this technique appeals to you, be certain that a disclaimer appears on your message boards notifying posters that all posts become your property and copyright). Use enough supporting material to make your case, and to demonstrate that, whatever angle you're promoting, it wasn't something you slapped together carelessly.

Next, a quote will help put in some perspective:

"I was surprised by the level of anger expressed in these messages," Smith said. "Teenagers are far more clued into this issue than most people would imagine."

Or, you might ask an expert for a quote:

"This demonstrates once again the need to teach young girls and boys about how to develop a positive self-image," said Jane Doe, author of I Like My Body Just As It Is. "theplace4vitamins.com has done a true service by bringing these attitudes to the public's attention."

Finally, spend a sentence or two describing your company and what you do:

theplace4vitamins.com was founded in 1997 to provide consumers with a wide choice of vitamins, supplements, and herbal products. The site offers a range of articles, research materials, and message forums for the health-conscious consumer.

This paragraph is known as the "boilerplate"—an old newspaper term meaning a block of standard text that's used over and over again (e.g., the explanation of symbols on the stock price page). In this case, it's text that you might use at the bottom of all your releases.

Place your boilerplate right above the # # #'s.

One more trick: below the ###'s, add a line that says something like:

If you'd like more information about this topic, or to schedule an interview with John Smith, please call Pat Brown at 555/555–2222 or e-mail Pat at pr@theplace4vitamins.com.

■ SOME KEY THINGS TO REMEMBER

Stay away from hype-bloated phrases like "breakthrough," "unique," "state-of-the-art," and so on.

Always write it from a journalist's perspective. Never use "I" or "we" unless it's in a quote.

Read lots of good newspaper writing, such as the *New York Times* or the *Washington Post* to get a feel for the style.

Shorter is better. If you can say it in two pages, great. If you can say it in one page, better.

■ ABOUT THE AUTHOR

Bill Stoller is a 25-year PR Pro helping others get their share of publicity and social media; editor and founder of *Free Publicity—The Newsletter for PR Hungry Businesses*. He has been referred to as the "encyclopedia" of publicity, public relations, and social media. He has worked with major brands and companies including Coca Cola, Hasbro, Nabisco, and FedEx.

Web Sites

www.publicityinsider.com

Primary Products or Books

Free Publicity—The Newsletter for PR Hungry Businesses

Chapter 41

Why I Changed My Coffee Religion

Scott Stratten

I have a morning ritual that I know many of you share. Coffee around here is a bit like a religion. You choose your brand, you pick your favorite, and then you stick with it. In the Toronto area, Tim Horton's is the church of coffee. It is a part of the culture up here, part of the vocabulary. When you say you're going for coffee, you go to "Tim's" or you're going to go to "Horton's."

I'm sure you have your own coffee chains in your area that have the same kind of following. They become a part of our routine. This has to be the ultimate goal for a business, whether it is service- or product-based. Work to become a part of somebody's routine. If you can, it is worth an incredible amount of money. The lifetime value of each and every somebody who spends $2 a day with your company is incredible. Think about that for a second—$2 a day equals more than $700 a year. Over 10 years you're looking at more than $7,000 in revenue from one person. Companies have a vested interest in making sure you become a regular, and you should be working hard to make your customers lifelong clients. Unfortunately, just like many personal relationships, when you become used to one another you take each other for granted, and companies do this far too often with loyal customers.

Tim Horton's had me. I was loyal as could be. But recently I have done something I never thought I would do. I changed brands. Being a loyal Tim Horton's customer, almost every day I would go and get my coffee from them. I didn't even think about it—that is just what I did. When any other coffee company came into the area, they were an afterthought. No way a new company was going to change my habit.

Slowly something happened. I started noticing cracks in the armor of my habit.

One misstep or one small issue will not lead to somebody changing a day-to-day habit. But when you begin to add up enough of those small things you open up the door to your competition. It is not usually extreme customer service issues that drive people away.

So here is the story of the small things that led me away from Tim Horton's. First, the servers wouldn't stir my coffee. The coffee was inconsistent, a small thing, but one that I know my fellow coffee drinkers out there will understand.

When you buy your coffee at the drive-through and start to drink it after you've pulled a mile or two away and find that it was not made or stirred properly, the experience is hurtful. For people like me who take three sugars in their coffee and order the same coffee every day, I really do notice the difference when it isn't made properly. Similarly, when there are mistakes in the order, when I can taste cream instead of milk, when there is sweetener instead of sugar, your customer will notice. These are little things. Mistakes happen, of course, but when they start happening more and more, your customer begins to wonder if this is how service will always be. Then the customer begins to doubt the quality of your service or product. This doubt creates a space where your customer is open to try something new.

Got gap?

Picture the image of a gap. It starts as a tiny crack. Your loyal customer has always been happy with your product or service and then slowly small doubts add up, and cracks begin to form. Until one day, the experience gap grows just big enough for one of your competitors to get through. The experience gap is the space between the best experience your customer has had with you and the worst. Ideally this gap doesn't exist or is as small as possible.

Businesses need to make buying their products easy. This was another issue with Tim Horton's that led me away from being a loyal customer. The company does not accept debit card payments. So their customers cannot pay for their coffee and doughnuts with a bankcard. This is rare today. As a matter of fact, the only reason I would ever take money out of the bank was so I could buy coffee from Horton's. (I think the only two businesses in the world that do not accept bank cards are Horton's and drug dealers. Although I think some of our local drug dealers here will take checks.)

Now the extra inconvenience of taking out cash was okay when my coffee was perfect, but adding this to the frequency of mistakes in my order was getting to be too much. Add in some other things I put up with in the name of my favorite coffee, such as the cumbersome lid that was impossible to open while driving, and the long wait times, and I was really open to the competition. I had been a loyal customer for 20 years. I figured that over the past 20 years I have spent upward of $15,000 with the company. I was at that point where all of these small negative experiences had come together, the perfect storm point, and I was open to give something else a try. It takes a lot for somebody to change anything, let alone change a part of their daily routine. I didn't really do it consciously, it just happened. All that it was going to take for another company to earn me as a new customer was quality that matched what I was used to and that gave me more convenience.

Enter McDonald's.

I was already a McDonald's fan. The company didn't have to begin at the start with me or get me to buy into its brand. But I didn't buy coffee there. My first real job was working at McDonald's when I was 15. As far as I could see back then, the only people who bought coffee at McDonald's were senior citizens at six in the morning. But now McDonald's was on a mission to prove that its coffee was worth buying on its own, a bold task considering the market already included heavy competition from Horton's and Starbucks.

A few years ago I wouldn't have even thought of trying the McDonald's coffee let alone switching over to it, but I had gotten to the breaking point as a customer. I was willing to at least try something different. Tim Horton's was taking my business for granted, but McDonald's was working for it.

McDonald's had a promotion to launch its coffee, and it was giving out free coffee to anybody during a certain time. So this was going to be the time I was going to try it. Unfortunately, the lineup of people to try the coffee when they found out it was free could have rivaled lineups for rides at Disney World. So I decided to hold off on giving it a try. A few weeks later I finally went in and tried it.

Compared with Tim Horton's, McDonald's had the same, if not more, drive-through locations, just the kind of convenience a lazy man like myself was looking for.

At this point the quality was important—no matter how much convenience or customer service I got, at this point if the product wasn't of the quality that I liked I wouldn't switch to it. This is really important to note. Quality is always important! No matter how much marketing or unmarketing you do, it doesn't make a difference if your product or service doesn't stand up. So I order the coffee and go to pay for it and the server takes my bankcard! I am allowed to use my bankcard to pay for the coffee—McDonald's earned one bonus point.

I get the coffee and I see that the coffee cup is double walled—meaning I don't have to put a sleeve on it! I don't have to ask for a second cup! McDonald's execs have spent some time thinking about their products and their customers and thought, "Hey, coffee is hot, people don't like to burn their hand" and come up with a solution—a double-walled cup. Genius.

I went to open it in my car, and the lid was amazing. You can open it with one thumb and it pops and locks open—no mess, no burned fingers, and another bonus point. The ease and convenience of the cup itself really improved my experience.

The location near my home also has a secret weapon. His name is David. At the Iroquois Shore Road location, in Oakville, Ontario, David is the guy you talk to in the morning in the drive-through. He's kind, considerate, happy but not the in your face that makes you hate him in the morning. Heck, he even makes the add-on suggestion of a muffin a pleasant occurrence. It's gotten to the point that I will go out of my way in the morning to have David serve me. Great service and a great new product. I never would've even known if it hadn't been for the dropping of the ball at the place I where was loyal.

This is exactly what your company does not want. You do not want your long-time loyal customer to be dissatisfied too many times and now in the hands of the competition and very, very happy. I then tasted the coffee, and it tasted great.

I get no reimbursement from McDonald's to say that I am not their affiliate. In all honesty, the coffee tasted great, even better than what I was used to. That did it. And now I look for McDonald's when I'm wanting a morning coffee or on the road. I may be just one customer, but my lifetime value is $20,000 or $30,000. How many people will it take for Tim Horton's to realize that understanding the needs and wants of the marketplace is a good thing to do all the time?

You need to know if your customers are happy, and if they aren't you need to know why and how you can change it. You need to know where you stand in the eyes of your customers. Are they happy, are they ecstatic, or are they just there holding on until someone better comes along? You do not want your brand to be in that zone with current customers where the experience gap has left a space for the competition. You cannot be complacent or inattentive leaving your hard-earned market ripe for the picking.

■ ABOUT THE AUTHOR

Scott Stratten is the president of UnMarketing. He is an expert in viral, social, and authentic marketing which he calls *UnMarketing*. It's all about positioning yourself as a trusted expert in front of a target market, so when they have the need, they choose you.

Formerly a music industry marketer, national sales training manager, and a professor at the Sheridan College School of Business, he now has over 80,000 people follow his daily rants on Twitter and was voted one of the top influencer's on the site with over 200 million users.

His book *UnMarketing: Stop Marketing. Start Engaging* (John Wiley & Sons, Inc., 2010) became a national best-seller before it was released, and recently a Globe and Mail number one business best-seller, and an Amazon.com, Amazon.ca, and Amazon UK best-seller as well as being named one of the top business books of 2010 by 1-800-CEO-READ.

His clients' viral marketing videos have been viewed over 60 million times even before YouTube existed.

Web Sites

www.un-marketing.com/blog

Primary Products or Books

UnMarketing: Stop Marketing. Start Engaging (John Wiley & Sons, Inc., 2010)

Chapter 42

Power of Psychological Triggers

Joe Sugarman

A desire to buy something often involves a subconscious decision. In fact, I claim that 95 percent of buying decisions are indeed subconscious.

Knowing the subconscious reasons why people buy, and using this information in a fair and constructive way, will *trigger greater sales response*—often far beyond what you could imagine.

I recall a time when I applied one of these subconscious devices by changing just one word of an ad, and response doubled. I refer to these subconscious devices as psychological "triggers." A psychological trigger is the strongest motivational factor any salesperson or copywriter can use to evoke a sale.

There are 30 triggers in all, some of which I will reveal to you in a moment. Each trigger, when deployed, has the power to increase sales and response beyond what you would normally expect.

There are triggers, for example, that will cause your prospects to feel guilty if they don't purchase your product. Let me give you an example. Whenever you receive in the mail a sales solicitation with free personalized address stickers, you often feel guilty if you use the stickers and don't send something back—often far in excess of the value of the stickers. Fundraising companies use this method a great deal. You receive 50 cents' worth of stickers and send back a $20 bill.

Another example is those surveys that are sent out asking for you to spend about 20 minutes of your time filling them out. Enclosed in the mailing you might find a dollar bill included to encourage you to feel guilty, and entice you to fill out the survey. And you often spend a lot more than one dollar of your time to do that.

Guilt is a strong motivator. I have to admit that I've used guilt in many selling situations, in mail order ads and on TV—with great success, I might add.

I call one of the most powerful triggers a "satisfaction conviction," which is a guarantee of satisfaction. But don't confuse this with the typical trial period you find in mail order; that is, "If you're not happy within 30 days, you can return your purchase for a full refund." A satisfaction conviction is different. Basically it takes the trial period and adds something that makes it go well beyond the trial period.

For example, if I were offering a subscription, instead of saying, "If at any time you're not happy with your subscription, we'll refund your unused portion," and instead said, "If at any time you're not happy with your subscription, let us know and we'll refund your entire subscription price—even if you decide to cancel just before the last issue."

Basically you're saying to your prospect that you are so sure that they'll like the subscription, that you are willing to go beyond what is traditionally offered with other subscriptions. This in fact gives the reader the sense that the company really knows it has a winning product and solidly stands behind the product and your satisfaction.

Is this technique effective? You bet. In many tests, I've doubled response—sometimes by adding just one sentence that conveys a good satisfaction conviction.

I received an e-mail from a company, a subsidiary of eBay, requesting my advice. They had an e-mail solicitation that wasn't drawing the response that they had expected. What was wrong?

Looking over what they had created, I saw several mistakes, many of which would have been avoided if they knew the psychological triggers that cause people to buy. Let me give you just one example.

In the subject line of most e-mails that have solicited me, I have been able to tell, at a glance, that the solicitation was for a specific service or an offer of something that I was clearly able to determine. Examples such as "Reduce your CD and DVD costs 50 percent," or "Lose weight quickly," pretty much told me what they were selling. Was this good or bad?

The problem with those subject lines is that the reader was able to quickly determine:

1. That it was an advertisement
2. That it was for some specific product or service

Most people don't like advertising. And most people won't make the effort to open their e-mail solicitation if they think they are getting an advertising message—unless they are sincerely interested in buying something that the advertisement offers.

The subject line of an e-mail is similar to the headline of a mail order ad, or the copy on an envelope, or the first few minutes of an infomercial. You've got to grab people's attention and then get them to take the next step. In the case of the envelope, you want them to open it. In the case of an infomercial, you want them to keep watching, and in the case of an e-mail, you want them open up the e-mail and read your message.

The key, therefore, is to get a person to want to open your message by putting something into the subject area of your e-mail that does not appear to be an advertising message—one that would compel them to take the next step. And the best trigger to use for this is the trigger of curiosity.

There are a number of ways you can use curiosity to literally force a person to take the next step. You can then use this valuable tool to put a reader in the correct frame of mind to buy what you have to offer.

Once again, all the principles apply to every form of communication—whether it be advertising, marketing, or personal selling. And to know these triggers is the key to more effective communication and most importantly, the avoidance of costly errors that waste time and money.

■ ABOUT THE AUTHOR

He's by no means "Your Average Joe." In fact, there's nothing average about him. No "Average Joe" could be such a creative, diverse, and successful entrepreneur. It's far from average to sell millions of people on products they didn't even know they needed, right?

No "Average Joe" could wear the many hats he has with style, grace, and excellence. Joe Sugarman, marketing legend, author and businessman, friend and father, husband and humanitarian . . . continues passionately helping others on his amazing journey.

Web Sites

www.joesugarman.com

Primary Products or Books

Triggers: 30 Sales Tools You Can Use to Control the Mind of Your Prospect to Motivate, Influence and Persuade (Delstar, 1999)

Advertising Secrets of the Written Word: The Ultimate Resource on How to Write Powerful Advertising Copy from One of America's Top Copywriters and Mail Order Entrepreneurs (Delstar, 1998)

Marketing Secrets of a Mail Order Maverick

TV Secrets for Marketing Success

The Seven Forces of Success

Five Guerrilla Marketing Weapons That Helped Increase My Business without Spending Any Money

Mike Tasner

The end of 2009 and into 2010 was proving to be a very difficult year for my company, Taz Solutions, Inc., a Web marketing, strategy, PR, and design firm. I discovered that the old ways of doing business were just not working in the new economy. I was used to charging $5,000 or more a month on retainer without anyone batting an eye as they saw the massive value we provided. This, however, seemed to turn overnight. $5,000 a month turned into $3,000, which turned into $2,000.

Rather than simply lowering the prices, I knew I needed to think outside the box. I decided to turn to the most well-known marketing brand in history—Guerrilla Marketing. I've been familiar with Guerrilla Marketing for years, but I had never really fully utilized its power. The whole essence behind Guerrilla Marketing is using time, energy, and imagination rather than money, which was simply perfect as I was strapped for cash! Instead of just reading some more of the materials, I decided to take some massive action—I flew out to Orlando and spent several days with Jay Conrad Levinson to become a Guerrilla Marketing Master Trainer. They were so impressed with my style and commitment, they made me the chief marketing officer for their whole company!

When I started delving deeper into the concepts of Guerrilla Marketing, I found that there were over 200 Guerrilla Marketing weapons that I could put into action. Rather than test out all 200, I tested about 30 of them. The following are my top five favorites that produced the best return.

1. *Designated guerrilla.* To keep our strategies organized and streamlined, I decided to make one person at my company the designated guerrilla. This person was responsible for the marketing calendar, and making sure that the Guerrilla Marketing weapons we were putting into place were being done correctly and tracked to the nth degree.

2. *Extra value.* I've never been a fan of dropping prices, especially since I never compete on price. Therefore, in order to make sure we started winning more deals, we began increasing the amount of value provided for clients. Here are some examples of what our clients now receive: a client-only event once a year (educational in nature), access to our training portal, and even a virtual assistant for 10 hours a week at no cost.

3. *Testimonials.* I had testimonials all over the place, but I wasn't leveraging them. I also discovered that using video testimonials, as opposed to just text, worked much better. Rather than just letting the testimonials sit dormant on the web site, I integrated them into the marketing materials as well as the sales process. This took the social proof factor up to a whole new level.

4. *Authoring a book.* A book is the best possible business card you can ever have. It took a lot more work than I expected, but the results have proven to be invaluable.

5. *Free public talks.* My favorite Guerrilla Marketing weapon is free public talks. I contacted various chamber of commerce organizations as well as some local business groups and offered to come and speak on various topics relating to web marketing, monetizing social media, and Web 3.0 marketing. They were thrilled because they were used to paying speakers, and I was happy because I was able to practice education-based marketing and contribute to the local business community. I did not even have to pitch my business to the crowd, which would have been a little tacky. People simply came up to me afterward asking for my business card.

If you're looking to generate some business without spending a lot of money, Guerrilla Marketing has worked wonders for me and my businesses.

■ ABOUT THE AUTHOR

An avid entrepreneur, author, speaker, investor, and charity proponent, Michael Tasner is fully dedicated to helping people achieve their dreams in life and goals in business. At 25, Michael has already written several books and started six businesses. Having since sold four of the latter, Mike is currently running two—Taz Solutions Inc., www.tazsol.com.

As the President of Taz Solutions, Inc., a highly successful web design and online marketing firm, Michael brings a wealth of experience to the table as an expert within the Internet marketing and business development space. His true specialty is his mastery of the Internet as a complete tool to both grow new businesses and help them to thrive in a very crowded playing field.

Michael has also aligned himself with the Guerrilla Marketing brand serving as their Chief Marketing Officer.

Michael created a blog that provides helpful tactics that boost site traffic and increase exposure. This blog is available at http://tazsol.com/blog.

Web Sites

http://michaeltasner.com

www.tazsol.com

www.college-butler.com

Primary Products or Books

Guerilla Marketing Coach

Marketing in the Moment

Chapter 44

Love and Logic Equals GREAT Marketing

MaryEllen Tribby

Every good marketer I know loves marketing. They read as much as they can about it. They understand the elements that make up a good marketing campaign and are thinking of ways to make each campaign better.

However, every great marketer I know not only loves marketing but also understands that marketing is a methodical process. That the science behind marketing is *more* important than creative-driven marketing.

And the greatest marketers of all are those who love marketing, use logic to track and read results, and understand the value of testing and live it every day.

■ KNOW YOUR ABTs

If you ask any great marketer the number one rule of marketing they will say, *"Always be testing!"*

It saddens me when I meet young marketers and they dismiss testing with a wave of the hand. They assume a single panel campaign they send to their prospects is the best way to go.

If you don't test, your business will not grow. Thinks about it: How can you possibly improve on your results if you do not go through the testing process—you can't.

Because this is one of the only ways to discover what your prospects want, let's start at the beginning.

■ WHAT IS TESTING?

In direct response marketing, testing is the process of two or more variations of a single variable offered to prospects simultaneously and coming to some conclusion based on responses.

Testing is a great way to tap into new audiences, explore a new market or niche, compare response rates on direct marketing fundamental elements, and get insight on a new concept or promotional package.

Testing is beyond theory and can be applied to almost any business and marketing channel. If you have been wondering, *Can I sell my product or service the way I want and at the price I want?*—testing gives you the answers.

You could be asking if you can charge more for your product, or whether a new marketing message will work to your target audience. You may want to see if you can cut costs by reducing the number of bonuses offered or changing your shipping and handling charges.

Generally, testing will fall into four categories. You should either be testing:

1. Copy
2. Product
3. Offer/Price
4. List/Media

■ COPY: THE MESSAGE BEHIND YOUR PRODUCT

When talking about copy tests, I am talking about any test where you change copy against your control. Don't be scared off by this thinking that it will be an expensive test and you have to have a full-blown new creative package against your control. This is not always the case. There are lots of ways for you to test copy.

The best copy tests are:

➤ Subject lines.
➤ Senders.
➤ You can test formats: long copy vs. short copy or text vs. HTML.
➤ You can test leads (the first two to three pages of your copy).
➤ You can test headlines.
➤ Background colors.
➤ Graphics.
➤ You can test closes (adding a P.S.).
➤ And you can test entirely new packages.

In the long run your biggest breakthroughs will come from completely new creative packages with new messaging and positioning.

Always ask yourself if your test is meaningful and will provide you with a significant boost in response. Do not test minor and frivolous things. Meaning always test things that *scream* not whisper.

■ PRODUCT: EVOLUTION IS A MUST

Good products are things that meet cretin needs and solve particular problems. But what solves a problem today is not necessarily what will work tomorrow.

A common mistake many entrepreneurs make is becoming very knowledgeable about a product without knowing how to market. Extreme product knowledge without marketing knowledge gives you a false sense of control because it allows you to answer all the questions. But in the long run, it is *not* as important as knowing how, when, and why customers buy.

Having market knowledge means that you understand the attractiveness of the product rather than the product itself. It means you understand its benefits, not just its features. It means that you know the customers' wants, needs, and desires so intimately that you can reinvent the product before they even realize it needs to be reinvented.

At that point you can test the products against each other. This part is hard because you have to assume you know nothing and let the market tell which product they want.

Being a market expert implies having a very good understanding of the selling process. Everything from how it's done, why it works, what is essential and what's not.

Rate yourself by answering these questions:

1. What is the most important psychological benefit your product offers?

2. What are the most common mistakes other marketers make when selling a similar product?

3. How have *your* customers' needs and desires changed in the recent past?

4. What changes have you made to accommodate those changes?

Products and services are not static things. They exist in relation to markets. And markets are a collection of individuals with changing needs, values, and perceptions. As time passes, these things change—and if your products/service doesn't change, you will be handing your market share to your competitor.

■ OFFER: IT CAN MAKE IT OR BREAK IT

The offer is the third make-it-or-break-it factor in the direct response world. When it comes to testing there are three main components to test. In order of importance they are:

Price: For example, you have published a special report on how to lose weight by eating three grapefruits a day. How much will people pay for it? Maybe $9.95 or $19.95 or $29.95? You just don't know until you test. Often you will be amazed at how many people place orders at prices you thought were sky high. Look at what your competition is charging to give you an idea of where your price points should be and test from there.

Term: Should you go for orders or leads? Should you offer a one-year and a two-year subscription or a one-year and five-year subscription? Do you offer three free bonuses or six free bonuses? Do you offer a physical product such as supplement holder or information on the benefits of a certain type of supplement? You just will not know until you test.

Refund policy: The "If you are not 100 percent satisfied, simply return this product to us within XX days and we will gladly refund 100 percent of your money" is really one of the most used refund policies.

But what is that magic number? Is it 30 days, 60 days, 90 days, one full year, or your lifetime? Generally speaking, the longer the refund period the lower the refund rate. But too many marketers are afraid to offer long-term refunds. So what do you do? *Test.*

■ LIST/MEDIA: THE BEST FOR LAST

List and media testing is something you will do when launching your online business and something you should continue to do with each mailing.

You will always be on the lookout for potential new lists of people to buy your products. List testing will reveal new segments of buyers and help grow your business. Here's how it works:

You may take the previously mentioned "Forget Cholesterol" package and test it on a variety of different health lists to see which list produced the better response. When you start your list research for a particular product, you will generally find the lists fall into different categories. For our example of a heart health product, you can break down the list universe into the following categories:

➤ Other alternative heart health products

➤ Other heart lists (subscriptions, fundraising)

➤ General nutritional health lists

➤ Specific condition alternative health lists

➤ Health newsletter list

Take the time to go through this exercise *before* your next mailing. Once you have categorized your lists, you will see which category has the most available names.

You should always consider the long-term implications of your testing. If you bring people in on a heavily discounted offer, that is what they will want to see in other offers from you. If you have tests that are premium intensive, then your customers will want to see those kind of offers again and again.

Consider this when you are setting up your tests. Be sure whatever copy you use is clear and specific.

The important thing is to be selective. Don't test everything. Don't overtest. Use testing only to increase your current response rates by *at least* 25 percent and up to 100 percent.

■ ABOUT THE AUTHOR

MaryEllen is a CEO, mom of three, best-selling author, wife, speaker, sister, daughter, business consultant, philanthropist, and friend.

MaryEllen not only recognizes what it takes to be a working mom, she also lives the life and is able to blend all of her roles with relative ease. She wants to supply the necessary tools all working moms need to live the life they have always dreamed of.

Today MaryEllen is the proud founder and CEO of Working Moms Only .com, the world's leading newsletter and web site for the empowerment of the working mom. Prior to founding WMO, MaryEllen was publisher and CEO of Early to Rise, where she was responsible for growing the business from $8 million in sales to $26 million in just 15 months. Before that, she served as president of Weiss Research where she led the company to $67 million in sales from $11 million in just 12 months.

Web Sites

http://workingmomsonly.com

Primary Products or Books

Changing the Channel: 12 Easy Ways to Make Millions for Your Business (John Wiley & Sons, Inc., 2009)

Chapter 45

The Importance of Being Different

Jack Trout

In 1960, an advertising agency chairman named Rosser Reeves was known as the high priest of hard sell. He wrote a very popular book titled *Reality in Advertising*. His book was translated into 28 languages and was widely used as a college textbook. In many ways it was the beginning of modern-day marketing.

In his book he introduced and defined a concept called the "unique selling proposition," or USP for short.

■ THE DEFINITION

To Rosser, the USP was a precise term so he gave it a three-part definition:

1. Each advertisement must make a proposition to the consumer. Not just words, not just product puffery, not just show-window advertising. Each advertisement must say to each reader: "Buy this product, and you will get this specific benefit."

2. The proposition must be one that the competition either cannot, or does not, offer. It must be unique—either a uniqueness of the brand or a claim not otherwise made in that particular field of advertising.

3. The proposition must be so strong that it can move the mass millions (i.e., to pull over new customers to your product).

He went on to say that most advertising in that day was "the tired art of puffery." There was no real message. Copywriters who did not understand reality wrote these advertisements.

Well, you might think that this was an argument of the past and that Mr. Reeves's ideas have long been accepted by today's advertising practitioner.

Wrong.

■ THE ARGUMENT STILL RAGES

What's stunning is that the argument still rages on Madison Avenue. A front-page article in *Advertising Age* that was published 37 years after Mr. Reeves's book proclaimed: "'Poets vs. killers': Perpetual ad debate—stress art or stick to hard sell?—is reaching fever pitch with fortunes hanging in the balance."

This article went on for pages and laid out the battle of the creatives that see their work as artful and emotional and the marketers who want advertising that is factual and rational.

One group wants to bond with the customer. The other group wants to sell the customer.

It's time we stopped arguing and faced not reality in advertising, but reality in the marketplace.

■ WHERE'S ROSSER NOW THAT WE NEED HIM?

When Mr. Reeves was talking about being different, the world was an easy place. Global competition didn't exist. In fact, by today's standards, real competition barely existed.

The concept of being unique or different is far more important in the year 2000 than it was in 1960.

While "to sell or not to sell" arguments have been raging, the New World Order has suddenly arrived. Today many companies have bigger sales than many countries have gross national products. The top 500 global companies now represent 70 percent of the world's trade.

Mergers and acquisitions are everywhere as the rich get richer and bigger. Not only is there more competition, there is tougher and smarter competition.

What this new competition is often able to exploit is the fact that buying behavior isn't just about people and income, it's also about how dissatisfied consumers are with present alternatives.

■ STEP 1 IN BUILDING BRANDS

There are books and books on branding, but very few books talk much about differentiation. And if it does get mentioned, rarely do authors go much beyond talking about the fact that branding is important to do.

Consider Young & Rubicam, a very large and talented global advertising agency that has developed a system they call "brand science." They say that "differentiation is first." It defines a brand and distinguishes it from all others. It is how brands are born and how they die as differentiation declines. (We do believe they've got it.)

But rather than really get into the subject, they quickly segue to things like relevance, esteem, knowledge, and brand power grids.

Well, good readers, we plan on going further. If differentiation is about the life and death of a brand, we feel it's worth your while to explore this subject in depth. (Good old Rosser would have wanted it that way.)

■ THE IMPORTANCE OF BEING DIFFERENT

Choosing among multiple options is always based on differences, implicit or explicit. Psychologists point out that vividly differentiated differences that are anchored to a product can enhance memory because they can be appreciated intellectually. In other words, if you're advertising a product, you ought to give the consumer a reason to choose that product. If you can entertain at the same time, that's great.

Unfortunately, the fact is that many advertising people don't appreciate the need to offer the prospect a unique selling proposition.

Most of these people feel that selling isn't cool and that people only respond to companies that don't try to sell them. Besides, many will argue, there often isn't enough "difference" to talk about in the products. What they ignore is the fact that, whether or not people like to be sold, in a sea of choice a prospect still has the problem of figuring out what to buy or not to buy. In other words, alternatives are but the raw material of decision making.

And decisions must be made.

■ HOW PEOPLE FIGURE THINGS OUT

Psychologists think a lot about how people solve problems. They've come up with four functions that come into play: intuition, thinking, feeling, and sensing. People tend to lead their decision-making process with one of these functions. Let's look at these functions from a selling point of view.

■ DIFFERENTIATING WITH "INTUITIVES"

People who use intuition concentrate on the possibilities. They avoid the details and tend to look at the big picture. This type of person would be very susceptible to a differentiating strategy based on your product being the next generation in its category. When the makers of Advil positioned their new ibuprofen as "advanced medicine for pain," they were differentiating themselves perfectly for the big-picture crowd.

Intuitives are very interested in the possibility of what's coming next. This is why selling to intuitives is often a very effective way to present a new type of product.

■ DIFFERENTIATING WITH "THINKERS"

Thinkers are analytical, precise, and logical. They process a lot of information, often ignoring the emotional or feeling aspects of a situation. While they may appear to be ruthless or uncaring, that isn't really accurate. They are just thinking (Henry Kissinger types).

These people are susceptible to a logical argument of facts about a product. BMW's differentiating strategy of "the ultimate driving machine" probably works very well with this crowd, especially when they present facts like ergonomic design, maneuverability, non-overweight engine, and lots of expert reviews on how BMWs drive.

■ DIFFERENTIATING WITH "FEELERS"

Feelers are interested in the feelings of others. They dislike intellectual analysis and follow their own likes and dislikes. They enjoy working with people and are capable of great loyalty.

This type of person is ideal for third-party endorsements from experts who look and sound real. The Miracle-Gro campaign that differentiates itself as the choice of experts is perfect for feelers. Nice people surrounded by beautiful flowers and talking about the wonders of Miracle-Gro is a perfect strategy.

■ DIFFERENTIATING WITH "SENSORS"

Sensors see things as they are and have great respect for facts. They have an enormous capacity for detail and seldom make errors. They are good at putting things in context.

Hertz's differentiating strategy of leadership (there's Hertz and not exactly) is a great program for the sensors, who instinctively know that Hertz is indeed number one. (Twenty-five years of telling us they are number one doesn't hurt.) To them it's just common sense that Hertz is the best.

What should be noted is that people often are a mixture of these functions. "Intuitives" and "feelers" both tend to dislike too much detail. "Thinkers" and "sensors" work with more information. But they all are trying to make a decision on what to buy, one way or another.

■ YOU CAN DIFFERENTIATE ANYTHING

Theodore Levitt, the Harvard marketing guru, wrote a book titled *The Marketing Imagination* (Free Press, 1984). He was definitely on Rosser Reeves's side when he stated in Chapter 4 of his book that you can differentiate anything.

His point is that products must be augmented by offering customers more than they think they need or have come to expect. This could be with additional services or support.

General Electric does this by advising customers on the nuances of doing business around the globe. GE also added service capability so its customers didn't have to keep service people on staff.

Otis Elevator uses remote diagnostics as a way to differentiate itself. In high-traffic office buildings, where servicing elevators is a major inconvenience to occupants and visitors alike, Otis uses its remote diagnostics capabilities to predict possible service interruptions. It sends employees to carry out preventive maintenance in the evening, when traffic is light.

Oral-B created a powerful source of differentiation with a toothbrush that tells customers when they need a new one (a patented blue dye in the center bristles).

■ DIFFERENTIATING COMMODITIES

Even the world of meats and produce has found ways to differentiate itself and thus create that unique selling proposition. Their successful strategies can be summed up in five ways:

1. *Identify.* Ordinary bananas became better bananas by adding a small Chiquita label to the fruit. Dole did the same for pineapple with the Dole label, as did the lettuce people by putting each head into a clear Foxy lettuce package. Of course, you then have to communicate why people should look at these labels.

2. *Personify.* The Green Giant character became the difference in a family of vegetables in many forms. Frank Perdue became the tough man behind the tender chicken.

3. *Create a new generic.* The cantaloupe people wanted to differentiate a special, big cantaloupe. But rather than call them just plain "big," they introduced a new category called Crenshaw melons. Tyson wanted to sell miniature chickens, which doesn't sound very appetizing. So they introduced Cornish game hens.

4. *Change the name.* Sometimes your original name doesn't sound like it would be something you would want to put in your mouth. Like a Chinese gooseberry. By changing it to kiwifruit, the world suddenly had a new favorite fruit it wanted to put in its mouth.

5. *Reposition the category.* Pork was just pig for many years. All that did was conjure up mental pictures of little animals wallowing in the mud. Then they jumped on the chicken bandwagon and became "the other white meat." A very good move when red meat became a perceptual problem.

Where there's a will, there's a way to differentiate.

■ ABOUT THE AUTHOR

Jack Trout is the acclaimed author of many marketing classics published in many languages: *Positioning: The Battle for Your Mind, Marketing Warfare,* (updated in the 20th Anniversary edition), *The 22 Immutable Laws of Marketing, Differentiate or Die, Big Brands, Big Trouble, A Genie's Wisdom,* and *Trout on Strategy.* Following the second edition of *Differentiate or Die,* he wrote *In Search of the Obvious: The Antidote for Today's Marketing Mess.* His most recent book is *Repositioning: Marketing in an Era of Competition, Change, and Crisis.*

He is president of Trout & Partners Ltd., an international marketing consultancy based in Connecticut. He has consulted for such companies as Hewlett-Packard, Southwest Airlines, Merck, Procter & Gamble, Papa John's Pizza, and many others. He has consulted with the State Department on how to better sell America and in 2006 helped the Democrats regain leadership of the U.S. Congress. He continues to advise the current administration on strategy.

Recognized as one of the world's foremost marketing strategists, Trout is the originator of Positioning and other important concepts in marketing strategy. He has over 40 years of experience in advertising and marketing, and became a boardroom advisor to some of the world's largest corporations and his worldwide consulting work gives him firsthand experience in a wide range of marketing scenarios. Jack Trout has gained an international reputation as a consultant, writer, speaker, and proponent of leading-edge marketing strategies.

Web Sites

www.troutandpartners.com

Primary Products or Books

Repositioning: Marketing in an Era of Competition, Change, and Crisis (McGraw-Hill, 2009)

In Search of the Obvious: The Antidote for Today's Marketing Mess (John Wiley & Sons, Inc., 2008)

Marketing Warfare (McGraw-Hill, 2005)

Positioning: The Battle for Your Mind (McGraw-Hill, 2000)

The 22 Immutable Laws of Marketing (HarperBusiness, 1994)

Chapter 46

The Five Most Important Words on Your Web Site

Nick Usborne

I hesitate to single out a handful of "must-have" words for your web site. It brings to mind the overblown promises of "power words" and the like. "Power words" strike me as being about as useful as "power naps" and "power lunches." Heavy on hype and light on content.

However, some words really can make a difference on your site. They are not "powerful" in isolation but, in the right context, can make an important difference.

■ NUMBER ONE: FREE

For those of us, myself included, who go on about how writing online is different, it is humbling to see how some things are exactly the same. "Free" is an extremely important word in the world of off-line marketing, and it's just as important online.

In fact, in some ways, "free" is even more important online. Much of the Web has grown up on the promise of free:

➤ Free browsers
➤ Free music
➤ Free software trials
➤ Free subscriptions

And so on. If you have any doubts about whether users of the Web are that interested in "free"—do a quick search on Google. I just did, and got 172 million results. The number one listing? "Adobe Acrobat Reader—Download."

So don't be shy about using the word. Offer free downloads, free subscriptions, free reports and papers, free trials, free shipping, free consultations.

The Web likes free (even if online publishers don't).

One caveat: Many people filter out e-mails that use the word "Free" in e-mail subject lines.

■ NUMBER TWO: SIGN UP

So it's two words. The point being that every site should be inviting its visitors to sign up or subscribe to an e-mail program or newsletter.

Why? Because you need to reach your prospects by e-mail.

People check their e-mail more frequently than they surf the Web. Much more frequently. As you already know, to your cost, conversion rates of first-time visitors to immediate purchasers is horribly low. And that person who bailed after spending a few seconds on your home page is unlikely to be coming back again anytime soon.

So instead of hoping that your visitors will make a purchase on their first visit, concentrate instead on collecting their e-mail addresses.

Caveat: Your e-mails or newsletters had better be good. Good content in their inbox will bring visitors back to your site again and again. Poor content will damage your chances of ever hearing from them again.

■ NUMBER THREE: BUY

You need to ask for the sale. It's amazing how many sites invest in presenting products and services, but fail to close the sale. Again, conversion rates online are nothing to write home about. So make sure that you actually ask for the sale at the right moment.

Make that BUY link prominent, both by positioning it close to the product or service in question, and by boosting it with a strong graphic treatment.

The word "BUY" is an instruction. It tells people to do something. So make that instruction jump out and grab their attention.

■ NUMBER FOUR: NOW

"Now" is good. "Later" is death. If someone digs deep enough into your site to find the product or service they want, and then just makes a mental note to come back again sometime, you've lost her.

The Web is an easy-come and easy-go environment. If you can't get people to act immediately, forget it.

So ask people to do things NOW:

➤ Sign up NOW
➤ Buy NOW
➤ Tell a friend NOW

Go further still with some incentives:

➤ Sign up NOW and receive a FREE report on [whatever].
➤ Buy NOW and get FREE shipping

■ NUMBER FIVE: THANK YOU

Okay, so it's two words again. But it's the thought that counts. When you sign up a subscriber or make a sale, the job is just beginning.

Just because someone signs up for your newsletter doesn't mean that they will read it.

And just because someone buys your product doesn't mean that they won't send it back.

When visitors become customers, your work is just starting. You have a relationship to build. And the first step in building that relationship is to say thank you. It's courteous. It's the right thing to say.

Maybe this will inspire you to go back to those automated "acknowledgement" e-mails you wrote a few years back.

Rewrite them, be personal, say thank you.

■ FINALLY

There are other important words to consider, but I can't think of any that top these five.

Look through your site, your e-mails, and your newsletters—and consider the places where these words could make a difference.

Then make some changes and test the results. As always, the proof is in the testing.

■ ABOUT THE AUTHOR

Over the course of a copywriting career spanning 30 years, offline and then online, Nick Usborne has worked with dozens of major companies, including Citibank, Apple, Chrysler, Franklin Mint, *TV Guide*, Diners Club International, J. Paul Getty Trust, MSN.com, Technogym, Encyclopedia Britannica, *New York Times*, Country Financial, Adorama, Reuters, WebEx, and others.

During his years as a direct-response copywriter he wrote direct mail by the ton, and earned more than his fair share of awards, both in Europe and North America.

In 1997, he abruptly stopped writing direct mail and has been working exclusively on writing online ever since.

He has also spoken at numerous conferences and has conducted in-house seminars and training sessions for many companies, including: Yahoo!, Intuit, Walt Disney Attractions, Association of American Publishers, Novartis Pharma, John Deere, National Cancer Institute, Merck & Co., Textron, and the Information Technology Media Advisory Council.

Web Sites

www.nickusborne.com

WebContentCafe.com

AskNickUsborne.com

Primary Products or Books

Writing Kick-Ass Website Sales Copy (WordTracker, 2008)

Net Words—Creating High-Impact Online Copy (McGraw-Hill, 2002)

Copywriting 2.0—Your Complete Guide to Writing Web Copy That Converts

Chapter 47

Crush It!

Gary Vaynerchuk

I've said over and over that if you live your passion and work the social networking tools to the max, opportunities to monetize will present themselves. I've also said that in order to crush it you have to be sure your content is the best in its category. You can still make plenty of good money if you're fourth-best in a category, or ninth-best, but if you really want to dominate the competition and make big bucks, you've got to be the best. Do that, be that, and no one will be able to touch you.

With one exception. Someone with less passion and talent and poorer content can totally beat you if they're willing to work longer and harder than you are. Hustle is it. Without it, you should just pack up your toys and go home.

Now, I'm betting that most people who pick up this book consider themselves hard workers. Many are probably just sick of the killer hours and inflexible schedules and demanding bosses often found in the corporate world and think entrepreneurship will somehow be less taxing. I hate to disappoint, but if you're looking for an easier time here, you're barking up the wrong tree. There might be a little more flexibility to your day, should you be at liberty to devote yourself full-time to building your personal brand, but otherwise, assuming you're doing this right, you'll be bleeding out of your eyeballs at your computer. You might have thought your old boss was bad, but if you want your business to go anywhere, your new boss had better be a slave driver.

Too many people don't want to swallow the pill of working every day, every chance they get. If you're making money through social media, you don't get to work for three hours and then play Nintendo for the rest of the evening. That's lip service to hard work. No one makes a million dollars with minimal effort unless they win the lottery.

The cool thing about hustle, though, is that it's one more thing that equalizes the playing field. Fifteen years ago you could have had a rock-solid idea of your DNA and your passion, but there was a billion to one chance of you actually crushing it in business—the platforms and channels were just too narrow and guarded by some pretty tight gatekeepers. Now we can take advantage of the explosion of tremendous, free digital platforms on the Internet, which are also making the gatekeepers more and more irrelevant. And now it's no longer a special interest story if you make it big without family connections or money or an education, because everyone can do it. The only differentiator in the game is your passion and your hustle. Don't ever look at someone else who has more capital or credibility than you and think you shouldn't bother to compete. You may only have a million-dollar business, and your biggest competitor may have a $50-million business, but if you can outwork him or her, you will win over time.

Anything insane has a price. If you're serious about building your personal brand, there will be no time for Wii. There will be no time for Scrabble or book club or poker or hockey. There will be time for meals, and catching up with your significant other, and playing with the kids, and otherwise you will be in front of your computer until 3:00 AM every night. If you're unemployed or retired and have all day to work, maybe you knock off at midnight instead. Expect this to be all consuming.

The thing is, if you're living your passion, you're going to want to be consumed by your work. There's no room for relaxation in the flop-on-the-couch-with-popcorn-and-watch-TV kind of way, but you won't need it. You're not going to be stressed or tired. You're going to be relaxed and invigorated. The passion and love for what you do will enable you to work the hours necessary to succeed. You'll lose track of the time, go to bed reluctantly, and wake up in the morning excited to do it all over again. You'll be living and breathing your content, learning everything you can about your subject, about your tools, about your competition, and talking nonstop with other people interested in the same thing you are.

As hard as you're going to push yourself, don't plan on seeing results right away.[1]

■ ABOUT THE AUTHOR

Gary Vaynerchuk has captured attention with his pioneering, multi-faceted approach to personal branding and business. After primarily

---

utilizing traditional advertising techniques to build his family's local wine business into a national industry leader, Gary rapidly leveraged social media tools such as Twitter and Facebook to promote Wine Library TV, his video blog about wine. As his viewership swelled to over 80,000 a day, doors opened to a book deal, several national TV appearances, and speaking engagements around the world. Gary's dual identity as both business guru and wine guy has made him the "Social Media Sommelier." He's been included in the 2009 Decanter Power List, an index of the 50 most influential figures in the industry.

Gary was named 18 on AskMen.com's Top 49 Most Influential Men of 2009.

Gary's remarks on personal branding, social media, and business at FOWA, Strategic Profits, and South by Southwest occasioned praise from established web denizens.

Gary also cofounded VaynerMedia with his brother AJ, a boutique agency that works with various Fortune 500 brands on community management and emerging tech.

Web Sites

http://garyvaynerchuk.com

http://tv.winelibrary.com

Primary Products or Books

Crush It! Why Now is the Time to Cash in on Your Passion (HarperCollins, 2009)

The Thank You Economy

Chapter 48

The Twenty-One Most Powerful Copywriting Rules of All Time

Dr. Joe Vitale

Writing copy is a key ingredient to successful and effective marketing. The following are notes for a full-length book on how to write copy that sells.

1. Know your USP.

USP = Unique Selling Proposition = a one-line statement (proposition) that explains (sells) how your product or service differs (unique) from the competition. You can't know it unless you research your product as well as your competition. What does Federal Express say? Dove soap? You must know your basic offer before you can begin to persuade anyone to accept it.

2. Use layout that supports copy.

Graphics, fonts, and layouts don't sell, but they can help bring attention to your sales message. Use proven formats. Look at the famous Maxwell Sackheim ad in my book, the *AMA Complete Guide to Small Business Advertising* (NTC Business Books, 1995). Consider an advertorial style. It can get 80 percent more attention than any other ad layout. You must know the form your sales message will take before you begin to draft your actual message. Knowing you are about to write a classified ad will lead you to write differently than if you were about to write a sales letter or a display ad.

3. Create a riveting and relevant headline.

Round up your prospects with a headline that makes them sit up and take notice. Best place to see good headlines is on the cover of *Reader's Digest*. See my AMA advertising book for 30 ways to write headlines. A headline *calls out* your readers. A change in headline can bring 19 times more response.

4. Write simply, directly, and in the conversational style of your prospects.

Who are you trying to reach? Housewives, business executives, children? You must know the type of person you are writing to. Write to one person from that group, and you will speak to all people in that group. Forget trying to impress people, win writing awards, or please a past English teacher. Good copy often violates the rules of English but still makes the sale.

5. So that—?

Write of the benefits, not the features. A feature generally describes a product; a benefit generally explains what the product does for you. A good way to write about benefits would be to keep saying *you get this . . . and the product does this . . . so that you get. . . .* Look at Kodak. People don't buy film for the pictures they create. They are buying memories. Look at their advertising and you'll barely see film anywhere. What you will see are family reunions, graduations, weddings, and so on. You get film, which helps you take pictures so that you get memories. Keep asking So that—? to dig up benefits. For example, *This computer is a 486 . . . so that . . . you get a computer that is twice the speed of other computers . . . so that . . . you can get twice the work done in the same amount of time . . . so that . . . you are free to have longer lunches, make more calls, or focus on something else.*

6. Use emotional appeal.

People buy for emotional reasons and justify with logic. Gene Schwartz wrote an ad that ran for 20 years and sold so many flowers it exhausted nurseries. It's packed with emotional appeal. It read in part:

> *When you put this into the Earth, and you jump back (quickly), it explodes into flowers. And everybody in your neighborhood comes and they look. And people take home blooms because you've got so many you could never find a house big enough to put them. And you've become the gardening expert for the entire neighborhood.*

7. Demolish the five basic objections within your copy:

    a. I don't have enough time.

    b. I don't have enough money.

    c. It won't work for me.

    d. I don't believe you.

    e. I don't need it.

8. Activate your writing.

Whenever you write the words "is," "was," "are," or "to be," train yourself to stop and change them to something more active. "The meeting is tonight" sounds dead; "The meeting starts at 7 PM sharp tonight" feels clear, direct, and alive. "Clair Sullivan is the finest promoter in the country" doesn't convey the excitement that "Clair Sullivan creates corporate events better than anyone else on the planet" does.

9. Tell them something they don't know.

Fascinate your readers. The more you tell, the more you sell. Long copy usually works better than short copy, as long as the copy holds interest. After all, people read whole books. They will read your copy *if* it interests them.

10. Seduce the reader into continued reading.

Keep your reader reading any way you can. Questions, unfinished sentences, involving statements, subheads, bulleted points, quizzes, all work. These techniques also handle the *skimmers* who just glance at your copy, as well as the word-for-word readers.

11. Say *collie*.

Be specific. Whenever you write something vague, such as "they say," or "later on," or "many," train yourself to stop and rewrite those phrases into something more concrete, such as: "Mark Weisser said . . . ," or "Saturday at noon," or "Seven people agreed." Don't say *dog* when you can say *collie*.

12. Overwhelm with testimonials

Get as many testimonials as you can. The more specific, the more convincing. In short, deliver proof that your claim is for real.

13. Remove the risk!

Give a guarantee. Less than 2 percent of your customers will ever ask for their money back, so offering a guarantee is a safe risk. Here's the guarantee from my book, *The Seven Lost Secrets of Success* (John Wiley & Sons, Inc., 2007):

> *Use these seven principles for six months. If you're out of work, you'll find a job. If you're employed, you'll get a raise. If you're in business, you'll see a whopping 25 percent jump in revenues—or return this book and your receipt for a full cash refund!*

14. Ask for the order.

Too much copy these days never asks anyone to buy anything. Sales copy should *sell*. Use a coupon as a way to signal readers that you want their business and to remind yourself to always ask for the order (or at least to ask people to contact you or remember you).

15. Use magic words.

There are certain words which have been proven to help get attention. If you just string these words together, they sound like fluff.

But weave them into your sentences, along with your facts, and they become powerful:

Announcing, astonishing, exciting, exclusive, fantastic, fascinating, first, free, guaranteed, incredible, initial, improved, love, limited offer, powerful, phenomenal, revealing, revolutionary, special, successful, super, time-sensitive, unique, urgent, wonderful, you, breakthrough, introducing, new, and how-to.

And consider the connotations of the words you use: *workshop* sounds like hard work while *seminar* sounds easier. *Read* sounds hard while *look over* sounds easy. *Write* sounds difficult while *jot down* sounds easy. Be aware of the psychological implications of the words and phrases you use.

16. Get pumped up!

Show your excitement for your product. If you aren't pumped up about it, why not? Enthusiasm sells.

17. Rewrite and test ruthlessly.

Test. Test. Test. A change of one word can increase response 250 percent. Sackheim tested his famous ad at least six times before he found the headline and format that worked. Most copy isn't written in one day. You have to write, rewrite, edit, rewrite, test, and test again. Keep asking yourself, *Would I buy this product?* and *Have I said everything to make the sale?*

18. State a believable deadline.

Most people won't take any immediate action unless there exists a sound reason to do so. Deadlines help, as long as your deadline sounds credible.

19. Instantaneous satisfaction!

Everything should be nearly instantaneous because we want instant gratification. Toll-free numbers and fax numbers help. If you're marketing on the Web, include a link or a "Buy Now" button that makes it easy for your readers to order.

20. Sincerity sells.

Don't offer fluff, mislead, or lie to your prospects. Tell them the truth. While rarely done, it actually helps sales to admit a weakness or a fault. Remember the ad, *These neckties aren't very pretty, but they're a steal at a nickel each!* Tell the truth in a fascinating way.

21. Copy your copy from the best.

Read excellent copy, write it out word-for-word in your own hand to get a feel for its rhythm, and memorize the following books:

➤ *The Copywriter's Handbook* (Holt, 2006) by Bob Bly

➤ *AMA Complete Guide to Small Business Advertising* (NTC Business Books, 1995) by Joe Vitale

➤ *Tested Advertising Methods* (Prentice-Hall, 1998) by John Caples

➤ *CyberWriting: How to Promote Your Product or Service Online* (Without Being Flamed) (AMACOM 1996) by Joe Vitale

BONUS TIP: The Easiest Way to Write Anything

I use the method described in my booklet, *Turbocharge Your Writing!* (Awareness Publications, 1989). I write in spurts. After you have decided what you want to accomplish with your writing, and you have completed your research, then write in 33-minute nonstop blasts. Then take a 10-minute breather, do some push-ups, get some air, dance, drink some coffee. Then write in another 33-minute spurt. This helps your left and right sides of your brain work in harmony.

■ ABOUT THE AUTHOR

Dr Joe Vitale is the author of way too many best-selling books to mention here. Some of them include *The Attractor Factor, Life's Missing Instruction Manual, The Key, Zero Limits, Attract Money Now,* and most recently *The Awakening Course.*

He's also recorded many audio programs, to name a few, "The Awakening Course," "The Missing Secret," "The Secret to Attracting Money," and his latest, "The Abundance Paradigm."

Joe has also been in several movies, including the blockbuster *The Secret.* He's been on Larry King Live and Donny Deutsch's TV shows.

He created a Miracles Coaching program and helps people achieve their dreams by understanding the deeper aspects of the law of attraction and the law of right action. This man was once homeless but today is a best-selling author who believes in magic and miracles.

For more information on Joe Vitale, go to www.mrfire.com.

Web sites

www.mrfire.com

Primary Products or Books

There's a Customer Born Every Minute (John Wiley & Sons, Inc., 2006)

AMA Complete Guide to Small Business Advertising (NTC Business Books, 1995)

Hypnotic Selling Secrets

The Hypnotic Marketing Institute

Search Engine Optimization Made Easy

Aaron Wall

Search engine optimization (SEO) is the art and science of publishing and marketing information that ranks well for valuable keywords in search engines like Google, Yahoo! Search, and Microsoft Live Search.

Search engines only show 10 results on the first page, and most searchers tend to click on the top few results. If you rank at the top business is good, but if you are on the second or third page you might only get 1 percent of the search traffic that the top ranked site gets.

The two most powerful aspects of search engine marketing are:

➤ Users type what they want to find into search boxes, making search engines the most precisely targeted marketing medium in the history of the world

➤ Once you gain traction in the search results the incremental costs of gaining additional exposure are negligible when compared with the potential rewards, allowing individuals and small businesses to compete with (and perhaps eventually become) large corporations

While many people consider SEO to be complicated, I believe that SEO is nothing but an extension of traditional marketing. Search engine optimization consists of nine main steps.

1. Market research
2. Keyword research
3. On page optimization
4. Site structure
5. Link building

6. Brand building

7. Viral marketing

8. Adjusting

9. Staying up to date

➤ Market Research

Do you have what it takes to compete in a market?

The first step is to search the major search engines to see what types of web sites are ranking for words which you deem to be important. For example, if mostly colleges, media, and government institutions are ranking for your most important terms it may be difficult to rank for those types of queries. If, on the other hand, the market is dominated by fairly average web sites which are not strongly established brands it may be a market worth pursuing.

You can extend out the research you get from the search results by using the SEO for the Firefox extension with the Firefox browser. This places many marketing data points right in the search results, and thus lets you see things like:

- ➤ Site age
- ➤ Google PageRank
- ➤ Inbound link count
- ➤ If any governmental or educational sites link at their site
- ➤ If they are listed in major directories
- ➤ If bloggers link at their sites

➤ Keyword Research

What keywords are people searching for?

Use the SEO Book Keyword research tool to search for popular and Long Tail keywords related to your industry. This tool cross references the Google Keyword Tool, Wordtracker, and other popular keyword research tools. Notice how our keyword tool provides daily search estimates and cross references other useful keyword research tools.

Keyword research tools are better at providing a qualitative measure than a quantitative measure, so don't be surprised if actual traffic volumes vary greatly from the numbers suggested by these tools. When in doubt you can also set up a Google AdWords account to test the potential size of a market.

In addition to looking up search volumes for what keywords you think are important also take the time to ask past customers how

WordTracker	WordTracker count	Google daily est	Yahoo! daily est	MSN daily est	Overall daily est
credit cards	2170	2,713	779	339	3,827
gift credit cards	441	551	158	69	778
prepaid credit cards	364	455	131	57	642
chase credit cards	344	430	123	54	607
best credit cards	335	419	120	52	591

📁export to CSV

Figure 49.1

they found you, why they chose you, and what issues were important to them in choosing you.

You can also get keyword ideas by doing things like the following.

➤ Checking your Web analytics or server logs

➤ Looking at page contents of competing web sites

➤ Looking through topical forums and community sites to see what issues people frequently discuss

■ SITE STRUCTURE

How should you structure your site? Before drafting content consider what keywords are your most important and map out how to create pages to fit each important group of keywords within your site theme and navigational structure based on:

➤ Market value

➤ Logical breaks in market segmentation

➤ Importance of ranking in building credibility and improving conversion rates

You may want to use an Excel spreadsheet or some other program to help you visualize your site structure. This miniscreenshot from an Excel spreadsheet shows example data for how you might align keywords for a section of a site focused on home-based businesses, start ups, and franchise opportunities.

topic	folder	filename	page title ideas	H1
startup opportunities	/opport	index.php	How to Start a Sm	Online Business Opportunity Ideas
buying a franchise	/opport	franchises.	Business Franchis	Franchises for Sale
buying an existing busi	/opport	buy-a-busi	How to Buy a Bus	Buying an Established Business
home based business	/opport	home-base	Small Home Base	Ideas for Creating Profitable Online

Figure 49.2

Make sure:

➤ Your most important categories or pages are linked to site-wide

➤ You link to every page on your site from at least one other page on your site

➤ You use consistent anchor text in your navigation

➤ You link to other content pages (and especially to action items) from within the content area of your web site

If you are uncertain how deep to make a portion of the site, start by creating a few high quality pages on the topic. Based on market feedback create more pages in the sections that are most valuable to your business.

■ ON PAGE OPTIMIZATION

It is hard to rank for keywords that do not appear in your page content, so each page should be organized around the goal of ranking for a specific keyword phrase, with some related phrases and related keywords mixed into the page copy.

Unique descriptive page titles play a crucial role in a successful search engine optimization campaign. Page titles appear in the search results, and many people link to pages using the page title as their link anchor text.

If possible, create handcrafted meta-description tags which compliment the page title by reinforcing your offer. If the relevant keywords for a page have multiple formats it may make sense to help focus the meta description on versions you did not use in the page title.

As far as page content goes, make sure you write for humans, and use heading tags to help break up the content into logical sections which will improve the scanability and help structure the document. When possible, make sure your page content uses descriptive modifiers as well.

Each page also needs to be sufficiently unique from other pages on your site. Do not let search engines index printer friendly versions of your content, or other pages where content is duplicate or nearly duplicate.

■ LINK BUILDING

Search engines view links as votes, with some votes counting more than others. To get high quality links (that help your site rank better), you need to participate in the social aspects of your community and give away valuable unique content that people talk about and share with others. The Google TouchGraph image shows a small graphic representation of sites in the search field that are related to SeoBook.com based on linking patterns.

Matt Cutts suggested that Google is getting better at understanding link quality. Search engines want to count quality editorial votes as links that help influence their relevancy algorithms.

■ LINK BUILDING TIPS

➤ Try to link to your most relevant page when getting links (don't point all the links at your home page)

➤ Mix your anchor text

➤ Use Yahoo! Site Explorer and other tools to analyze top competing backlinks

➤ Don't be afraid to link out to relevant high quality resources

■ LINK BUILDING STRATEGIES

➤ Submit your site to general directories like DMOZ, the Yahoo! Directory, and Business.com

➤ Submit your site to relevant niche directories

➤ Here is more background on directories and SEO

➤ If you have a local site submit to relevant local sites (like the local chamber of commerce)

➤ Join trade organizations

➤ Get links from industry hub sites

➤ Create content people would want to link at

➤ Here is a list of 101 useful link building strategies at www.seobook .com/archives/001792.shtml

■ BRAND BUILDING

Brand-related search queries tend to be some of the *most targeted*, *best converting*, and *most valuable keywords*. As you gain mindshare people will be more likely to search for your brand or keywords related to your brand. A high volume of brand-related search traffic may also be seen as a sign of quality by major search engines.

If you build a strong brand when people search for more information about your brand and other web sites have good things to say about your brand, these interactions help reinforcing your brand image and improving your lead quality and conversion rates.

Things like advertising and community activity are easy ways to help improve your brand exposure, but obviously branding is a lot more complicated than that. One of my favorite books about branding is Rob Frankel's *The Revenge of Brand X*.

■ VIRAL MARKETING

Link building is probably the single hardest and most time consuming part of an effective SEO campaign, largely because it requires influencing other people. But links are nothing but a remark or citation. Seth Godin's *Purple Cow* is a great book about being remarkable.

The beautiful thing about viral marketing is that creating one popular compelling idea can lead to thousands of free quality links. If your competitor is building one link at a time and you have thousands of people spreading your ideas for you for free then you are typically going to end up ranking better.

In SEO, many people create content based around linking opportunities. Many of us refer to this as *Link Baiting*. You can learn link baiting tips from:

➤ SEO Book

➤ Stuntdubl

➤ Performancing

➤ Copyblogger

➤ Wolf Howl

You can search social news or social bookmarking sites like Digg or Del.icio.us to see what stories related to your topic became popular.

■ MEASURING RESULTS

"Half the money I spend on advertising is wasted; the trouble is I don't know which half."

—John Wanamaker

How can I tell if my SEO campaign is effective? The bottom line is what counts. Is your site generating more leads, higher-quality leads, or more sales? What keywords are working? You can look at your server logs and an analytics program to track traffic trends and what keywords lead to conversion.

Outside of traffic another good sign that you are on the right track is if you see more web sites asking questions or talking about you. If you start picking up high-quality, unrequested links you might be near a tipping point to where your marketing starts to build on itself.

Search engines follow people, but lag actual market conditions. It may take search engines a while to find all the links pointing at your site and analyze how well your site should rank. Depending on how competitive your marketplace is it may take anywhere from a few weeks to a couple years to establish a strong market position. Rankings can be a moving target as at any point in time including:

➤ You are marketing your business

➤ Competitors are marketing their businesses and reinvesting profits into building out their SEO strategy

➤ Search engines may change their relevancy algorithms

■ KEEPING UP TO DATE

How do you track the changes in the SEO market? In my SEO tools I also offer Google Gadgets, which makes it easy for you to embed keyword, competitive, and link research tools inside any web page. You can track your ranking changes using this free keyword rank checker.

If you want to keep up with how the SEO market as a whole is changing consider using any of the following resources

➤ SEO Conferences

➤ SEO Blogs

➤ SEO Forums

We also offer guides to blog SEO and charity SEO. And if you want an up-to-date training program consider joining our SEO training program.

Best of luck with your sites!

■ ABOUT THE AUTHOR

Aaron Wall is an American-based Search Engine Optimization expert and Internet entrepreneur. He is most recognized for his popular online SEO training program that helps web masters to optimize their web site to achieve better search engine rankings. In addition to having taught over 10,000 students, Aaron publishes a portfolio of profitable web sites outside of the internet marketing vertical.

Chapter 50

What Is Marketing?

Allen Weiss

We thought it would be good to balance out some recent talk on the Web about what is marketing. Here's our view.

We've noticed that on a well-known marketing web site (actually, it's on the ClickZ.com web site), there is an article with a similar title—just what is marketing? This is a very good question, and the answer typically ends up (as it is in the aforementioned article) being a lot of tactics, like advertising, brand management, sales, service, pricing, e-mail marketing, and so on. That's a good start, but far from complete.

And that's one of the problems with the Web. There are lots of web sites out there with people claiming to be knowledgeable about marketing. In fact, if you go to search engines like Google and type in marketing, you'll come up with over 16 million web pages! By the time you've got that many people claiming to be experts in marketing, it's difficult to even know what *marketing* means.

■ MARKETING IS NOT TACTICS

When most people think of marketing, they think of marketing tactics. People associate marketing with tactics, partly because they're fun. Advertising is fun, promotions are fun, and so is sending out e-mail campaigns and every other similar tactic. But tactics, while the most salient aspects of marketing, are similar to the tactics of sport. They're very important, but useless without having a sound basis of knowledge.

And so it is with marketing. Marketing is far more than tactics. Marketing is analysis, and a sound marketing strategy is based on this analysis.

■ OBVIOUSLY, MARKETING IS ABOUT CUSTOMERS

What type of analysis are we talking about? Well, analysis about customers, for example. Having a solid understanding of customers means having a solid understanding about how customers behave, their motivations, their perceptions, and preferences. It means segmenting the market correctly and not in the way that most companies think about segmentation (if they ever do).

It means having a profound understanding of customers' attitudes, their knowledge, and their emotions. Without this knowledge, the tactics of marketing are just blowing in the wind. You'll hope that the tactics work, but be blissfully unaware about whether anyone would want to pay attention or listen.

■ WHAT ABOUT COMPETITIVE ANALYSIS?

Rarely do we see marketing sites deal with competitive analysis (we do!). Marketing is also about understanding competition. But not just listing off who the competitors are. It means thinking about their competitive reactions, their objectives, and their capabilities. It means understanding competitive forces in an industry as well.

Too often I see firms acting as though they were monopolists, as though their competitors were unlikely to react or had little interest in capturing a market. The Internet is a good example of this. How many Internet companies really seriously thought about the potential competitive reactions of the entrenched players? Did any of them consider long-term competitive reactions? What about putting together plans that were robust to future competitive reactions?

No, marketing is also about competitive analysis, not just the interesting and fun tactics that permeate the Web.

■ WHAT ABOUT COMPANY CAPABILITIES?

Once again, to think about marketing you also need to think about a company's abilities to actually survive in the market. I'm not talking about financial abilities, although that is part of the story. What about a culture, the sales force compensation, the relationships with distributors, suppliers, and so on?

Some companies focus squarely on customers and even think about competitors. But these same companies often forget about their ability to provide what customers need, or the incentives in their distribution system to actually get the job done.

No, marketing is not just about tactics, it's also about understanding your own company and its abilities and weaknesses.

■ SO, WHAT IS MARKETING?

Marketing is, in fact, the analysis of customers, competitors, and a company, combining this understanding into an overall understanding of what segments exist, deciding on targeting the most profitable segments, positioning your products, and then doing what's necessary to deliver on that positioning.

How do you deliver on a positioning? Well, this is where the tactics come in. You deliver by branding correctly, by advertising correctly, by communicating via e-mail, letters, or whatever, but all done in a way that is consistent with the analysis that marketing is really responsible for.

If you want to get involved in tactics, that's fine. But just think about artists, sports figures, doctors and scientists, and ask yourself whether in these other areas (which all, by the way, are as creative as marketing), it is just necessary to understand tactics. I think what you'll find is that tactics alone won't get you very far, but tactics along with a strategy based on great analysis will get you exactly where you want to go.

So before you go hiring consultants and network with other marketers (as suggested in this "other article"), make sure you understand what marketing is so you don't just become a tactical pawn, but someone who can ultimately direct the entire marketing campaign.

■ ABOUT THE AUTHOR

Allen Weiss founded MarketingProfs in 2000 and continues to provide strategic direction for the company. He's currently a professor of marketing at the University of Southern California. Prior to MarketingProfs, he served as a professor at Stanford University and a member of the technical staff at Bell Labs. His research and consulting expertise is in the marketing of high technology products and Internet marketing. He has consulted with leading technology companies, including Texas Instruments, Intel, IBM, and Hughes Space and Communications. Allen holds a BS in electrical engineering from the University of California, Santa Barbara, and a PhD in marketing from the University of Wisconsin.

Web Sites

www.marketingprofs.com

Additional World Class Marketing Resources

In addition to the great resources provided in the main section of our book, we have included information on 55 additional experts for you to review. Each one of them has proven expertise in marketing.

1. Akin Arikan

   Akin Arikan works at Unica, an IBM company. He is responsible for ensuring customer satisfaction with Unica's web analytics and Internet marketing offerings. The analytics space has captivated him since 1999 where he has served clients across many industries.

   Previously, he developed analytical enterprise applications at business intelligence software vendor MicroStrategy. It was through the great people of MicroStrategy that Akin received his professional introduction to business intelligence and data warehousing practices.

   He is frequently on the road participating in panels or speaking sessions at such trade shows as Search Engine Strategies, DMA, eMetrics Marketing Optimization Summit, net.finance, and Web 2.0 Expo.

   Web Sites

   www.multichannelmetrics.com

   Primary Products or Books

   Metrics and Methods for On and Offline Success (Sybex, 2008)

2. Al Ries

   Al is a legendary marketing strategist and the best-selling author (or coauthor) of 11 books on marketing including *Positioning* (McGraw-Hill, 2000), *Marketing Warfare* (McGraw-Hill, 2005), *Focus*, (Harper, 2005), *The 22 Immutable Laws of Branding* (Harper-Business, 1994), *The Fall of Advertising & the Rise of PR* (Harper

Paperbacks, 2004), and his latest *War in the Boardroom* (HarperBusiness, 2009).

Al worked in the advertising department of General Electric before founding his own advertising agency in New York City, Ries Cappiello Colwell in 1963. In 1972, Al coauthored the now-infamous three-part series of articles declaring the arrival of the Positioning Era in *Advertising Age* magazine. The concept of positioning revolutionized how people viewed advertising and marketing. Marketing was traditionally thought of as communications, but successful brands are those that find an open hole in the mind and then become the first to fill the hole with their brand name.

Al currently writes a monthly marketing column for AdAge.com and appears on the RiesReport.com.

Web Sites

www.ries.com

www.riesreport.com

Primary Products or Books

War in the Boardroom (HarperBusiness, 2009)

The Fall of Advertising & the Rise of PR (Harper Paperbacks, 2004)

The 22 Immutable Laws of Branding (HarperBusiness, 1994)

3. Alex Carroll

Alex got his first interviews by mortgaging his last credit card and putting an ad in a radio guest resource publication called *Radio TV Interview Report* (RTIR for short). They came up with a pitch for him, wrote his ad, and mailed out the magazine. The calls rolled in. When it was all said and done, 50 radio shows had booked him for an interview. Alex has done *1,264 radio interviews*, grabbed more than *$4,500,000 worth of free radio airtime*, and raked in *$1,526,000 in direct sales* in the process.

Web Sites

www.radiopublicity.com

Primary Products or Books

The Millionaire Package

Radio Publicity Program

4. Alex Mandossian

Since 1991, Alex Mandossian has generated over $233 million in sales for his clients and partners via "electronic marketing" such teleseminars, radio, TV and the Internet. . . .

Alex has personally consulted Dale Carnegie Training, NYU, 1ShoppingCart Corp., Mutuals.com, Trim Spa, and Sam's Club.

He has hosted teleseminars with many of the world's top thought leaders such as Mark Victor Hansen, Jack Canfield, Stephen Covey,

Les Brown, Harv Eker, Donald Trump, Brian Tracy, Harvey Mackay, and many others.

He is the CEO of Heritage House Publishing, Inc.—a boutique electronic marketing and publishing company that "repurposes" written and spoken educational content for worldwide distribution.

He has trained over 14,300 teleseminar students since 2002 and claims that practically any entrepreneur can transform their annual income into a weekly income once they apply his principle-centered electronic marketing strategies.

Web Sites

www.alexmandossian.com

www.marketingonlinelive.com

Primary Products or Books

Teleseminar Secrets (Heritage House Publishing, 2005)

Marketing Minute

Personal Action Secrets Audio eCourse

5. Alexander Hiam

For more than 14 years, Alexander Hiam has been a successful manager, speaker, consultant, educator, and writer who dedicates his professional life to sharing valuable management techniques. He has lectured in MBA programs at Western New England College and American International College and was on the faculty of the School of Business at U. Mass Amherst for five years as a visiting professor.

He also has trained hundreds of government employees for the City of New York and Calgary, the U.S. Coast Guard and other organizations, and has been a keynote speaker at various business functions across the country.

He contributed to magazines such as the *Harvard Business Review*, and wrote his first book, *The Vest-Pocket CEO: Decision-Making Tools for Executives* (John Wiley & Sons, Inc., 2010). He worked with Ken Blanchard, Bob Nelson, and Roy Lewicky, and was interviewed by the *New York Post, USA Today, Training & Development Magazine, Futurist,* and the *Los Angeles Times.*

Web Sites

www.alexhiam.com

www.tspectrum.com

Primary Products or Books

Marketing For Dummies (For Dummies, 2009)

The Wizard's Guide to Taming the Conflict Dragon (Alexander Hiam & Associates, 2000)

The Manager's Pocket Guide to Creativity (HRD Press, 1999)

6. Anne Holland

A multiple award-winning marketer and publisher, Holland is president of Anne Holland Ventures Inc., a media company publishing web sites, including WhichTestWon.com and Subscription Site Insider, which feature practical research for business people.

As founder and past president of MarketingSherpa Inc., Holland published pragmatic research studies such as annual *Search Marketing and E-mail Marketing Benchmark Guide*s and the best-selling *Landing Page Handbook*.

Holland has been a featured speaker, and often keynote, at more than 100 industry conferences including E-mail Summit, Business-to-Business Lead Generation Summits, eTail shows, Affiliate Summit, Direct Marketing Association events, Microsoft Worldwide Partner Conferences, Online Marketing Summit, and Ad-Tech conferences (for which she is also a former advisory board member).

An award-winning marketer herself, since 1992 she has served as a judge for many industry awards including the Testing Awards, the Viral Marketing Hall of Fame, the Ad-Tech Awards, the Electronic Retailing Association Awards, MarketingSherpa's E-mail Awards, and the Interactive PR & Marketing Nettie Awards.

A 25-year business veteran, Holland's past credentials include advising such brands as *The Economist* and Bacardi on online strategies. As head of marketing for Phillips Business Information, a $100-plus million media company, Holland led the launch team for one of the world's first profitable subscription web sites in the mid-1990s.

Web Sites

http://whichtestwon.com

http://subscriptionsiteinsider.com

Primary Products or Books

Search Marketing

E-mail Marketing Benchmark Guides

Landing Page Handbook

7. Armand Morin

Armand Morin, an author, self-made multimillionaire, and best-selling recording artist, is one of the most well-known Internet marketers in the world today. Having started online in 1996, his personal online businesses alone have generated over $76 million in online revenue since then. This doesn't include the millions of dollars his students have produced from his teachings.

Armand has taught tens of thousands of people his amazingly unique and proprietary Internet business building principles and strategies, as well as his unconventional, no-nonsense life design and management skills, which work without fail for every single person or business who has implemented them.

Each year, Armand appears at live business trainings and seminars all over world. Last year alone, Armand has spoken in front of and personally trained well over 200,000 people.

Web Sites

www.armandmorin.com

Primary Products or Books

Generator Software

8. Bill Chiaravalle

Bill Chiaravalle's experience in branding and design spans more than 20 years of involvement and the direct creation of literally hundreds of brand identity programs. His background includes serving in Landor Associates (a world-renowned agency and pioneer in brand strategy and design), both as design and creative director for over a decade. While at Landor, Bill worked on numerous comprehensive branding programs for companies such as American Express, AT&T, Bacardi, Danone, Delta Airlines, FedEx, Gatorade, Hyatt, IBM, Microsoft, NEC, P&G, Smucker's, Sunkist, and Trinchero Winery.

He founded Brandnav in 1999.

Web Sites

www.brandnavigation.com

Primary Products or Books

Branding For Dummies (For Dummies, 2006)

9. Bill Glazer

Bill Glazer is president of Glazer-Kennedy Insider's Circle, Professional Speaker, a highly regarded Marketing Strategist and much sought-after copywriter. After 30 years of in-the-trenches work with his own hugely successful businesses he perfected his unusually effective advertising, which he has termed OUTRAGOEUS, and combined it with Direct Response marketing that routinely receives outstanding responses.

Primary Products or Books

Outrageous Advertising (Morgan James Publishing, 2009)

10. Brian Halligan

Brian Halligan is CEO and cofounder of HubSpot, a marketing software company he cofounded four years ago to help businesses transform the way they market their products by "getting found" on the Internet. Since its founding, HubSpot has already accumulated over 3,000 customers. He is author of two books: *Inbound Marketing: Get Found Using Google, Social Media, and Blogs* (John Wiley & Sons, Inc., 2009), which is in its fourth printing and has been translated into six languages, and *Marketing Lessons From the Grateful*

Dead (John Wiley & Sons, Inc., 2010), published in August 2010. He is also an Entrepreneur-in-Residence at MIT. In his spare time, he sits on a few boards of directors, follows his beloved Red Sox, goes to the gym, and is learning to play guitar.

Web Sites

www.hubspot.com

Primary Products or Books

Marketing Lessons from the Grateful Dead: What Every Business Can Learn from the Most Iconic Band in History (John Wiley & Sons, Inc., 2010)

Inbound Marketing: Get Found Using Google, Social Media, and Blogs (John Wiley & Sons, Inc., 2009)

11. Brad Fallon

Brad Fallon is the CEO of Smart Marketing, Inc., a network of wholesale and retail e-commerce businesses. Beginning with a $2,000 start-up investment for My Wedding Favors, Brad's online businesses grew from $1.2 million in first-year revenue to $7.8 million in 2005 and $32 million in 2006.

Brad is the author of *Creating Customers out of Thin Air: Secrets of Online Marketing for Offline Businesses* and the host of Search Engine Radio, one of the first online radio shows dedicated to SEO.

In October 2006, Brad cofounded StomperNet with Andy Jenkins, the leading subscription-based Internet marketing training program. StomperNet provides DVD courses and online training classes from expert faculty members, an online portal community, proprietary software, and quarterly live conferences. StomperNet's launch on October 3, 2006, set the first day sales record for online sales of information products.

Web Sites

www.stompernet.com

Primary Products or Books

Creating Customers Out of Thin Air: Secrets of Online Marketing for Offline Businesses

12. Chet Holmes

Chet Holmes has worked with over 60 of the Fortune 500 companies as America's top marketing executive, trainer, strategic consultant, and motivation expert. He has identified and developed the 12 core competencies that are proven to provide the main structure of truly great companies, and he has developed more than 50 proprietary methods for implementing to see his and your ideas actually take root and grow.

The realization of Chet's discoveries came to full fruition while running nine divisions of a company for Charlie Munger (on the

Forbes "Billionaires" list, partner of Warren Buffett). Chet Holmes doubled the sales volume of each division, most within only 12 to 15 months, continuing strategic growth in several divisions and again doubling sales for several years consecutively. Charlie has called Chet, "America's greatest sales and marketing executive."

Web Sites

www.chetholmes.com

Primary Products or Books

The Ultimate Sales Machine (Portfolio Trade, 2008)

Business Growth Masters Series

Mega Marketing and Sales

13. **Chip and Dan Heath**

Chip Heath is the Thrive Foundation of Youth Professor of Organizational Behavior in the Graduate School of Business at Stanford University. Dan Heath is a Senior Fellow at Duke University's CASE center, which supports social entrepreneurs. They are the coauthors of *Switch: How to Change Things When Change Is Hard* (Crown Business, 2010), which debuted at number one on the *New York Times* and *Wall Street Journal* best-seller lists. The Heath brothers previously cowrote the critically acclaimed book *Made to Stick* (Random House, 2007), which was named the Best Business Book of the Year, spent 24 months on the *BusinessWeek* best-seller list, and has been translated into 29 languages, the last of which was Slovak.

Web Sites

http://heathbrothers.com

Primary Products or Books

Switch: How to Change Things When Change Is Hard (Crown Business, 2010)

Made to Stick (Random House, 2007)

14. **Dan O'Day**

Dan O'Day is a highly opinionated radio advertising guru and radio talent coach, waging war against bad commercials and bad radio. He is despised by mediocre radio pros worldwide.

Web Sites

http://danoday.com

Primary Products or Books

The Psychology of Management (O'Liners Production, 1993)

How to Get Past the Gatekeeper: Advanced Strategies for Sales Professionals CD course

How to Attract, Hire & Keep Sales Superstars CD course

15. Danny Sullivan

Danny Sullivan is the editor-in-chief of Search Engine Land, a blog that covers news and information about search engines, and search marketing. Search Engine Land is owned by Third Door Media, of which Danny Sullivan is partner and chief content officer. Third Door Media also owns and operates other search-related companies, including Search Marketing Now, which provides webcasts and webinars, both live and on demand, about web marketing; and Search Marketing Expo, a search engine marketing conference. SMX: The Search Marketing Expo Conference Series, SMXOur Brands, Third Door Media.

Web Sites

http://searchenginewatch.com

www.squidoo.com/dannysullivan

Primary Products or Books

Search Engine Land: News about Search Engines & Search Marketing Sphinn: News, Discussion Forums, Networking for Search and Internet Marketing Professionals

16. Dave Evans

Dave is the author of best-selling *Social Media Marketing: An Hour a Day*, as well as *Social Media Marketing: The Next Generation of Business Engagement*. Dave is a frequent keynoter and leads workshops with the American Marketing Association as well as Social Media Executive Seminars, a C-level business training provider. Dave writes a social media column for ClickZ.

Dave has worked in social technology consulting and development around the world: with India's Publicis|2020media and its clients including the Bengaluru International Airport, Intel, Dell, United Brands, and Pepsico and with Austin's GSD&M| IdeaCity and clients including Southwest Airlines, AARP, Wal-Mart, and the PGA TOUR.

Web Sites

www.digital-voodoo.com

Primary Products or Books

Social Media Marketing: The Next Generation of Business Engagement (Sybex, 2010)

Social Media Marketing: An Hour a Day (Sybex, 2008)

17. David Ogilvy

David MacKenzie Ogilvy (June 23, 1911–July 21, 1999), CBE, was a notable advertising executive. He has often been called "The Father of Advertising." In 1962, *Time* called him "the most sought-after wizard in today's advertising industry." He was known for a career of expanding the bounds of both creativity and morality in advertising. Ogilvy's advertising mantra followed these four basic principles: research, professional discipline, creative brilliance, and results for clients.

Primary Products or Books

Confessions of an Advertising Man (Southbank Publishing, 2004)

Ogilvy on Advertising (Vintage, 1985)

18. Dharmesh Shah

   Dharmesh Shah is chief technology officer and founder of HubSpot.

   Prior to HubSpot, Dharmesh was founder and CEO of Pyramid Digital Solutions, an enterprise software company selling to large financial services companies. Pyramid was a three-time winner of the *Inc.* 500 award and an industry leader in providing innovative web applications available to millions of consumers. The company was acquired by SunGard Data Systems in 2005.

   Prior to Pyramid Digital Solutions, Dharmesh held a number of technology management and development positions. Dharmesh also runs OnStartups.com, an online community for entrepreneurs, which is one of the top 10 most read startup blogs and receives over a thousand visitors a day. Dharmesh holds a BS in Computer Science from the University of Alabama and an MS in the Management of Technology from MIT.

   Dharmesh is author of a book entitled *Inbound Marketing: Get Found Using Google, Social Media, and Blogs* (John Wiley & Sons, Inc., 2009).

Web Sites

www.hubspot.com

www.OnStartups.com

Primary Products or Books

Inbound Marketing: Get Found Using Google, Social Media, and Blogs (John Wiley & Sons, Inc., 2009)

19. E. Haldeman-Julius

   E. Haldeman-Julius (né Emanuel Julius) (1889–1951) was an American socialist writer, atheist thinker, social reformer, and publisher. He is best remembered as the head of Haldeman-Julius Publications, the creator of a series of pamphlets known as "Little Blue Books," total sales of which ran into the hundreds of millions of copies, and as the editor of *Appeal to Reason*, a socialist newspaper with a large national circulation

Primary Products or Books

The Militant Agnostic (Prometheus Books, 1995)

My First Twenty-Five Years (Haldeman-Julius Publications, 1949)

My Second Twenty-Five Years (Haldeman-Julius Publications, 1949)

20. Eban Pagan

Eben Pagan is an American author and entrepreneur. At a very young age, he shot to fame with his *Double Your Dating eBook*. Today, he ranks among those who are extremely trusted and looked upon, in the industry. The 38-year-old entrepreneur makes over $25 million per year.

Web Sites

http://promotedprofits.com

http://ebenpagan.wordpress.com

Primary Products or Books

Wake Up Productive

Guru Mastermind Course

21. Erik Qualman

Erik Qualman is the author of *Socialnomics: How Social Media Transforms the Way We Live and Do Business* (John Wiley & Sons, Inc., 2010).

Qualman is international speaker of the Fortune 500 and has been interviewed in numerous media outlets, including: *Business-Week*, the *New York Times*, CNET, *San Francisco Chronicle*, *Mashable*, *USA Today*, *Forbes*, CBS Nightly News, and the *Huffington Post*. He has shared the stage with Alan Mulally (Ford CEO), Lee Scott (CEO/ chairman of Wal-Mart), Jose Socrates (prime minister of Portugal), Olli-Pekka Kallasvuo (Nokia CEO), Julie Andrews (Actress), Al Gore (former vice president), and Sarah Palin. He is also the video producer of 2010's "Social Media Revolution" and "Social Media ROI."

For the past 16 years Qualman has helped work in the online marketing and eBusiness organizations of Education First, Cadillac, EarthLink, Yahoo!, Travelzoo, and AT&T. He is a columnist for ClickZ, while also owning the social media blog socialnomics.com. He is currently the global vice president of Online Marketing EF Education.

Web Sites

http://socialnomics.net

Primary Products or Books

Socialnomics: How Social Media Transforms the Way We Live and Do Business (John Wiley & Sons, Inc., 2010)

22. Gary Halbert

Gary Halbert was one of the most respected marketing minds and was often hailed as one of the greatest copywriters ever. Gary was a prolific writer that talked about everything from marketing strategy, copywriting, direct marketing, and entrepreneurship on his web site

The Gary Halbert Letter. He had a signature writing style that pounded in real-world wisdom and life lessons into every issue he wrote.

Web Sites

www.thegaryhalbertletter.com

Primary Products or Books

The Gary Halbert Letter

23. Harry Beckwith

Harry has addressed or advised 31 Fortune 200 companies in 17 countries, including Target, Wells Fargo, and Microsoft, and over 60 start-ups.

His four books have earned over $21 million in sales in 24 translations. His first, *Selling the Invisible* (Business Plus, 1997), spent 36 consecutive months on the *BusinessWeek* best-seller list, and appears on numerous "best business books of all time" lists. He also is featured in *The Ten Secrets of World's Best Business Communicators* and dozens of other business books.

Web Sites

http://beckwithpartners.com

Primary Products or Books

The Invisible Touch (Business Plus, 2009)

What Clients Love (Business Plus, 2003)

Selling the Invisible (Business Plus, 1997)

24. Joel Comm

Joel Comm is an entrepreneur, best-selling author, public speaker, social media evangelist, and mobile marketing innovator. Joel has been building profitable and cutting-edge Internet ventures since founding InfoMedia in 1995. He is the best-selling author of *The AdSense Code* (Morgan James Publishing, 2010), *Click Here to Order: Stories of the World's Most Successful Internet Marketing Entrepreneurs* (Morgan James Publishing, 2008), and *Twitter Power* (John Wiley & Sons, Inc., 2009). The leading authority on new media marketing tactics, Joel has appeared in the *New York Times*, on Jon Stewart's *The Daily Show*, on CNN online, and on Fox News, and continues to be the media's go-to expert when talking about social media and Internet marketing. Joel is the leading innovator in the world of Internet marketing and continues to diversify and lend his talents to exciting new markets and ventures. Joel lives with his family in Loveland, CO.

Web Sites

http://joelcomm.com

www.nextinternetmillionaire.com

www.toponereport.com/about

Primary Products or Books

The AdSense Code (Morgan James Publishing, 2010)

Twitter Power (John Wiley & Sons, Inc., 2009)

Click Here to Order: Stories of the World's Most Successful Internet Marketing Entrepreneurs (Morgan James Publishing, 2008)

25. John Jantsch

John Jantsch is a marketing and digital technology coach, award-winning social media publisher, and author of *Duct Tape Marketing* (Thomas Nelson, 2008) and *The Referral Engine* (Portfolio Hardcover, 2010).

He is the creator of the Duct Tape Marketing System and Duct Tape Marketing Coach Network that trains and licenses small business marketing coaches around the world.

His blog was chosen as a *Forbes* favorite for marketing and small business and his podcast, a top-10 marketing show on iTunes, was called a "must listen" by *Fast Company* magazine.

He is the featured marketing contributor to American Express OPENForum and is a popular presenter of workshop and webinars for organizations such as American Express, Intuit, Verizon, HP, and Citrix.

Web Sites

http://johnjantsch.com

www.ducttapemarketing.com

Primary Products or Books

The Referral Engine: Teaching Your Business to Marketing Itself (Portfolio Hardcover, 2010)

Duct Tape Marketing (Thomas Nelson, 2008)

26. John Reese

John Reese is an Internet marketing pioneer and will help you start or grow your business online. Thousands of entrepreneurs look to him for advice on the latest online strategies and techniques.

Web Sites

www.marketingsecrets.com

Primary Products or Books

Marketing Secrets

27. Jonathan Mizel

Jonathan Mizel is the owner of CyberWave—a leading marketing company that provides Internet marketing insights and related products.

Jonathan Mizel is a true marketing expert as he understands completely the concept that givers gain. He gives you so much solid, sound information for free that you realize that his paid information is well-worth accessing.

As well as his Internet marketing advice, newsletters, and occasional speaking engagements Jonathan also has some products to his name including the popular "Amazing Pop Up" software.

Web Sites

www.jonathanmizel.net

www.marketingletter.com

Primary Products or Books

Traffic Evolution

The Online Marketing Letter

28. Marlon Sanders

Marlon Sanders has spoken at 120 seminars around the world, including London and Birmingham in the UK, the gorgeous Gold Coast of Australia, Bermuda, Hawaii, and all over the United States, including Seattle, San Francisco, LA, San Diego, Miami, Atlanta, Raleigh, Nashville, St. Louis, Dallas, Houston, Seattle, Philly, New York, Chicago, Cincinnati, and other cities.

In a strange twist of irony, his Amazing Formula has been featured before in the Mensa (the organization for people with genius IQs) online catalog.

Web Sites

www.marlonsanders.com

Primary Products or Books

Amazing Formula

The Big Course!

Push Button Letters

29. Marti Barletta

Marti Barletta's dynamic style, command of her subject, and passion for her topic make her a popular speaker at corporations and conferences. Combining gender expertise, marketing experience, and a lively sense of humor, she delivers eye-opening insights and practical "how to" pointers that audiences find enlightening, entertaining, and easy to apply. She regularly writes a column for *AdAge.com*, *Marketing Profs*, and *The Boomer Project* and has been quoted on CBS Evening News, ABC Money Matters, and *The Today Show* on NBC, as well as in the *Wall Street Journal*, *New York Times*, *Fast Company*, *BusinessWeek*, *Entrepreneur*, and many other publications worldwide.

Prior to launching The TrendSight Group, Marti was VP, director of Frankly Female at Frankel, a leading brand marketing and promotion agency.

Web Sites

http://trendsight.com

Primary Products or Books

Primetime Women: How to Win the Hearts, Minds, and Business of Boomer Big Spenders (Kaplan Business, 2007)

Marketing to Women: How to Understand, Reach, and Increase Your Share of the World's Largest Market Segment, 2nd ed. (Kaplan Business, 2007)

Trends—Recognize, Analyze, Capitalize

30. Matt Cutts

Matt Cutts joined Google as a software engineer in January 2000. He is currently the head of Google's Webspam team.

Before Google, Matt worked on his PhD in computer graphics at the University of North Carolina at Chapel Hill. He has an MS from UNC–Chapel Hill, and BS degrees in both mathematics and computer science from the University of Kentucky.

He wrote the first version of SafeSearch, which is Google's family filter, and he's worked on search quality and webspam at Google for the last several years.

Web Sites

www.mattcutts.com/blog

31. Mike Filsaime

Mike Filsaime has learned a lot of marketing and sales experience in the automotive field. He handled much of the advertising for his dealership. And in the past he was the head sales trainer for a 13-store auto group. He has taken many courses on sales and negotiating and phone selling skills.

Mike has been able to apply many of the sales and marketing tactics he's learned over the last 14 years and implement them into his online marketing. His online success has come very quickly.

He started online marketing in October of 2002. His first purchase was a product called Instant Internet Empires. It taught him how to get started and was really good for the newbie. But he had to learn many of the other techniques on his own. He is a student of "How to" books and self-improvement.

Web Sites

www.ButterflyMarketing.com

http://mikefilsaime.com

https://the7figuresecrets.com/index.php?

Primary Products or Books

The 7 Figure Secrets (www.7figuresecrets.com, 2005)

Butterfly Open Source Code

32. Mike Koenigs

Mike Koenigs (pronounced "kay-nigs") is the creator of Traffic Geyser, a Web 2.0 syndication service that simplifies the distribution of marketing content and a coaching course called Main Street Marketing Machines 2. Koenigs became interested in computers at an early age and has been involved in Internet marketing since 1991. He has played many different roles over the years—marketer, video producer, speaker, and trainer, to name a few—and one of the most versatile, legitimate Internet marketing gurus around.

Web Sites

www.trafficgeyser.com

Primary Products or Books

Traffic Geyser

Main Street Marketing Machines 2

33. Paul Colligan

Paul Colligan helps busy people leverage the technologies of new media to get their message out to more people, with less effort, and for greater profit. He is CEO of Colligan.com Inc. and manages several popular Internet properties that include YouTube Secret Weapon, Automate Sales, The New Media Inner Circle, and PaulColligan.com.

Mr. Colligan has played a key role in the launch of dozens of successful Web and Internet marketing strategies that have seen tens of millions of visitors and dollars in revenue. Previous projects have included work with Peak Potentials, Heritage House Publications, InternetMCI, the Oregon Multimedia Alliance, Rubicon International, Microsoft, Traffic Geyser, The Electronics Boutique, Traffic Geyser, and Pearson Education.

Web Sites

www.paulcolligan.com

Primary Products or Books

YouTube Secret Weapon

Automate Sales

The New Media Inner Circle

34. Paul Hartunian

Paul Hartunian is a wiz at showing people how to get mountains of free publicity for their online and offline businesses. He has shown tens of thousands of people how to use publicity to make sales, get leads, rocket businesses to all time highs, and even become celebrities.

His techniques require no special skills, no "insider contacts," and little or no money.

Paul and his publicity students have been featured on CNN, Paul Harvey News, the *New York Times*, the *Regis Philbin Show*, *Smart Money*, *Forbes*, *New Jersey Monthly*, *Money magazine*, *USA Today*, the *Wall Street Journal*, and over 1,000 other radio and TV talk shows.

Web Sites

www.hartunian.com

Primary Products or Books

How to Get $1 Million Worth of Publicity . . . FREE!

Paul Hartunian's Million Dollar Publicity Strategies

35. Pete Cashmore

Pete Cashmore is the 24-year-old CEO and founder of Mashable.com, a Technorati Top 10 blog worldwide. He founded Mashable in a small Scottish town in 2005 at age 19.

In 2009, Cashmore was chosen as one of *Inc. Magazine*'s 30 Under 30, *Forbes'* Top 25 Web Celebs and the *Huffington Posts'* Top 10 Game Changers 2009. He writes a weekly column on technology and media at CNN. He is one of the top 40 most-followed Twitter users, with more than 1.7 million followers.

Mashable itself has been chosen as a must-read by *Fast Company* and *PC Magazine*, and *BusinessWeek* has featured the site as one of the world's most profitable blogs.

Web Sites

www.mashable.com

36. Ralph Wilson

Dr. Ralph F. Wilson is widely recognized as one of the top international authorities in the area of Internet marketing. *BusinessWeek* called his popular WilsonWeb.com web site "bar none the best e-commerce resource out there." Business 2.0 profiled him as one of the savvy dot-com survivors. The *New York Times* named Dr. Wilson "among the best-known Internet Marketing publishers and consultants who preach the responsible use of e-mail for marketing."

He is the founder and editor-in-chief of *Web Marketing Today*, the grandfather of the Internet marketing ezines, published continuously since 1995. Currently it is sent to 101,000-plus confirmed opt-in subscribers.

He is a winner of the Tenagra Award for Internet Marketing Excellence and the author of hundreds of articles and numerous books, including *Planning Your Internet Marketing Strategy* (John Wiley & Sons, Inc., 2002), *The E-Mail Marketing Handbook* (2nd ed., 2005), and The Shopping Cart Report.

Web Sites

www.wilsonweb.com

Primary Products or Books

Planning Your Internet Marketing Strategy (John Wiley & Sons, Inc., 2002)

The E-Mail Marketing Handbook

The Shopping Cart Report

37. Rand Fishkin

Rand Fishkin is the CEO and cofounder of SEOmoz, a leader in the field of search engine optimization tools, resources, and community. He coauthored the *Art of SEO* (2009) from O'Reilly Media and was named on the 40 Under 40 List and 30 Best Young Tech Entrepreneurs Under 30. Rand has been written about in the *Seattle Times*, *Newsweek*, and the *New York Times* among others and keynoted conferences on search around the world. He's particularly passionate about the SEOmoz blog, read by tens of thousands of search professionals each day. In his miniscule spare time, Rand enjoys the company of his amazing wife, Geraldine.

Web Sites

www.seomoz.org

Primary Products or Books

The Art of SEO (O'Reilly Media, 2009)

38. Rick Radditz

Rick Raddatz is a genuine Internet marketing pioneer. He is the genius behind the AudioGenerator and InstantVideoGenerator services that make inexpensive audio and video streaming from web sites a reality allowing professionals and marketers to use the power of their voice and personality on their web sites and in their e-mail messages.

Before founding AudioGenerator and InstantVideoGenerator, Rick spent 10 years at Microsoft Corporation specializing in everything from product management to marketing and PR. He was on the original MSN team that helped develop Microsoft's e-mail newsletter marketing strategy. Rick has given closed-door presentations to Bill Gates and Steve Ballmer as well as to numerous Fortune 500 decision makers, and he is pleased to talk to the Real Estate CyberSpace Society on Real Estate CyberSpace Radio about new and powerful Internet voice marketing strategies that can help members boost their visibility and income.

Primary Products or Books

Instant Teleseminar

Xiosoft Audio

Lead Generator

39. Robert Collier

Robert Collier's sales letters and marketing strategies are so powerful and so hypnotic that they are probably "plagiarized" more by the world's top copywriters than anything else.

He had the amazing writing ability to sell everyday commodities, such as books, raincoats, fertilizer machinery, stocks, neckties, and tires, all by U.S. mail (he even sold coal by the carload).

As a result, he literally dumped hundreds of millions of dollars into clients' pockets.

Primary Products or Books

The Secret of the Ages (Kessinger Publishing, 2010)

Riches within Your Reach (Robert Collier Publications, 1947)

40. Russell Brunson

Russell Brunson is one of the top Internet marketing gurus. He is the founder and president of DotComSecrets.com, which intends to assist others build and promote their online businesses.

Russell is also an accomplished author, renowned speaker, software developer, and business consultant. He has clients in dozens of countries all around that range from the stay-at-home entrepreneur all the way up to huge multimillion dollar corporations. He has been featured in magazines, on TV, and speaking in front of some of the largest audiences in the world.

Web Sites

www.russellbrunson.com

www.dotcomsecrets.com

Primary Products or Books

Dotcomsecrets University

41. Ryan Deiss

Ryan Deiss is a 10-year Internet marketing veteran, and by the age of 30 Ryan had become a widely followed and respected IM guru releasing countless reports and courses on subjects ranging from social media to continuity programs and SEO.

In 2009 Ryan started Idea Incubator LP, under which he uses his expertise to market, advertise, and distribute Information products online. Idea Incubator currently contains six companies offering products in the health market, relationship market, IM market, and even household green cleaning products.

Ryan hosts a live seminar in Austin, Texas, each year called the Traffic & Conversion Summit where he gives the most up-to-date and comprehensive look at how to marketing online for any business. In 2010 Ryan was excited to welcome over 750 guests.

Web Sites

http://drivingtraffic.com

Primary Products or Books

The Perpetual Traffic Report

Rank Mogul

Domain Scalping

42. Seth Godin

Seth Godin has written 12 books that have been translated into more than 30 languages. Every one has been a best-seller.

American Way Magazine calls him "America's Greatest Marketer," and his blog is perhaps the most popular in the world written by a single individual. His latest book, *Linchpin*, hit the Amazon top 10 on the first day it was published and became a *New York Times* best-seller.

Yoyodyne, his first Internet company, was acquired by Yahoo! in 1998. It pioneered the use of ethical direct mail online, something Seth calls permission marketing. He was VP of direct marketing at Yahoo! for a year.

His latest company, Squidoo.com, is ranked among the top 125 sites in the United States (by traffic) by Quantcast. It allows anyone (even you) to build a page about any topic you're passionate about. The site raises money for charity and pays royalties to its million-plus members.

Web Sites

www.sethgodin.com

www.squidoo.com

Primary Products or Services

Linchpin: Are You Indispensable? (Portfolio Hardcover, 2010)

Tribes: We Need You to Lead Us (Portfolio Hardcover, 2010)

Meatball Sundae (Portfolio Hardcover, 2007)

43. Shawn Collins

Shawn Collins has been an affiliate marketer since 1997.

Shawn is a cofounder of the Affiliate Summit, the leading industry conference for affiliate marketing, which regularly sells out and features the biggest names in performance marketing.

He is also the coeditor-in-chief of *FeedFront Magazine* and founder of GeekCast.fm.

His book, *Successful Affiliate Marketing for Merchants* (Que, 2001) is the best-selling book in the space, and it is considered to be required reading by affiliate managers.

He publishes the annual AffStat Report, a research, analysis, and benchmarking report for the affiliate marketing industry. The data in the AffStat series is widely quoted by trade publications, including Internet Retailer and Jupitermedia properties.

Shawn writes a daily blog on affiliate marketing news and opinion at his Affiliate Tip site, and posts regularly to his Affiliate Tip TV channel on YouTube.

Web Sites

http://blog.affiliatetip.com

Primary Products or Books

Successful Affiliate Marketing for Merchants (Que, 2001)

44. Stephen Pierce

Stephen Pierce is an Internet marketer who first broke into the industry with his book the *Whole Truth and Nothing but the Truth About Internet Marketing . . . under Oath*. Since then, he's released many training programs that focus on the overall strategy rather than on tactics and techniques. Rather than focus on business alone, he strongly advocates developing a strong mind-set and working on yourself to improve your success in businesses.

In addition to teaching Internet marketing, Stephen is also a speaker and a personal development coach. That gives him a unique stance in knowing what it takes to succeed and what causes people to fail in their business. A lot of the teachings on his blog and web sites cover both personal development and business strategy.

Web Sites

www.stephenlive.com

www.makerealmoneyontheinternet.com

Primary Products or Books

The Whole Truth And Nothing But The Truth About Internet Marketing . . . Under Oath

Make Real Money on the Internet

45. Steve Harrison and Bill Harrison

Steve Harrison is the chief instructor for most of our training programs and the company's "Mr. Outside." A graduate of Davidson College, Steve was first bitten by the media bug in high school while working as a freelance writer for the local newspaper. A 2:44 marathoner in his younger days, today Steve's running around is mostly limited to the tennis court.

Bill Harrison is the company's "Mr. Inside" and serves as its chief executive officer, overseeing the day-to-day operations, marketing and strategic partnerships. A graduate of Haverford College, Bill began his career as a freelance photojournalist and covered such notables as Jimmy Carter, Ronald Reagan, George H.W. Bush, Ted Kennedy, Jimmy Connors, Bill Cosby, Cheryl Tiegs, Bob Hope, and others. His photos appeared in *Newsweek*, Gannett Newspapers, and on the United Press International wire service.

Web Sites

www.freepublicity.com

www.reporterconnection.com

46. Ted Nicholas

At age 21, and $96,000 in debt, Ted started his own candy business called "Peterson's House of Fudge." It was here where he began to learn the ropes of how to successfully market a business.

Through much determination and hard work Ted grew his candy business from 1 store in the beginning to ultimately 30 retail candy store franchises.

It was around this time Ted got the idea for his first book, titled *How to Form Your Own Corporation without a Lawyer for under $50* (Kaplan Business, 1999).

With the success of *How to Form Your Own Corporation without a Lawyer for Under $50* Ted built a book publishing empire called Enterprise Publishing, eventually leading to 14 other best-selling business books. He also created an incorporating service company called The Company Corporation. TCC grew to become the largest incorporating company in the world.

Web Sites

www.tednicholas.com

Primary Products or Books

How to Form Your Own Corporation without a Lawyer for Under $50 (Kaplan Business, 1999)

Dream Information Publishing Seminar DVD Home-Study Course

Success in the Sun Home Study Course

47. Tim Ash

Tim Ash is the president and CEO of SiteTuners and its parent company Epic Sky. He is the author of Amazon.com e-commerce best-seller *Landing Page Optimization: The Definitive Guide to Testing and Tuning for Conversions* (Sybex, 2008). During his 20-year involvement with the Internet, Tim has worked with American Express, Sony Music, Verizon Wireless, American Honda, COMP USA, Harcourt Brace & Co., Universal Studios, Eaton, American Red Cross, Texas Instruments, 1-800-Flowers, Red Envelope, SAIC, Pyxis, and B.F. Goodrich Aerospace to develop successful Internet initiatives.

He has chaired Internet conferences and spoken internationally at industry events including Search Engine Strategies, eMetrics, Affiliate Summit, PPC Summit, eComXpo, PC Expo, and Internet World. Tim is the "By the Numbers" expert columnist for Search Engine Watch, and has written articles on harnessing the power of the Internet for business. He is a contributing columnist for several industry publications including *Web site Magazine*, *Electronic Retailer Online Strategies*, and *Visibility Magazine*.

Web Sites

http://sitetuners.com

Primary Products or Books

Landing Page Optimization: The Definitive Guide to Testing and Tuning for Conversions (Sybex, 2008)

48. Willie Crawford

In 1996, while still serving in the Air Force in Hawaii, Willie decided to start his own Internet-based business. By the time he retired in 2003, Willie had built that into a six-figure part-time income.

Willie is now one of the world's leading Internet marketing experts, having spoken at dozens of seminars in the United States, Malaysia, Singapore, and the UK.

Willie has created dozens of information products, written over 1,300 articles and 50 ebooks on ecommerce. He's hosted seminars and now hosts his own radio show several times per week.

Willie has an incredible 1,600 web sites, some of which get over 1 million unique visitors per month.

Willie often serves as a middleman or a joint venture broker. He's also Executive Director of The International Association of Joint Venture Brokers.

Willie has written several books. including a best-selling soul food cookbook (featured in The Soul Food Museum in Atlanta, Georgia) and an inspirational biography, *Git Off the Porch*.

Web Sites

http://williecrawford.com

Primary Products or Books

Git off the Porch (Profits Publishing, 2006)

Soul Food Recipes Learned On a North Carolina Tobacco Farm (self-published, 2001)

Index